A KIND OF MAGIC

MAKING THE ORIGINAL
HIGHLANDER

JONATHAN MELVILLE

POLARIS
PUBLISHING

This paperback edition first published in 2022 by

POLARIS PUBLISHING LTD
c/o Aberdein Considine
2nd Floor, Elder House
Multrees Walk
Edinburgh
EH1 3DX

www.polarispublishing.com

First published in hardback in 2020

Distributed by
BIRLINN LIMITED

Text copyright © Jonathan Melville, 2020, 2022

ISBN: 9781913538446
eBook ISBN: 9781913538156

British Library Cataloguing-in-Publication Data
A catalogue record for this book is available on request from the British Library.

Designed and typeset by Polaris Publishing, Edinburgh
Printed in Great Britain by MBM Print SCS Limited, East Kilbride

CONTENTS

For Mum and Ron

INTRODUCTION

The first time I saw *Highlander* was in a cinema, but not on its original UK release in August 1986.

At that time I was ten-years-old and in the month the film was released here I'd moved from the family home in the city of Edinburgh to a new life in the Highlands of Scotland. The nearest cinema was in Inverness, a couple of hours away by train or car, and we didn't have a car. We also didn't have a video recorder, although the film wouldn't arrive on VHS until 1987 and the choice of titles available to rent in the local corner shop was limited to seemingly endless *Police Academy* sequels and low-budget action films.

Not that it mattered much as I don't recall hearing about the film at school. It would be a few years before I started reading *Starburst* magazine, a title that would become my gateway into the world of science fiction and fantasy news, previews and reviews years before the internet arrived. Instead, it would take eight years from its UK release for this cinemagoer to discover the film back in Edinburgh, where I'd moved back to as a student in 1994.

Rather than spend my evenings in the student union stocking up on cheap pints and vodka, I was more likely to be found in my flat, watching videotapes of old sci-fi series or more recent action films, either on my own or with flatmates. One of them was far more up on his horror films than me, and his nocturnal trips to the local garage for cigarette papers and tobacco meant he was usually to be found watching videos until the wee small hours.

Study time often became cinema time at our local, the Cameo, an Edinburgh institution which prided itself on its eclectic programme of films, and it was here I'd see the likes of *Shallow Grave*, *Ed Wood*, *Pulp Fiction* and *The Limey* in their opening weeks, while trips to the now long-gone Odeon in South Clerk Street were reserved for bigger films like *Die Hard With a Vengeance*, *The Rock* or *The Matrix*. I'd like to say I spent just as much time seeking out the latest Peter Greenaway or Werner Herzog, but in those days I was devouring *Empire* magazine rather than *Sight & Sound*.

One memorable aspect of the Cameo's eclectic scheduling was its series of weekend late screenings on Friday and Saturday nights in Screen 1. For just £3.50 you could turn up from 11.30 p.m. and expect a double bill of vaguely thematically linked films, such as *Reservoir Dogs* and *Miller's Crossing*, *Dazed and Confused* and *Slacker* or *Goldfinger* and *Dr No*. It was on 29 October 1994 that I headed along to the Cameo with my flatmate to witness one of the finest double bills ever scheduled: *The Crow* and *Highlander*.

The Crow was only a few months old at this point and had made headlines thanks to the tragic death of its star, Brandon Lee, in a freak on-set accident, something which gave its plot an added poignancy. In the film, Lee's character, Eric Draven, is killed by thugs before returning from the dead to avenge both his own death and that of his fiancée.

The Crow's partner that night was an update of the traditional sword-and-sandal epic which combined battle scenes in medieval Scotland with skirmishes in 1985 New York, throwing in a thumping soundtrack from the world's biggest rock band, Queen. The American-born, Swiss-raised actor Christopher Lambert played the Scottish Connor MacLeod, while local lad Sean Connery (born just around the corner from the cinema in Fountainbridge) was the Egyptian Ramirez, complete with strong Edinburgh accent. Wrapped in the astonishing visuals of Australian director Russell Mulcahy, in *Highlander* you had a film ready to collapse at any moment under the weight of its own ambition.

Needless to say, I loved it.

Stumbling out into the bracing October night at 3 a.m. and heading back to my flat, my head was spinning with imagery and ideas from both films, realising that although each was rooted in fantasy, they also spoke to the universal themes of death, fear, hope and love. They also had some pretty cool fight scenes and Sean Connery looked amazing, so there was something for everyone.

Much as I loved the original *Highlander*, I never became an obsessive fanboy, for a few reasons. Firstly, in the nineties it was hard, though not impossible, to find others with similar niche interests in a particular film. The internet wasn't easy to access, and even if you could you weren't guaranteed that anyone had created a web page about something you were interested in.

Secondly, the sequels just weren't very good. I remember renting *Highlander III: The Sorcerer* (or whatever it was called that week) on VHS soon after its release in 1995 and being underwhelmed by the plot and the action scenes, while it took me another few years to see *Highlander II: The Quickening* and to be equally disappointed. I appreciate that saying a *Highlander* film isn't great in a book about *Highlander* may not be a good sales technique, but it's best to be honest from the start. If this leads to me having a yoke tied to my back and being forced out of the metaphorical Highland village by *Highlander III* fans, then so be it.

In 2000 I headed to Australia for a year and, fearing homesickness for Scotland, took a copy of *Highlander* on VHS along with me in my backpack. In hostels from Brisbane to Coober Pedy I'd suggest my fellow travellers relax with a few beers and a screening of the film, if not reminded of home by Christopher Lambert's accent, then certainly by the visuals of lochs and mountains. Looking back, I can see that a picture book of Scottish vistas may have been more appropriate to take with me, but it would have been far less enjoyable.

Fast-forward ten years or so and by the early 2010s I was a freelance film journalist and wannabe author, dabbling in writing features for *SFX* magazine on films such as *Tremors* and *Short Circuit* while working for various arts-related companies. Whether that meant writing blog posts, penning a weekly column for a local newspaper or organising a film festival for a mobile cinema travelling the Highlands and Islands of Scotland, there was usually a film connection. I'd even started my own film website, looking at film and TV from a Scottish perspective.

One thing that always struck me about Scotland's attitude to cinema was that we were forever looking over our shoulders at what had gone before while fretting about the future. Despite much hand-wringing about the state of Scottish film production, Scotland has never had a film studio. We've been content to host productions from around the globe while our own film-makers struggle for funding from national bodies such as the British Film Institute or Screen Scotland and Creative Scotland, while the BBC, STV and Channel Four nurture local talent in fits and starts depending on their budgets.

We've always had plenty of talented writers, directors, actors, producers, camera operators and best boys, but we haven't necessarily always had a glut of productions to keep them all gainfully employed throughout any given year. The early 1980s saw a bright light flicker briefly in the shape of writer-director Bill Forsyth, whose unique brand of whimsy had seen films such as *That Sinking Feeling*, *Gregory's Girl* and *Local Hero* appear between 1979 and 1983, before he made a few films in America towards the tail end of the decade.

While these films stand shoulder to shoulder with anything produced outside of Scotland, they remain something of a high-water mark for Scottish cinema, a period regularly referred to as a Golden Age by writers including myself. "Where's the next Bill Forsyth?" we ask, whereas we probably mean, "When will we have some successful homegrown films again?" That's not to denigrate the work of current independent production companies who are working hard to bring new films and TV to our screens, it's just a comment on the fact that few of them have had the global success of *Local Hero*, which to this day has fans around the world keen to travel to Scotland to visit *that* phone box.

All of which means that we Scots embrace almost any film that has a local connection, including *Whisky Galore!* (an Ealing Studios production shot on location on the island of Barra), *Braveheart* (which had a few scenes filmed in Scotland while the majority was shot in Ireland) and *Brave* (the Disney animated film set in Scotland). It's not so much that we ignore the questionable attempts at Scottish accents or decisions to mess around with historical fact to make the fiction more exciting, more that we revel in seeing some sort of reflection of ourselves on the cinema screen rather than yet another superhero film set in New York.

Though *Highlander* is about as Scottish as *The Simpsons'* Groundskeeper Willie or *Star Trek's* Scotty (actually, we'll claim them for our own as well), and despite being savaged by critics through the years (the *Los Angeles Times* announced it was "stultifyingly, jaw-droppingly, achingly awful" on its release in 1986, while *Variety* reckoned director Russell Mulcahy couldn't decide whether he was "making a sci-fi, thriller, horror, music video or romance"), we still hold it close to our hearts.

If it really is so bad, why has *Highlander* refused to simply disappear into the Scotch mist since its somewhat bungled initial release? Despite Russell Mulcahy being accused of directing "little more than an everlasting [music] video", why did the Edinburgh International Film Festival celebrate the film's 30th anniversary in 2016 with a premiere for a newly restored version of the film, complete with an appearance from star Clancy Brown? And why do fans from all around the globe still make pilgrimages to Eilean Donan Castle each year to see the 'birthplace' of Connor MacLeod, before heading further west to run along a remote beach in the footsteps of their hero?

These are just a few of the questions I've been curious about since I started writing about Scottish film, and to answer them I decided to talk to the men and women who put months of their lives into making the film back in 1985.

Jonathan Melville
Edinburgh
September 2020

ONE

CREATING THE LEGEND

To walk through the corridors of the Tower of London is to walk through a thousand years of history. It was in the late 11th century that William the Conqueror, the first Norman king of England, ordered the Tower's construction, an opportunity to show Londoners that their new rulers meant business.

In subsequent centuries it would be known variously as a palace, a prison and a fortress, while in the 15th century a royal armoury was established to procure equipment in times of war. Opening to the public as a tourist attraction in the 16th century, its displays of armour were immediately popular with visitors, and by the 20th century the Tower allowed visitors from around the world to marvel at weapons of war and oppression, before stopping off in the cafe for tea and scones.

One tourist who wandered the corridors and anterooms in 1980, gazing at relics from centuries past, was an 18-year-old high school graduate, Gregory Widen, a native of Laguna Beach, California. "They have the world's largest collection of armoury," explained Widen many years later. "I was walking through it and I thought, *What if you owned all this?* Then I thought, *What if you wore all this?* And then I thought, *What if you never died and you were giving someone a tour saying you owned all this?*"

Despite the teen's interest in the military history surrounding him, it could easily have been a passing thought, instantly forgotten as he left the building and continued with his holiday, before he headed home to California.

Already one of the youngest paramedics in Laguna Beach, Widen now had his sights set on becoming a firefighter, a competitive role not commonly held by teenagers. In Southern California, the fire department and the ambulance service were one and the same, meaning the same people who rode on the fire engines also drove ambulances. With paramedic training under his belt, Widen impressed those in charge of admissions and duly won his place as a firefighter.

By 1981, following stints as a disc jockey and broadcast engineer for ABC TV, Widen decided to sign up to UCLA's (University of California, Los Angeles) advanced graduate course in screenwriting, paying for his education by working as a firefighter. Said Widen, "On the one hand, I was going into burning buildings, then I was going to class talking about Japanese cinematographers."

Looking back on the work of his one-time student, Professor Richard Walter explains that each week for ten weeks during the academic quarter (of which UCLA has three annually instead of the more traditional two 15-week semesters), Widen and seven other young screenwriters would meet under the tutelage of various instructors, including Walter himself, whose credits include the earliest drafts of 1973's *American Graffiti*.

According to Walter, who describes himself as a "working stiff" writer, all instructors are members of the Writers Guild of America West, and "all bring to the table a vantage that is not exclusively intellectual and analytical, but also a hands-on familiarity with the nuts and bolts and slings and arrows and meat and potatoes that constitute the professional writing life". The group would work on their assignment, a feature-length screenplay, with Walter emphasising the importance of economy in a script. The professor explains that he and his colleagues are "story hard-liners" who think that success in dramatic narratives is all about writing a strong story. "My teaching also involves one-on-one tutorial sessions in which the writer and I review the notes I've made after reading his or her pages."

Searching for ideas to turn into his first screenplay, Gregory Widen settled upon memories of the trip to England he'd made a few years earlier, specifically to the Tower of London where he'd been surrounded by swords and armour. The young writer was also inspired by the 1977 film, *The Duellists*. Directed by Ridley Scott from a Gerald Vaughan-Hughes script, itself based on a Joseph Conrad short story, the film follows two soldiers in the French Hussars, Keith Carradine's d'Hubert and Harvey Keitel's Feraud, who become mortal enemies after a seemingly minor altercation. The pair end up fighting each other in numerous duels at various points through the subsequent decades.

Feraud is the traditional 'baddie', although Keitel avoids the temptation to play him as an over-the-top villain. Carradine's d'Hubert, the younger of the pair, is as baffled as the audience by the reasons behind the feud and it's him that the viewer spends most time with. "To me, that was a very classic dilemma for the main character, how you interact with a person like that," said Widen. "Could you be that person in another guise?"

Combining the themes of *The Duellists* with the idea of someone living forever, a classic concept stretching back to Greek myth, led Widen to start his script, initially titled 'Shadow Clan'. Another likely source of inspiration for Widen was American author Joseph Campbell, who in his 1949 book *The Hero With a Thousand Faces* outlined the journey taken by heroes found in world myth. Campbell's theory – that the hero begins his journey in his everyday life, before he's introduced to "a region of supernatural wonder", encounters strange forces, wins a victory and returns from his adventure a better man – fits the basic plot of 'Shadow Clan' perfectly.

In his 1992 book *The New Screenwriter Looks at the New Screenwriter*, one of Widen's former tutors, William Froug, painted a picture of a serious student who rarely spoke in class but listened attentively. Wrote Froug, "There was earnestness about him, and self-assurance without arrogance, that let you know that he was a man who kept his own council [sic]." According to Froug, Widen's early work also showed self-confidence. "As a teacher I knew he would come in with a solid, workable screenplay, and indeed he did."

Recalling one of the first rules of screenwriting, to "write what you know", Gregory Widen cannily used his London holiday as material for a new script, outlining a plot that would see a young 15th-century Scottish clansman, Conor MacLeod, realise that he was no ordinary warrior, but an Immortal destined to battle his way through the centuries against an evil foe, the Knight.

Where the script veered away from more typical sword and sorcery fodder was in the decision to set much of the story in present-day Washington DC, juxtaposing MacLeod's early life as a novice Immortal with that of a more world-weary veteran who had lived, loved and lost and who displayed the scars, mental and physical, of a long life. The hero was tormented by the presence of the Knight, whose only goal was to kill his rival and become the last Immortal.

As well as attending classes, Widen also spent some time with Richard Walter in one-on-one tutorial sessions, during which the pair reviewed notes made by the tutor on the 'Shadow Clan' script, teasing out some elements and discarding others. Though Walter recalls that his student's writing was "overly descriptive", he felt that it still worked and that it was his favourite kind of script: a rule-breaker. "It was a gripping read from the start and I told him he should keep on doing whatever he was doing. Widen was a standout among standouts."

While there are numerous differences between 'Shadow Clan' and what would later become *Highlander*, it's clear to see what fascinated Richard Walter about his student's work and the following overview is designed to highlight some of the similarities and differences between the earliest draft and the finished film. One of the biggest differences is the spelling of the lead character's first name, which is Conor here rather than the Connor of the film – he'll be referred to as Conor in this chapter.

The plot

Opening in present-day Washington DC with a brief confrontation between Conor MacLeod and fellow Immortal Iman Fasil in an alley outside some side street porno houses, the former takes his rival's head in decidedly unheroic fashion; it's dark and the pair can barely make each other out.

The first flashback takes the reader to MacLeod's home in 15th-century Scotland and introduces his father, Ian, his mother and a young child who is almost certainly his brother. MacLeod's father is keen to send him to battle for the Duke against the Clan Sutherland, and he's soon sent off with some clansmen to make his family proud. Unfortunately, the Knight is also on the battlefield and he attempts to kill MacLeod, whispering a phrase before he does so that would go through some subtle alterations in subsequent drafts: "There can be but one."

The fight is intercut with police officers, led by Detective Lt. Moran, in Washington apprehending Richard Taupin (MacLeod's 1980s persona) in an alley after they find him near the headless body from the start of the script. From here, the film flips back and forth through time between Scotland and Washington, the Highlander meeting his mentor Juan Cid Romirez and discovering his true potential, while the police in the 1980s investigate a spate of murders involving headless corpses and query the possible involvement of Richard Taupin.

Taupin's/MacLeod's 1980s love interest is Brenna Cartwright, the niece of the District Attorney, who is working as a historian at the Smithsonian museum. MacLeod must face the Knight as part of the Gathering, their final battle taking place at the Jefferson Memorial.

Had Widen's script been faithfully adapted for the screen, it's likely it would have been a curious modern take on the sword and sorcery epic. Rather than a *Conan the Barbarian*-style rampage through a faux-Middle Age backdrop, with limbs being chopped off by muscle-bound actors, Widen adds depth to his central character while also throwing in obligatory fight sequences. It's questionable whether a mainstream audience would have responded well to the dialogue-heavy nature of the film, but Widen's version would undoubtedly have found a welcoming fan base.

Conor MacLeod

While *Highlander* fans will see much that is familiar in Gregory Widen's vision of the universe, there are also many subtle differences, particularly with regard to familiar characters.

Conor MacLeod was born on 11 December 1408 in the village of Ardvreck on the Highland plain of Strathnaver. In reality there is no village named Ardvreck in Scotland, though there is an Ardvreck Castle in Sutherland, which may have been Widen's reference point. MacLeod has parents who worry after him and his first love interest is Mara.

Having been apprehended by police following the discovery of Fasil's body, Taupin/MacLeod is interrogated by Moran at the police station, during which he admits he has American citizenship – Fasil is identified as having been Syrian. More of MacLeod's backstory is revealed by Widen, with a number of flashbacks filling in gaps in his life. He tells Brenna that he has "served in the armies of twelve nations, married nine women, fathered 38 children and buried them all".

At one point, MacLeod assumes the role of Major Dupont, a member of the French infantry in the 18th century, who encounters another young Immortal, Private Mulet, during an inspection. When Mulet confronts Dupont about them both being the same, Dupont warns him about threatening a senior officer, to which Mulet retorts: "Threats and nothingness. It's what we live for."

More light is cast upon MacLeod's early life when the story moves to the small Pennsylvanian town of Worstick. MacLeod lived in Worstick in the 1800s as William Taupin, earning himself a reputation as a ladies' man and antagonising local men who feel he's stealing their girlfriends and wives. By the 1980s, Taupin lives in New York and runs an antiques shop, with at least one member of staff, a receptionist who is given no name and who could be male or female.

The Knight

The story in Widen's script belongs to MacLeod, with the Knight showing up at inopportune moments to remind the young Immortal that he's only alive because the Knight allows him to be. Going by the alias Carl Smith, the Knight is a believer in tradition and knows Latin, which he recites in church after a fight with MacLeod which leaves him badly wounded. No backstory is given for the Knight; he's simply fighting to be the last Immortal and has no qualms about it.

The nature of the ongoing battle between MacLeod and the Knight is addressed by the Scotsman in an exchange with Brenna, who wonders what could be worth all the murder and destruction. "Sometimes I think it's just for something to do," admits Conor. "A conquest to be the last. Something to hold on to while everything else around you withers and blows away. Something to replace the love that can never work."

Romirez

Juan Cid Romirez introduces himself as "chief surveyor and alchemist" when he first meets MacLeod at the latter's blacksmith shop five years after he left his village. The Spaniard had been sent to Inverness by the King of Spain as a consultant on matters of metal, learning during his travels of MacLeod's recovery from certain death "by powers not of this Earth".

Romirez recognises MacLeod because of a flow that he feels pushing against him. Immortals feel this when another is nearby and the sensation lessens. "We are brothers," says Romirez to MacLeod at the latter's home. The Spaniard explains MacLeod's place in the world and introduces him to The Game, "the one continuity and tradition" Immortals know, before skewering him through the heart with his sword and "killing" him for three days.

Romirez goes on to tell MacLeod that as long as they are alive then the Knight cannot have it all. MacLeod learns more basic rules from his mentor, including the need to avoid attracting attention to himself and to "keep his soul sewed to the earth" by avoiding greed. Says Romirez, "Life without morality, without the ability to truly taste the sweetness of wine and love, is no life at all." Soon after, the Knight finds Romirez inside MacLeod's home, severing his head and escaping just before the younger Immortal returns and begins sobbing.

Exploring the Immortals

It's fascinating to get a glimpse into Widen's take on the concept of Immortals fighting through the centuries to be the last man (there don't appear to be any female Immortals) standing. In Widen's script, once a head has been chopped off, bodies simply fall to the ground.

However, there's more to a beheading than meets the eye, with Romirez helpfully explaining to MacLeod that there is a power divided between each Immortal "like cuts in a pie", though Conor and the Knight have more power than most. By staying alive, Conor is preventing the Knight from prevailing.

MacLeod bumps into Ling Kahn, an Asian Immortal who knew to look for the former in a bar that sold lager and lime, the Highlander's drink of choice. Kahn enjoys getting drunk with MacLeod each time they meet and the pair spend some time kicking around Washington after dark, reminiscing about the old days. "Tasting and enjoying life is the only thing of value we have,"

explains Kahn to MacLeod; "everything else is just marking time."
The Knight kills Kahn off-screen later in the script, presenting his
head to MacLeod before they fight.

The final battle

As the final battle between the Knight and MacLeod at the
Jefferson Memorial begins, the Highlander has little fight left in
him, resigned to the fact that he's in the weaker position. The
Knight still believes in tradition, and demands the "little boy" fight
him properly.

MacLeod is injured early in the fight, the Knight slicing through
his shoulder, chest and stomach. It's thanks to the intervention of
Detective Lt. Moran, who shoots two bullets into the Knight, that
the Immortal is weakened. Though Moran dies by the Knight's
sword, MacLeod is able to surprise his foe, slicing into his chest
before putting his sword to the Knight's throat and reciting Latin,
"Requiescat in pace" or "Rest in peace" before cutting the Knight's
head off with his sword. This doesn't stop the Knight's headless
body from grabbing Brenna, while his head smiles at her from the
floor before dying.

Later, having closed up his shop and home for good, MacLeod/
Taupin meets Brenna at the Washington Mall, and explains to her
that rather than inheriting power and control, he now has a better
understanding of life, and he can also die.

```
                    TAUPIN
    Life is only life when it is bounded by
  death. The inheritance is death. The gift
  is the finality of life. To be part of the
              fabric. The inside.
              (turns to Brenna)
            I love you Brenna.
```

He then goes on to state that:

TAUPIN

It will be horrible. The future. I may
die tomorrow or 10,000 tomorrows. I can
promise you nothing. Nothing but a moment.
Maybe two. But a moment of love, is that
not worth a lifetime?

The pair then hold each other, as a jogger runs past them, "unaware of any life but his own".

Selling the script

Gregory Widen's script was renamed 'Highlander' during a brainstorming session with his two UCLA roommates, Ethan Wiley and Fred Dekker, who would both go on to collaborate on the screenplay for 1987's *House* and forge their own successful careers in writing and directing. "We went through endless lists of titles," revealed Widen to *Cinefantastique*. "We originally had a joke one – *Sword of Bad*, which you have to say fast to appreciate."

Despite the script's originality, it was still only a class project, read by a handful of fellow classmates and his tutor. Luckily for Widen, Richard Walter liked what he was reading in the early drafts and as it neared completion was its biggest supporter. "I knew after reading the first half of the first page that Greg was a writer who was engaging and compelling," Walter tells me. "By mid-script I was on the phone to a major agent suggesting he let Greg send him the script."

In Walter's screenwriting book, *Essentials of Screenwriting*, he discusses his feelings about the script and even includes the query letter written by Widen that helped secure representation. "I was always taught that you can only get an agent through a referral," said Widen. "But I didn't know any better, so I got a list from the Writers' Guild and literally sent 'Highlander' out with a cover letter. I said, 'Hi, my name is Greg. Please represent me.' And a handful of them wrote back."

At the same time as Widen was busying himself looking for an agent who would help him get his script seen by producers, those same producers were keeping an eye on what was happening at LA's film schools.

Two such men were the team of Peter Davis and William [Bill] Panzer, who had been working together since the mid-1970s, after being introduced by an ex-partner of Davis. Davis was a former New York City mergers and acquisitions lawyer who had also run a steel company, while Panzer was a graduate of New York University Film School who had worked as a cameraman and editor, but who was keen to move into feature films. Each man brought different skills to the partnership, with Davis' financial nous complementing Panzer's production knowledge on their first picture, 1976's *The Death Collector*, which the pair produced for just $175,000.

Films such as *Stunts* (1977), *Steel* (1977), *Gas* (1981) and *O'Hara's Wife* (1982) followed, the pair turning down offers to work for film studios, preferring to go independent with their own company, Davis-Panzer Productions. "Early on we recognised that we are just not corporate types," explained Panzer to *Screen International* in 2005. Davis-Panzer were determined to find an original work that they could bring to the sales market circuit and raise the necessary funds for their next film. "We learned by going to the markets that it pays to be making a film that is original," continued Davis. "These types of projects take a long time to sell, and you don't want to be pushing a flavour of the month."

Bill Panzer's introduction to Gregory Widen's script began with lunch at the legendary Hollywood Boulevard restaurant, Musso & Frank's, during a conversation with agent Harold Moskowitz, who according to Panzer used to cruise film schools looking for material. "He said, 'I don't think this is the best script I've ever read, but [it's] a really good idea.' It did have some of the principal characters in it and the idea of immortality, the idea of Immortals in conflict, but it was much darker. And it was less romantic."

"We like adventure movies and 'Highlander' seemed to have a lot of elements that coalesced well to appeal to a wide audience," added Peter Davis. "The script spans every area – fantasy, romantic adventure, contemporary comment, even period comedy."

Davis-Panzer went on to option the rights for $1,500 from Widen in 1982, with the writer noting that "the option money for *Highlander* was very, very minuscule". Widen would receive a few thousand dollars a year from the producers until they managed to set the picture up with a studio. Any deal that followed would go on to make him substantially more money, with his payment index linked to the film's eventual budget. This payment would only be made when the film finally went into production.

Bill Panzer and Peter Davis' next move was to take the bare bones of the original 'Highlander' script and craft it into something more palatable for the sales market, who in turn had their sights firmly set on audiences sitting down to enjoy a movie at the cinema on a Friday night.

TWO

REWRITING HISTORY

"Happy to provide the real story of *Highlander*," emails screenwriter Larry Ferguson in response to my request for an interview, "since much of what's out there is just patently wrong."

It's the summer of 2017, and as we exchange details to arrange a suitable time to chat by conference call with him and his one-time writing partner, Peter Bellwood, I learn that the 77-year-old Ferguson has left behind the bright lights of Hollywood and is living on the edge of a rainforest in his native Oregon. "I came here to write a novel, which is nearly finished, and I'm going to stay."

Ferguson has come home after decades spent as a screenwriter in California, though his early life on a farm near Klamath Falls didn't hint at a career in show business. After graduating from the University of Oregon's College of Arts and Sciences in the early 1960s, he moved to California to pursue a career as an actor and wound up repossessing cars. He then found himself cast in a play at the University of California, Davis, west of Sacramento, before enrolling there on an MA in Theatre and Dance. After a few seasons at the American Conservatory Theater in San Francisco, the 1970s found the actor moving to New York to work on Broadway, before Hollywood came calling.

"An agent from Los Angeles saw me, and said, 'You should be a movie star.' I moved my family from New York to LA, and was excited about the whole idea of it. I called the agent when I got there, but he didn't remember who I was and told me to come back later." Undeterred, Ferguson opened a conservatory in Los Angeles and penned his own screenplay, which he eventually sold to Paramount for $125,000.

English-born Peter Bellwood had studied History at Cambridge University at the tail end of the 1950s, before going on to join Footlights Dramatic Club in 1959 after impressing its president with his ukulele playing skills. Bellwood became Footlights president in 1960, the same year John Cleese arrived at Cambridge, becoming friends with Peter Cook just as the club's fame grew with the establishment of the *Beyond the Fringe* stage revue featuring Cook, Dudley Moore, Jonathan Miller and Alan Bennett.

After his time at Cambridge, Bellwood moved into advertising, making TV commercials for soap company Procter & Gamble until he was invited by Peter Cook to write and perform with *Beyond the Fringe* when it moved from London to New York. When that finally closed its doors and returned to England, Bellwood remained in New York, continuing to write scripts for TV specials while also becoming a theatre producer, moving into screenwriting in the 1970s. It was as a screenwriter that Bellwood first encountered producers Peter Davis and Bill Panzer on the 1979 drama, *Steel*.

By the end of the 1970s, Ferguson and Bellwood had joined forces and were hired by Davis and Panzer to write a script based on the real-life events leading up to the eruption of Mount St. Helens in Washington in 1980. The aptly named *St. Helens*, starring Art Carney and David Huffman, was filmed between November 1980 and April 1981 and broadcast as an HBO TV movie on the first anniversary of the disaster, 18 May 1981.

Happy with the collaboration, Davis and Panzer approached the two screenwriters again in late 1982 to work on a rewrite of Gregory Widen's 'Highlander' script. "We were given an outline and we turned it into a green-light movie," states Ferguson simply, referring to the industry term for a studio deciding to go forward with production on a new film. "In other words, they had secured the rights but they did not have a whole bunch of finances and said, 'It's a great idea; can you turn it into a commercial screenplay?'"

Widen was ready for changes to his script long before Peter Davis and Bill Panzer came calling. Film school may have been a place to learn about the craft of screenwriting, but it was also somewhere to learn about the realities of trying to get a project moved from words on a page to flickering images on a screen. "I was a young, green college kid and the producers ultimately didn't trust my instincts," said Widen matter-of-factly. "That is their right."

Richard Walter, Widen's UCLA teacher, tells me that he advises students to "pray their work will be taken from them and changed for the big screen. The worst thing that can happen to a writer is to be ignored. Screenwriting is collaboration. That is not its downside but its special nature, its joy. If you can't stand that, write novels. Collaborate comes from 'co' which means 'with' and 'labour' which means 'work'. Screenwriting is about working with others: directors, actors, editors, costume designers, hairdressers, carpenters, electricians and even lawyers."

"We were in a position where we're taking a 62-page document that was Widen's and turning it into a script of epic proportions," says Peter Bellwood. "Which is the reason the film has done so well, if I may be so bold as to say."

Ferguson and Bellwood have an easy rapport, with the former doing most of the talking during our conversation. Although neither is keen on using online services to chat ("Over the years I've made a ton of concessions to tech, but I've drawn the line at Skype," states Ferguson), I'm using it to call them, leading to a couple of unfortunate program crashes which don't faze them. "One of the reasons we're talking to you is that once the pop culture really began to embrace the movie, there were people who were secretaries to somebody who was a driver who claimed credit for a lot of stuff on that film," explains Ferguson.

When I ask about the pair's working process, Ferguson is quick to respond. "I don't think in a million years I could describe to you how magical it was. We each had different roles. Peter could type so much faster than I could, so I'd walk around and talk and supposedly he was writing down what I was saying. But I would say something like, 'George answers no' and 15 minutes later Peter was still over there typing, and I knew he was putting in something more than 'George answers no'. It was one of those things where it just clicked for us."

In early 1983, the pair began to forensically dissect the original 'Highlander' script, spitballing a number of potential directions in which the film could go. Initially they considered more of a science fiction approach, but that was quickly rejected by Panzer and Davis. "I think by page three, we'd spent around $200 million," says Ferguson. Although unwilling to be drawn any further on the finer details of the draft, clarifying that it was "more of a template to do a lot of different things", he does add that he recalls "entering the room, looking at [the producers] and they didn't have any blood in their faces".

Making changes

Following their hastily aborted science fiction approach, the decision was made by the writers to be more faithful to Gregory Widen's vision without being sentimental about any single part of it. If it made sense to retain something then so be it, otherwise they'd try something fresh.

For their earliest drafts, the writers started addressing the characters, making changes to names, backstories and motivations. As a result MacLeod's first name changed from Conor to Conner (which is how he'll be referred to in this chapter), while his 1980s alter ego changed from Richard Taupin to Russell Nash. "With Taupin, I think one day Peter asked me, 'Isn't that a pig?'" laughs Ferguson.

It was decided that the Knight would become the Prussian Count Von Krohn, while his 1980s alter ego was now Victor Kruger. Other characters to receive name changes included MacLeod's first love, who now became Kate instead of Mara; his modern-day love interest was no longer Brenna Cartwright but Brenda Wyatt; the Asian Ling Kahn swapped race to become the African Sarto Kastagir; and Juan Cid Romirez was now Juan Sanchez Ramirez. They also introduced a new love interest, Heather. In addition, the MacLeods now battled the Clan Fraser in flashbacks, erroneously spelled 'Frazer' in the script.

The action was moved from present-day Washington DC to New York, for the simple reason that the Big Apple is a more cinematic backdrop, with the opening confrontation between MacLeod/Nash and Iman Fasil expanded to give viewers a more energetic introduction to the world of the Immortals. Rather than taking place outside a porno house, the first scene was established at Madison Square Garden during a hockey match between the New York Rangers and the Edmonton Oilers.

The fight between MacLeod and Fasil is short and violent, leading to cars being pulverised and stone columns being bathed in a shower of sparks. While the confrontation is already more action-packed than Gregory Widen's draft, it also differs in the aftermath of Fasil's beheading by MacLeod. Rather than simply falling to the ground, a crystal-green cloud floats from Fasil's body, enveloping him. "He starts to glow," says the script, as the pair of Immortals are witnessed by a group of teenagers.

As in Gregory Widen's script, the storyline continues to switch between 16th-century Scotland and 1980s New York, with MacLeod being stopped by police as he tries to leave Madison Square Garden, before we meet him in 1536 in a flashback. MacLeod's place of birth changes from Ardvreck to Loch Shiel, in the shadow of Glamis Castle. Clearly this is some alternate universe version of Scotland, as in reality Glamis Castle is more than a three-hour drive from Loch Shiel, but if the reader is willing to accept immortal warriors then anything is possible.

As they began to immerse themselves in the finer details of the story, Bellwood and Ferguson knew they had to make changes to the overall tone of the piece. "It was just unalterably grim. People don't mind going into the darkness, but there has to be a reason for it and there was never any reason for what Gregory Widen had written as the Knight."

When Count Von Krohn is introduced he is reminding the clan chief, Lord Murdoch, that he's helping the Frasers on the condition that Conner MacLeod is his. When Von Krohn later drives his sword into MacLeod's stomach on the battlefield, MacLeod responds by "piledriving his sword into Von Krohn's armour, opening him like a tin can" before the enemy retreats into the mist, reminding the Scotsman that "in the end, there can only be one", a slight change from Widen's "there can be but one".

In the present day, Detective Frank Moran is introduced alongside Leon Brewster and Walter Bedsoe as three of the officers investigating Fasil's beheading. As news crews jostle for a view of the carnage, the cops are joined by Brenda Wyatt, assistant director in the Department of Forensics, along with her assistants, Greg and Ralph.

While MacLeod/Nash waits to be interviewed by police back at the station, he has a flashback to Nazi-occupied Budapest in 1942, where under the name Wallingford Benoit he's trying to help save the lives of 11 children who are hiding under a trapdoor in an apartment. MacLeod/Benoit bursts into the apartment, killing soldiers before securing travel permits for the family from a Gestapo officer, Vogel. As Benoit attempts to push the soldiers into the trap, Vogel states that Benoit will need to shoot him first. "Whatever you say, Jack. You're the master race," replies Benoit, before killing Vogel and kicking him into the trapdoor.

Later, as MacLeod/Benoit attempts to move the family across the Swiss border, he's shot by soldiers in front of one of the children. Hurling himself on top of the girl, the blood on Benoit's body reverses itself and the wounds disappear. "Why didn't you die?" asks the girl, to which Benoit replies, "Don't be afraid. It's a kind of magic." One of the children saved by Benoit/MacLeod is Rachel Ellenstein, who stays with MacLeod and becomes his surrogate daughter. By the time of the Gathering, Rachel is 60-years-old and working as his secretary.

The police interrogation from Gregory Widen's script turns up in the new draft, this time carried out by Detective Moran and Brewster, with some of the script's most offensive language cropping up as Brewster asks, "Are you a faggot, Nash?" before asking if he's "cruising for ass?" This scene would broadly remain the same in subsequent drafts.

Introducing the Quickening

An Immortal who receives more attention in Bellwood and Ferguson's script than Widen's is Ramirez, who reveals that his real name is Tak Ne, born in Egypt 2,437 years earlier, rather than Spain.

Ramirez is a useful tool for the screenwriters, providing an explanation for the strange energy clouds that depart the body of Immortals once they are beheaded, and the odd feeling that comes over them when another of their kind is nearby, occurrences known as the Quickening. This is a Ferguson and Bellwood concept that didn't exist in Gregory Widen's script, an idea that adds another layer of mysticism to the idea of immortality.

"The Quickening has a literal meaning: it's the first movement of a child in the mother's womb," explains Larry Ferguson. "Evidently a lot of people who talk about the movie didn't know that. I remember Peter and me discussing the Quickening and what it was. We were able to come up with something that had a meaning if somebody wanted to check it out."

A few years after creating the Quickening, the writers elaborated on its meaning in a memo entitled 'The Legend of The Prize' to Bill Panzer, Peter Davis and director Russell Mulcahy dated 15 April 1985. According to Ferguson and Bellwood, "each Immortal, at the moment of his death, surrenders all his Quickening to his opponent. It is this transfer of telepathic Quickening that is dramatised in the energy exchange between a decapitated Immortal and the victor." The memo notes that "nature has created an indeterminate number of Immortals. These Immortals are not the result of extraterrestrial influences . . . they are a natural phenomenon, the result of genetic misfunction. These Immortals can all be killed by a sword chopping off their heads, and each possesses a 'sixth sense' called 'The Quickening'. 'The Quickening' is a TELEPATHIC PHENOMENON".

Bellwood and Ferguson's April 1985 memo outlines the path to the Prize, making it clear that the only way it can be won is for the last six Immortals remaining in the world – each one possessing the telepathic energy of the Immortals they have killed – to take part in the Gathering. "THE PRIZE" IS 100% OF THE TELEPATHIC PIE – 100% OF "THE QUICKENING".

The first draft not only added more depth to the Immortals than existed in Gregory Widen's script, it also introduced new Immortals that wouldn't find their way into the film itself. Firstly, mention is made of a Bulgarian Immortal killed by Von Krohn in New Jersey, Osta Vazilek. In one scene, Von Krohn pulls out a vellum envelope with photographs of four Immortals described in the script as:

```
No. 1. Yung Dol Sing, an Oriental on a
freighter in New York Harbor.
No. 2. Sarto Kastagir, a suave African
leaving the Russian Tea Room.
No. 3. Russell Nash, hailing a cab on
Park Avenue.
No. 4. Ivan Timoshenko, a security
guard, sitting at TV monitors under a
sign: MALABAR, INC.
```

Von Krohn, disguised as a guard, opts to pursue Timoshenko at the Malabar building, while MacLeod, having escaped Bedsoe at the museum, is revealed to be fighting Yung Dol Sing in an abandoned warehouse by a river. At one point, despite having the upper hand, MacLeod/Nash shows that he's not interested in winning by refusing to kill Sing, saying:

                              NASH
To hell with the Prize. 400 years' killing
   is enough. I give you your life. Take it
                       and leave.

Sing doesn't take him up on the offer and tries to kill MacLeod as
he walks away. The Scotsman is too fast for his rival and takes his
head, a crystal-orange cloud rising from the corpse and engulfing
MacLeod, who begins to glow.

   Back on the 40th floor of the Malabar building, Von Krohn goads
Timoshenko into destroying desks, phones and a coffee machine.
"You fight like an old woman," says the Prussian before taking
the Russian's head. A crystal-blue cloud rises from Timoshenko,
causing Von Krohn to glow.

   Later, MacLeod again makes it clear that he's not interested in
the Prize, suggesting to Sarto Kastagir that the pair join forces to
fight Von Krohn. When Kastagir asks about tradition, MacLeod/
Nash replies:

                              NASH
Screw tradition. Sometimes I think I'm
  losing my mind. I never know where I am.
   Past, present and future – they're all
                     jumbled up.

Kastagir LAUGHS, sitting on a swing.

                           KASTAGIR
   I feel the same. It goes with the
   territory. My memory's always being
          triggered by something.

This could be seen as a metatextual comment on the style of both
the script and the editing of what would be the final film. While
the constant flashbacks and flashforwards are a visually interesting

way of telling the story, it seems they're also a glimpse into the head of Conner MacLeod, a way to understand what being an Immortal might mean to the subject's mental process. Unfortunately for MacLeod, Kastagir isn't keen on his proposal, and the latter comes to a nasty end by Von Krohn's sword, emitting a crystal-orange cloud when he dies.

Fleshing out the characters

In one scene, MacLeod, Brenda and Rachel have dinner, the latter encouraging the Highlander to tell the story of the time he fought a duel with a man called Bassett on Boston Common in 1797. At one point Rachel shows Brenda some of MacLeod's wealth, accumulated through the centuries and stored in banks around the world. Apparently he's lost track of how many. Rachel is also given her own subplot when she meets Detective Moran for the first time in MacLeod/Nash's shop. He asks her out for a drink, which she accepts towards the end of the script, though they enjoy a cold beer together at Moran's apartment after Rachel burns down MacLeod's shop, part of his plan to leave his old life behind.

Larry Ferguson mourns the loss of a moment between Conner and Brenda, which referenced the work of cardiac surgeon Christiaan Barnard, who performed the world's first heart transplant in 1967. It comes soon after MacLeod has given her a dagger to hold, before he takes her hand and plunges it into his heart to prove his immortality. The pair then have dinner and make love, resulting in Brenda confronting MacLeod about the difficulty he's had falling in love with another woman after losing Heather centuries before.

"We had a discussion between the two of them where she's talking about the fact a guy has invented a way of transplanting a human heart," explains Ferguson. "MacLeod says, 'I don't have heart problems,' and she says, 'Yes you do.'" Brenda explains that while Barnard couldn't guarantee a long life for his patients, he could guarantee them freedom from pain. "What is your point?" asks MacLeod.

BRENDA
My point is, Ramirez was wrong. Just one year of love, though it ends in death, is better than an eternity alone.

Brenda's dialogue riffs on one of the last lines in Gregory Widen's script, which found MacLeod asking Brenna "A moment of love, is that not worth a lifetime?", and it clearly resonated with Bellwood and Ferguson. "The beauty I found, and could never duplicate, was the extreme fun that I had with Peter when we were sitting there talking about what is a metaphor for this man and what is happening to him," says Ferguson. "He's being drawn back into something he's sworn he will never experience again. It's one thing, as Gregory Widen did, to have him say something, but it's another thing for him to take and put a dagger in her hand and pull that dagger straight to the stabbing of his heart. That's a wonderful metaphor."

MacLeod and Brenda's relationship is given more depth in the script, the pair walking through Bronx Zoo as Brenda opens up to MacLeod and explains that she'd had a plan to move on from forensics into a lectureship at Columbia, before marrying and having a couple of kids.

Gregory Widen had created a romantic subplot for MacLeod in the shape of Katherine, but the new writers opted to replace all events that took place in the town of Worstick, instead introducing a new love interest, Heather. One of the most important decisions made by Ferguson and Bellwood was to add a short scene emphasising the effect that the death of a human might have on an Immortal. Taking place in MacLeod and Heather's hut, the couple look back on their life together as Heather wishes she could have given her husband children, her life gradually ebbing away as he cradles her in his arms.

In more new dialogue, MacLeod recalls his friend Ramirez as he buries Heather:

```
                  MACLEOD
   You were right, haggis. I cheated her.
  Robbed her of a full life. There will be
                  no more.
```

MacLeod vs Von Krohn

In Gregory Widen's script the final confrontation between MacLeod and the Knight took place at Washington DC's Jefferson Memorial, but the move to New York required a different location. This time, Von Krohn lures MacLeod to Coney Island Amusement Park, where the pair proceed to demolish roller coaster pilings, arcades and Ferris wheel chairs, battling beneath a giant fruit with the words 'Fun in the Big Apple' emblazoned upon it.

During the course of their fight, MacLeod realises that his opponent is scared of him and that rather than running away from Von Krohn through the centuries, it was actually Von Krohn who was running from the Scotsman, terrified to face him. "You're not the perfect killing machine. You're a coward," says MacLeod to Von Krohn, before slicing off his enemy's head and watching a crystal-purple cloud leave the Prussian's corpse and swirl around MacLeod's body. Brenda then watches as MacLeod glows all the colours of the rainbow. According to the script, "His hair stands on end. Color erupts from his eyes. He's like a Roman candle against the waves. The wind howls."

In Ferguson and Bellwood's 1985 memo, they have more to say about the Prize, noting that each Immortal "has within him the combined Quickening of all his fallen opponents, and their fallen opponents, and their fallen opponents, and so on . . . [MacLeod] gets it all. He gets 'The Prize'. It doesn't come in manageable portions. It overwhelms him in one, mind-bending blast: TOTAL

TELEPATHIC AWARENESS. Billions upon billions of thoughts, feelings, instincts, wishes, dreams, secret desires, all jumbled and tumbling and boiling over in one great ROAR!"

In the script, MacLeod states that he is "the global brain. The night air is my breath. The life-force smothers me. I can feel everything."

Towards the end of the script, MacLeod and Brenda are travelling on an ocean liner, with the former explaining that he's now able to control the Quickening, turning it up and down and tuning in to different stations. Says Larry Ferguson, "Peter and I had something we both loved and cared about, which was that [MacLeod] could hear everyone's thoughts on the planet and that it was really, really loud and it made him a little crazy, but he was carefully learning how he could turn the volume down."

As scripted, MacLeod explains that there's a man and woman living in adjoining houses in Paris who are in love with each other, but who never speak. Elsewhere, a man in Honduras is planning a coup to overthrow the government. MacLeod suggests he and Brenda go to Paris to introduce the neighbours to each other.

As the pair fall deeper in love, MacLeod says to Brenda that "just one year of love is better than a painful eternity alone", echoing her comment from earlier, before Brenda produces a bottle of 1976 plum brandy, leading MacLeod to recite facts to her about the year's events, including *One Flew Over the Cuckoo's Nest* winning five Academy Awards and the discovery of a new atomic particle by US scientists. Brenda then quotes from Dylan Thomas' *Fern Hill*, before the pair state their love for each other, kiss, and the liner sails away.

The (almost) final draft

Larry Ferguson and Peter Bellwood's early drafts of the script were effectively stepping stones from Gregory Widen's version to what would become the final shooting script. Following discussions with producers Peter Davis and Bill Panzer, it was agreed that another draft was required, which would further refine the screenwriters' vision of a world inhabited by Immortals.

Though a script exists in the vaults of the British Film Institute dated 6 February 1985 that is theoretically the final draft, it also includes further changes printed on pink pages dated 25 March 1985. By this point some characters' names had changed, including MacLeod, whose first name clearly caused the writers some confusion – on white pages he's Conner, while on some pink pages he changes to Connor, the latter version continuing through to the film itself (and how he'll be referred to in this book going forward). Ramirez's name is extended slightly to become Juan Sanchez Villa-Lobos Ramirez, and Sarto Kastagir becomes Sunda Kastagir.

Perhaps the most significant name change came while Ferguson and Bellwood continued their meticulous research process. Count Von Krohn would soon go through a metamorphosis. "One day the two of us were scrolling through some history books and we came across a group of people on the Russian Steppes who were terrifying," says Ferguson. "They would throw babies into a pit with wolves to see if the baby could survive, and they were called the Kurgans. That always made much more sense to us than the Knight, who had no character. I remember the two of us really having a lot of fun with his character in particular."

This draft saw Connor's family grow, with Dugal and Angus now identified as his cousins, rather than simply his friends. New dialogue, such as Angus admitting he "peed his kilt" the first time he rode into battle, made its first appearance here.

Another debut is a line of dialogue that existed in earlier drafts in a different form, but which would go on to be the most quoted from the film. Gregory Widen had the Knight whisper, "There can be but one," while in Bellwood and Ferguson's early drafts Von Krohn shouts, "There can only be one." By the final draft the writers had decided to tweak it once more. Says Ferguson, "Peter and I would walk past each other saying, 'Can there only be one?', 'Can there be only one?', and we came up with 'There can be only one', which I felt poetically lifted the film out of a kind of B-movie into something else."

The characters of Yung Dol Sing and Ivan Timoshenko are merged into one and renamed Yung Dol Kim, with Kim's fight now taking place in the office against the Kurgan. The fight at the docks detailed in the earlier draft was now removed for good.

The relationship between MacLeod and Kastagir is given an extra dimension, as the pair are followed from Central Park to a New York bar by Bedsoe, who is tailing the Highlander. The Immortals are aware of the policeman's presence and proceed to blow his cover and get him drunk, before MacLeod tells him about his encounter with Bassett on Boston Common and the script presents the reader with a flashback to their sword fight.

Moran (now a lieutenant) and Rachel's romantic subplot remains in later drafts, the pair still meeting in the antiques shop and culminating in Rachel meeting Moran on the sidewalk as Nash's shop burns towards the end of the film. The pair agree to go for a coffee. After this, Bedsoe receives a delivery of MacLeod's aquarium which has been saved from the burning building, referencing an earlier scene in which the pair met in MacLeod's shop.

The ending also remains, with MacLeod and Brenda professing their love for each other before sailing away on a cruise liner.

After multiple drafts and discussions with producers Peter Davis and Bill Panzer, Peter Bellwood and Larry Ferguson had a script that could be shopped around to potential funders. The only question now was whether anyone would be interested in such a quirky story that jumped between time periods and mixed comedy with historical drama with a dash of romance.

THREE

KING OF THE POP PROMO

The history of music videos can be divided into two distinct eras: BRM (Before Russell Mulcahy) and ARM (After Russell Mulcahy).

MTV exploded onto American TV screens at 12:01 Eastern Time on Saturday 1 August 1981, ushering in a new way of discovering and listening to music. Running for 24 hours a day, seven days a week, the first video played was 'Video Killed the Radio Star' by British band The Buggles, an ironic statement by the new station's owners that the old medium was about to be replaced by something bigger, in your face and, most importantly, in your living room.

The song had been written in 1978, but it wasn't until September 1979 that the band recorded and released it, complete with a music video shot by the 27-year-old Australian director Russell Mulcahy on a one-day shoot in south London. Years later, Mulcahy recalled that on the day "no one really knew what they were doing, including me". In 1979 the music video hadn't established itself as a promotional tool around the globe: on MTV's opening night, the channel's co-founder, Bob Pittman, estimated there were just 250 music videos in existence, and MTV didn't even have them all.

Not that Mulcahy was completely in the dark. Back in Australia he'd been working in TV since the early 1970s, editing news programmes on the Seven Network. Although his love of the moving image stretched back to his teenage years – his mother buying him an 8mm camera at the age of 14 sparked his passion for making films – he entered the industry with the type of resourcefulness that would define his career. On approaching a TV station on the off-chance of work and being asked if he'd ever edited a 16mm film, Mulcahy confirmed that he had, despite never having touched it. "I learned everything in roughly half an hour. I've bluffed a lot of things in my life."

The young editor made the most of Seven's facilities, arriving in the editing room at three in the morning and cutting his own films on 16mm. Mulcahy happened to be working at the channel at the same time as former radio DJ Graham Webb was putting together a weekly music show for teenagers, *Sounds Unlimited*, later shortened to *Sounds*. In need of new clips of bands performing, Webb approached Mulcahy and asked that he film a batch for him. "My early promos were like little frustrated features. I was running round in an old beat-up station wagon with a tripod and camera and that was the company."

Mulcahy's inspiration in his teenage years came mainly from European film-makers such as Federico Fellini, Ingmar Bergman and Ken Russell's early work, noting that "they had a freedom in their work, which I liked. They broke the rules; the camera crossed the line and it didn't matter." When a couple of Mulcahy's narrative films won the Sydney Short Film Festival for two years in a row, he used the prize money to set up his own company, later stating proudly, "I invented the pop promo in Australia."

Making it big

Having worked full-time on music videos with Australian groups such as AC/DC and Hush, Mulcahy made his way to London in 1978 to direct a video for Birmingham group Garbo and the Death Eaters, followed by the comedy documentary film *Derek and Clive Get the Horn* starring Peter Cook and Dudley Moore. He was soon earning £50 a week working alongside music video director and producer Jon Roseman, before teaming up with conceptualist Keith Williams, who would go on to dream up ideas for videos such as Ray Parker Jr's 'Ghostbusters' and Bonnie Tyler's 'Holding Out for a Hero'. The pair would work well into the night on their latest projects, Mulcahy sleeping on the couch of Williams' Ladbroke Grove flat.

The process for developing a new video was relatively simple for Mulcahy, with bands sending him a cassette of the song, him listening to it with his eyes closed, before he came up with an idea that would enter production a few days later. "It really was just grab what you can and do it . . . Ultravox gave me a cassette of their song 'Vienna'. I listened to the song and told them, 'I have this idea of you guys in gondolas.' I was a typical Australian, not knowing anything about Europe. They said, 'No, it's Vienna, not Venice!'"

Next, Mulcahy formed a production company, MGMM, with three other music video pioneers: directors David Mallet and Brian Grant, and producer Scott Millaney, going on to direct for acts such as Ultravox, Spandau Ballet and Supertramp while winning plenty of awards in the process for his experimental style. It was his work on Kim Carnes' 'Bette Davis Eyes' that cemented his reputation as the king of the music video. The video went into heavy rotation on American television, helping the single stay at number one in the charts for nine weeks and becoming Billboard's biggest hit of 1981.

"It broke every rule of what is and what isn't allowed on television; it was the most creative thing I'd ever seen on TV," said fellow music video director Marty Callner after catching 'Bette Davis Eyes' on pay cable station, the Z Channel. Mulcahy's director of photography, Daniel Pearl, stated that "Russell was a visionary. The whole genre was kind of his baby," going on to describe his directorial style as "organised chaos . . . we had a policy not to break the rules, but to blow up the fucking rules."

Cinematographer Tony Mitchell, who worked with Mulcahy on multiple videos, describes the 1980s as a "great time for music.

It was a brilliant time for fashion. It was a brilliant time for TV. And it was a great time for young film-makers. Go out and be fucking great, come up with a good fucking idea. MTV changed everything."

Mitchell remembers that working with Mulcahy meant decisions were often made on the spur of the moment, no matter the budget. "We were in London, shooting Tina Turner. We were at the office of MGMM and I'm there with Russell, a production manager and a producer having drinks. It's getting late and we all went down into the basement and started watching black-and-white movies. [We were talking] and we rewrote the script the day before the shoot. We snorted coke and drank all night, went from there to the studio with a whole new script, showed it to Tina and the agents. Everybody freaked out a little bit and that's what we shot. I don't remember half the things I did to be honest."

"We would work 17-hour days," says Mulcahy from his home in California. After a year of emailing back and forth, we're finally sitting down to discuss those heady music video days. "I remember doing 'I'm Still Standing' and we finished at 5 a.m., then I got on a bus or ferry back to England and we did 'I Guess That's Why They Call it the Blues', then it was straight on to a film. They were crazy days, but days I cherish."

By 1982, Mulcahy was one of the hardest-working directors in music videos, with a slew of his three-minute epics being beamed into homes around the globe and acting like calling cards for the one-man video industry. Following a collaboration between the director and British New Wave band Duran Duran on their debut video, 1981's 'Planet Earth', Mulcahy was called upon to shoot the video for the forthcoming 'Hungry Like the Wolf'. Courtesy of record label EMI, the production headed for Sri Lanka in the spring of 1982 to film a storyline described simply by band member Andy Taylor as "Indiana Jones is horny and wants to get laid".

Thanks to a slump in the British film industry during the 1970s, a new breed of director had emerged from the country's TV commercial industry, learning the ropes on small-screen budgets.

By 1983, the likes of Ridley Scott (*Alien*, 1979), Alan Parker (*Midnight Express*, 1978) and Adrian Lyne (*Flashdance*, 1983) had successfully transitioned to the big screen and found international success. By 1983, the pop promo was the new commercial and young directors such as Russell Mulcahy were perfectly placed to transfer their kinetic style to feature films.

When 'Hungry Like the Wolf' made its debut on MTV in the summer of 1982 it was soon being shown four times a day, leading to increased radio airplay and, ultimately, a place in the top five of the Billboard Hot 100. By 1983, the video had also caught the eye of an Australian producer, Hal McElroy, who knew Russell Mulcahy. "[He] rang me up in London and said, 'Do you want to come and do a movie in Australia?' I was a frustrated moviemaker and I went, 'Oh my God, yes, yes!' Then I said, 'What's it about?' and he said, 'Oh, it's about a giant killer pig.' And I said, 'Great!' and I went off to make *Razorback*."

Going hog wild

Set in the barren Australian outback, *Razorback* pits man against pig as a giant boar attacks Jake Cullen (Bill Kerr) in his home and steals his grandson, leading locals to doubt his story. When an American wildlife reporter, Beth Winters (Judy Morris), heads to the area to investigate potentially illegal goings-on at a pet food factory, she too is killed by the boar, forcing her husband, Carl Winters (Gregory Harrison) to follow in her footsteps. When Winters discovers that wild pigs are becoming unusually aggressive, he decides to get to the bottom of the problem and finds himself coming face to snout with the razorback.

Mulcahy may have been something of a veteran when it came to music videos, but a 90-minute feature with a \$A5.5 million budget was a very different proposition. On arriving in the outback a day before principal photography began on the eight-week shoot, he was overwhelmed by the responsibility that rested on his shoulders.

Admitting that the crew, which included cinematographer Dean Semler, initially doubted his capabilities until they saw the first day's rushes, the director likened the shoot to a roller coaster: "There was just no stopping it and you went with the flow."

At one point during the shoot Mulcahy was concerned about the ending and offered to pay for a reshoot out of his own pocket to the tune of $A20,000, something Warner Bros. refused. The studio may have stumped up a portion of the film's budget in exchange for US distribution rights, but after a disastrous preview in Los Angeles they dropped the film from their release schedule. The preview cards highlighted that the audience felt the experience of viewing *Razorback* was like watching a two-hour MTV video, something the director acknowledged. "I know I'm always going to be categorised by working in pop promos and there really isn't much I can do about that. It will be like a millstone around my neck for the rest of my life."

One of the most interesting glimpses into Mulcahy's approach to film-making came towards the end of an interview with *Starburst* magazine, when along with reflecting on the influence of directors Alfred Hitchcock and Stanley Kubrick and his love of fantasy films, he noted that his painting background inspired his colour sense and composition. He also told how his old collaborator Keith Williams said that the film "looked like someone had told me it was to be my first and only film, so sling everything in you can".

Despite giving *Razorback* everything he had, the film failed to set the box office alight, with middling reviews helping to keep the audience away, as well as a poor marketing campaign. Mulcahy succinctly summed up what he thought was the biggest issue, the question of who actually wants to go and see a film about a giant killer pig. Unlike the producers, he never saw it as a potential box-office smash, but a "thriller for horror fans . . . who were sick to death of seeing the same old splatter. As entertaining as possible with the interest kept at a dynamic level whenever the story showed signs of flagging. As far as I'm concerned, *Razorback* was one from the heart."

After his adventures Down Under on *Razorback,* Mulcahy went back to the familiar routine of travelling back and forth between England and America shooting more music videos. "It wasn't until I did another Duran Duran video called 'The Wild Boys' a couple of years later that they rang me up and said, 'Do you want to come and do *Highlander?*'"

Finding a backer

Once they'd received a script they were happy with from screenwriters Peter Bellwood and Larry Ferguson, producers Peter Davis and Bill Panzer had started trying to drum up interest in *Highlander* from financiers.

Thanks to a deal they'd struck with 20th Century Fox, the pair were assured of guaranteed distribution in the United States on six films. Though Fox wouldn't put up any production funding, they would distribute Davis-Panzer films on a "very aggressive basis", allowing the producers to secure total funding from elsewhere. The theory was that any investor would be enticed by a strong release in the US.

The person tasked with finding a willing investor was Michael Ryan, who started his career in the UK TV industry in the 1970s, before co-founding J&M Entertainment in 1978 and becoming a distribution sales agent for independent films. By the early 1980s, Ryan's J&M Film Sales company was working with Davis-Panzer on their latest project, 1983's *The Osterman Weekend.*

When it came to *Highlander*, Ryan found a receptive audience in British production company Thorn EMI Screen Entertainment (TESE) in late 1984, explaining to *Screen International* that "they took the world outside the US for *Highlander* and covered the budget". Talking in 1985, Peter Davis explained that EMI "thought it was terrific. That, plus an unusual distribution deal in the US and the belief that they could do very well in the foreign marketplace and with worldwide video, coalesced their interests."

A press release announcing the deal was issued by Davis-Panzer on 6 November 1984, noting that the film was budgeted at $13.8 million and that it would be shot in early 1985 in Scotland, London and New York locations.

The history of TESE – formerly known as EMI, MGM-EMI and Anglo-EMI – stretched back to the early 1930s, the result of numerous mergers and demergers that saw it become involved in television broadcasting, retail/rentals, defence, music and consumer electronics. Films such as Lionel Jeffries' *The Railway Children* (1970), Joseph Losey's *The Go-Between* (1970) and Mike Hodges' *Get Carter* (1971) were funded and distributed by EMI in its early years, with the success of 1974's *Murder on the Orient Express* – on a budget of $1.5 million it grossed more than $19.1 million in US rentals alone and became the ninth highest grossing British film of the 1970s – cited as the point the traditionally British company became a transnational company.

Despite EMI's successes with films such as the Oscar-winning *The Deer Hunter* in 1979 and David Lynch's *The Elephant Man* in 1980, the decision to invest in the musical comedy, *Can't Stop the Music* (1980) proved to be a flawed one when the film bombed at the box office. Internal strife followed at Thorn EMI as new management tried to get their finances in order, with ex-*Doctor Who* producer Verity Lambert hired as head of production in 1982, while also remaining as the head of Thames Television subsidiary, Euston Films. Along with newly arrived chief executive Gary Dartnall, the pair oversaw a slew of lower budget productions.

"*Highlander* was a huge investment," says David Semple, business affairs administrator at Thorn EMI from 1982 to 1986. Unsure of his company's latest project, one weekend in 1985 he decided to take home a copy of the film's script. "The reason I read it was because I said, 'What the fuck are we investing in?' You work in a company and you hear all these rumours about the film, and the accountants keep coming up and saying, 'You see what they're spending on?' and I thought we were spending a hell of a lot of money on a hell of a lot of films; how were we going to make this back? I didn't think that we'd negotiated a good deal on that because we were 100% financing the film but we weren't getting 100% of the world market. I think it was originally around £12 million and went up to £19 million."

According to Semple, Thorn EMI forecast that the film would earn around £25 million in worldwide sales. "EMI had to put up more money, but the completion guarantor put in money too. 20th Century Fox had the theatrical rights in the States and I believe TV rights, but EMI had the video distribution rights, Thorn EMI HBO video in the United States. We handled direct video distribution in a lot of territories and then we had licences for the other territories."

For Gregory Widen, who had been receiving cheques for a few thousand dollars per year while his script was being rewritten and touted to different funders, the deal meant he finally received a more substantial payment of around £250,000.

Thanks to the tax cuts and other benefits that came from *Highlander* qualifying as a British film, it meant a certain quota of actors and members of the production team had to be from the UK, while producers Peter Davis and Bill Panzer had to live in England for the 14-month production period. Noted Panzer, "We were socially comfortable in Europe, we liked being there. We liked having people with a different point of view than you just get in this five-mile area in Hollywood. The idea of basing ourselves in England and shooting in England and in Scotland, and a little bit in New York . . . was very attractive, because British [crews have] always been great."

Davis and Panzer's search for a director had begun when 20th Century Fox asked them who they were planning to helm the film. They'd worked with the great Sam Peckinpah on *The Osterman Weekend*, but as Bill Panzer stated, "Many of my favourite directors were dead." As they started asking agents to suggest names of potential directors, one film they were encouraged to watch by Michael Ryan was the recently released *Razorback*.

Ryan's J&M Film Sales had bought and distributed *Razorback* in the foreign marketplace. Impressed by the film, the producers then tracked down some of Russell Mulcahy's music videos, and were soon convinced of the director's talent. "There were certain aspects [of *Razorback*] we didn't like," admitted Panzer, "but I think that pointed to the story and the material rather than to Russell's work in it. You could really see he had a very unique style of shooting."

After debating whether to go down the route of playing it safe with the film, trusting a more experienced director to deliver a competent final print with little controversy, or to take a chance on something less conventional, the producers opted for the latter. "*Highlander* cried out for a willingness to roll the dice and go for it," said Davis. "To really take someone who could take very interesting material and bring a great visual style that would enhance the material."

With the blessing of Fox President and CEO, Larry Gordon, who had also seen and enjoyed *Razorback*, Panzer and Davis set up a meeting with Russell Mulcahy at a London hotel to discuss the script. Mulcahy quickly hit it off with the producers, running through some of the ideas he had about the project. "All of a sudden I'd got the job," he recalls. "It was such a passion project because I thought the script was a combination of adventure, romance, tragedy and everything combined. Thank God for Greg Widen who wrote the original."

"In *Highlander* [Russell] got his first chance to tell a story with human beings rather than rock stars or a pig," noted Bill Panzer in 1986.

As screenwriter Peter Bellwood remembers, it was Panzer who phoned to let him know that Mulcahy had been offered the job, explaining that he'd recently finished a series of videos for Duran Duran. "I said to Bill, 'Has he made any movies?' and Panzer said, 'Yeah, he made one movie.' When I got off the phone I called Larry [Ferguson] and said, 'They're going to hire this guy, Russell Mulcahy,' and Larry said, 'Great, what's he done?' and I said, 'Well, he's only made one movie, it's called *Razorback* and at the climax of the movie, the heroine is eaten by a giant warthog.' There was a long pause and Larry said, 'This may be our guy!'"

A press release announcing the hiring of Mulcahy was drafted on 18 December 1984. "I had a great working relationship with Larry Ferguson and Peter Bellwood, who were just the most wonderful gentlemen," says the director.

Though developments at Thorn EMI in the spring of 1985 would lead to more changes in the company's management team that would have a major effect on *Highlander*, this wasn't of much concern to Davis-Panzer who were getting ready to enter pre-production.

FOUR

SETTING THE SCENE

Not everyone who works on a film gets the credit they deserve. They might turn up day after day on locations far from home, work long hours and not see much of their friends and family for months on end, but when it comes to the end titles of a film, their name somehow drops off the list.

Scan the end titles of *Highlander* and you won't see the name Joe Haidar scrolling past, but pay a visit to the film's listing on IMDb and you'll find the words: Joe Haidar – storyboard artist (uncredited).

A commercial animator in his native Canada, Haidar had travelled to London in the early 1980s to work in the city's vibrant animation industry as "it seemed all the really great stuff was being done out there". At just 24-years-old, Haidar didn't have much experience, but he was encouraged by the fact that Richard Williams, another expat Canadian animator dubbed England's own Walt Disney, was working there.

Haidar had always wanted to try his hand at storyboarding a live action film, sketching out each scene from a script to help the director and production team better visualise the picture they were about to make. Through a series of personal and professional connections, Haidar met Allan Cameron, an English production designer who was making the transition from working on television to films, including Michael Radford's visually impressive *1984*, released in 1984. "[Allan] was doing a movie at the time called *Lady Jane* and he needed a storyboard artist. He ultimately turned me down because I wasn't in the union," recalls Haidar.

Six months later, the film gods smiled on the still unemployed Canadian when he sat down to dinner at Grunts, a Chicago pizza restaurant in Covent Garden which sat patrons at tables with other people. Haidar found himself sitting with a complete stranger, who turned out to be a set designer. "We started chatting and the only person I knew in the live action world was Allan Cameron. I mentioned him and he said, 'Oh my God, you really must call him right now; he's looking for a storyboard artist!' I thought that was really insane, but I called him the next day."

During the call, Cameron explained that due to the value of the British pound suddenly being on a par with the US dollar, a raft of American productions had flooded England and hired all the available storyboard artists. Desperate for work, Haidar accepted the offer of a job on Cameron's new film, before being invited to Twickenham Studios to meet production manager, Eva Monley. Thanks to his lack of industry experience, Haidar had no idea how much to quote the producer for his work, adding £50 to his usual animation salary. "Everyone in the room, including Allan Cameron, broke out laughing. Eva said, 'Oh, I think we can do better than that,' and gave me twice what I asked for, which blew me away. Later on I discovered it was half of what a storyboard artist earned at that time."

With his family hailing from the west coast of Scotland, 40-year-old Allan Cameron's interest had been piqued a few weeks prior to Haidar's call when he'd heard rumblings that a film called *Highlander* was about to go into pre-production in London. He was surprised to receive a phone call from Russell Mulcahy, inviting him to Blakes Hotel in South Kensington for a chat. "I'd never met him before," said Cameron years later in a DVD featurette, though he was aware of Mulcahy's pop promo work, in particular 'The Wild Boys'. "We got on pretty well . . . I read the script and loved it and about a week later, he said, 'Would you like to do the film?'"

A memo from Peter Davis dated Tuesday 19 February 1985 confirms Cameron's hiring, also noting that Eva Monley had been retained as associate producer and noting that he and Bill Panzer "continue to be extremely excited about Russell Mulcahy. The ideas and freshness he brings to the project are quite extraordinary."

"Allan came in early and we sat down and did thumbnail sketches," explained Mulcahy in an interview for the film's press notes carried out in 1985. "Then we began doing drawings even before we had been to Scotland. Surprisingly enough, we drew villages and the forge on the hills and we have been able to find them pretty well how we envisaged them and without even knowing what we were going to shoot."

Though Mulcahy had the final say on working with Allan Cameron, the director's initial talk to the production designer was born out of a legal requirement necessitated by the producers' decision to source their funding from a British film distributor, Thorn EMI Screen Entertainment. For the same reason, Mulcahy's first choice for a cinematographer, his *Razorback* colleague Dean Semler, fell through at an early stage, though not before he visited Scotland on a location shoot in April 1985. "That wasn't going to work because of the quotas, which kind of pissed us off at the time," said Bill Panzer of the decision.

Another early choice of Mulcahy's was the New York-based Tony Mitchell, the music video veteran who had worked with him on numerous productions. "When Russell first got *Highlander* he asked me if I'd shoot it," says Mitchell. "I didn't even think about how big it was. It was just Russell asking me to shoot another big fucking project for him. We'd worked with each other for years. I said, 'What are you talking about, you're crazy, of course I'll do it.' And then the producers didn't want me because I'd never shot a movie."

Once again the producers looked at British cinematographers who might be interested in working on the film, their attention falling on Gerry Fisher. Contemporary production notes claimed that hiring Gerry Fisher was Sean Connery's idea following a plane journey that the pair shared en route to England from Switzerland.

Connery and Fisher had previously worked together on Sidney Lumet's 1973 film, *The Offence*. Connery is quoted as saying of British cameramen: "We know they are probably the best. One doesn't say that because one is British, but it is recognised as such. Nobody seems to be able to give a really good reason why."

Fisher was a veteran of British cinema who had worked on films such as Richard Fleischer's *See No Evil* (1971) and William Peter Blatty's *The Ninth Configuration* (1980). After being called for an interview with the *Highlander* director, Fisher familiarised himself with *Razorback*, later stating he thought the film was "really wild, kind of like a pop video . . . I could also see that he had a very sharp sense of editing, and a lot of sense of fun too, so the thing progressed and they asked me to do it". Mulcahy was keen to carry over the style he used on *Razorback* to *Highlander*, forcing the more experienced Fisher to adapt to a new way of working. Mulcahy made it clear he was looking for constant movement in scenes and a heightened state of reality.

Despite the 57-year-old Fisher giving his all professionally to the film, art director Tim Hutchinson, brought onto the production to work alongside Allan Cameron, isn't convinced that Mulcahy's pop video sensibilities and pace of working were a perfect match. "Gerry was always quite a miserable person, I thought. There was quite an age gap between him and Russell, whereas Allan Cameron, Russell and I were all much closer in age."

Joe Haidar hadn't heard of Russell Mulcahy before he started work on *Highlander*, but he was aware of his company, MGMM, and knew of *Razorback*. "He seemed only a few years older than me, and he took me under his wing at Twickenham Studios; he kept me inside his office and I really didn't know what I was doing. I don't know how I survived that time."

Thanks to Allan Cameron's personal knowledge of Scotland's west coast, after reading through the script he soon had ideas about which exterior locations the production could visit in the spring of 1985. On Tuesday 19 February, Cameron and Tim Hutchinson took an early morning flight from London to Glasgow to meet location manager Brian Donovan, before driving to Fort William to kit themselves out in suitable clothing for the cold weather. That evening, the trio headed west to a snowy Kyle of Lochalsh to take the ferry across to Skye, a decade before the opening of the Skye Bridge.

After a spin around the island, taking in the Cuillin Hills and in particular the Cioch Buttress on Sron Na Ciche, the team headed to the tiny village of Dornie, home to Eilean Donan Castle. "The castle is fabulous," says Hutchinson. "It was the first time I'd been and Allan knew exactly where we were going. He suggested that it would be Glamis Castle, that we could dress the bridge and that's where we'd first see MacLeod."

The next day saw Cameron, Hutchinson and Donovan visit locations including Loch Shiel, Glen Nevis and Loch Insh, before arriving at Glencoe, which Cameron felt would work well for the battle and the exterior forge where MacLeod is exiled. On the evening of Friday 22 February the three men travelled to the town of Kingussie, where they stayed overnight at the Osprey Hotel, before Cameron and Hutchinson headed back down to Glasgow via Stirling on the Saturday for a flight home to London. Although they visited Scotland for less than a week, they took hundreds of photos back with them to show a delighted Russell Mulcahy, Peter Davis and Bill Panzer at Twickenham Studios, who agreed to almost all of the suggestions.

Allan Cameron may have been one of the team taking care of the look of the film, but costume designer James Acheson was brought aboard to focus on the appearance of the actors. He'd made a name for himself at the BBC in the 1970s, most notably on the long-running science fiction series, *Doctor Who* (1963–), but by the early 1980s he had moved into features on films such as *Time Bandits* (1980) and *Monty Python's The Meaning of Life* (1983). By early 1985, Acheson was looking for work and aware of Russell Mulcahy's growing reputation.

"I chased the job because I don't think I had an agent at the time and I remember I really enjoyed the 'Wild Boys' video with this guy chained to a windmill," says Acheson. "It was all really strange and moody and it was directed by Russell Mulcahy. I remember thinking, 'I'd really like to work with that guy,' and then I discovered he was making *Highlander*. I got a hold of him but he'd already found somebody: he got rid of the guy who was doing it and gave it to me. I think he'd seen a film I did called *Brazil* and because of that I got the film."

Another early addition to the crew came about when film editor Peter Honess (*Electric Dreams*, 1984), who was working on another film at Twickenham Studios while pre-production was under way on *Highlander*, heard that *Razorback* director Russell Mulcahy was working nearby. Having seen and enjoyed Mulcahy's giant pig creature feature, he made himself known to the director and the pair quickly hit it off. "He took me through the storyboard that he was working on and offered me the movie." Unlike other members of the crew, Honess didn't start work on the film until reels of film came back from the first day of shooting.

Introducing Silvercup

Just as a recce was required for the Scottish sequences, one was also carried out for New York, with a small team including Russell Mulcahy and Allan Cameron heading out in February 1985. As well as visiting Central Park and looking for suitable exteriors for MacLeod's antiques shop, Cameron was keen to visit a selection of New York apartments to help influence his design for MacLeod's spacious loft.

Since they would be building the apartment in London, it also meant adding windows that looked out over the Manhattan skyline, something Cameron achieved by collaborating with the New York crew during his recce. Cameron organised for large cameras to be placed on the roofs of buildings around the city so that they could then be developed back in England as translights, large illuminated backdrops that could be erected outside windows to trick viewers into thinking they were looking out at New York.

At the end of Larry Ferguson and Peter Bellwood's *Highlander* script, the final battle between the Kurgan and MacLeod took place at a collapsing roller coaster at Brooklyn's Coney Island amusement park. Having tried hard to work out a way to make the sequence work, Cameron had come to the conclusion that the logistics and cost would be too prohibitive for his budget. Luckily a solution presented itself during their New York visit. "Russell and I had been driving across one of the bridges and we saw the Silvercup in the distance," said Cameron, referencing the old Silvercup Bakery building which had recently been converted into a film studio. "We both looked at each other [and said], 'Maybe we should stage it on that and the sign could fall down.'"

The decision to alter the location meant that Ferguson and Bellwood were required to work on more rewrites in March, submitting their script dated 3 April to producers Bill Panzer and Peter Davis on 8 April. The rewrite was accompanied by a letter from the writers explaining that they had even more ideas for changes. These were to incorporate new research that had been carried out on the way metal is folded in Japanese swords, along with new geographical information about the true seat of the Clan MacLeod. This latter information never made it into the script, with the real clan associated with the Isle of Skye rather than Glenfinnan.

This new draft incorporated requests for the use of Silvercup as the backdrop to the final fight, with the Kurgan properly introducing himself to Brenda having kidnapped her and brought her to the building.

KURGAN

I am Kurgan. Warrior eternal. I have carved my name in the flesh of Venetian princes, raped the daughters of Attila the Hun and set ablaze the Seven Hills of Rome.

On his arrival, MacLeod forces the Kurgan onto the roof for their sword fight, demolishing chimneys and air-conditioning units as they go. Having shattered a water tower and fallen into the building below, the pair fight inside a vast kitchen, with MacLeod exhausting his enemy so that the Kurgan has no energy to raise his sword.

                    MACLEOD
For Heather, Ramirez, Kastagir and all the
    others I never knew. And last, for the
  Highlander MacLeod of the Clan MacLeod —

He raises his Samurai.

                    MACLEOD
      There can be only one.

MacLeod then cuts off the Kurgan's head, "centuries of pent-up energy released in a mind-bending EXPLOSION", stretches out his arms and experiences "a THUNDERING waterfall of light – red, purple, yellow and blue clouds" swirling around him as he experiences what he calls the Prize. His body transforms into different people – Ramirez, Fasil, the Kurgan and unknown figures – as voices echo around him. The final scenes were now set back in Scotland, with the dialogue largely similar to that of the earlier scripts.

This draft also introduced a new opening sequence, still set inside Madison Square Garden, but now featuring a wrestling match instead of a hockey game. The decision to change sports was a result of the National Hockey League denying the request, as they felt it would show hockey as a violent sport.

The scripted fight was between real-life wrestlers Sergeant Slaughter and The Iron Sheik, real names Robert Rudolph Remus and Hossein Khosrow Ali Vaziri respectively, two major names in the early 1980s. "We realise it may not be practical to have them fight just for this movie," wrote Bellwood and Ferguson in a note to the producers, "and that you will be shooting whatever the card is on the night you're in the Garden."

As the crowd chants, "Iran sucks," Connor MacLeod watches dispassionately as in his mind the Sheik becomes a 15th-century Highlander wielding a broadsword. The writers were clearly uneasy about the change to wrestling, noting in their memo that it was "wholly appropriate" for hockey sticks to become broadswords in MacLeod's mind and remind him of a battle, while wrestling could be "something grafted on to the action arbitrarily". They also questioned at which point the first flashback should be incorporated into the action, wondering if it would be less confusing for the viewer if it was during the fight with Fasil in the car park.

It appears that the writers were asked to explain why MacLeod was at a wrestling match in the first place, the theory being that he was too sophisticated to attend one. "We don't think this is necessary," stated Ferguson and Bellwood. "It manages to offend everybody and is an attempt to explain something that doesn't need explanation. MacLeod/Nash is there to fight Fasil. Period."

The other major change in the April draft was that the final scenes of the film were relocated from a cruise liner to the Highlands of Scotland in the present day, MacLeod having taken Brenda back to the old forge where he'd once lived with Heather. Much of the dialogue was the same as in earlier drafts, with a coup in Honduras and a couple who were in love but who had never spoken to each other referenced. The pair kiss as "the sun breaks through the clouds, turning everything to gold".

At the sharp end

For a film that featured swordplay as a vital element of its action sequences, ensuring the actors could convincingly handle their weapons was a challenge for Russell Mulcahy and the producers. Fortunately, they were able to call on the services of two men who worked as an unofficial tag team on numerous films stretching back to the early 1950s: Bob Anderson and Peter Diamond. Anderson would become *Highlander*'s swordmaster, responsible for training the actors on the use of swords, while Diamond became the film's stunt coordinator and an uncredited stunt performer.

Taking up fencing while serving in the British Army during World War II, Bob Anderson became a fencing champion after the war and competed in the 1952 Olympics. It was during training that he was asked to train Errol Flynn on how to use a sword for the 1953 film *The Master of Ballantrae*, introducing him to the film industry that he'd be associated with for the next 50 years. "The sword is the ultimate weapon," explained Anderson to the *Los Angeles Times* in 1995. "It's not so threatening shooting at someone 20 or 30 paces away or while hiding behind things. When you get into a sword fight, you're standing toe to toe with someone who's trying to kill you and you're looking him in the eye – now that's thrilling."

Peter Diamond had trained as an actor at the Royal Academy of Dramatic Art (RADA), graduating in 1952 and almost immediately going on to coordinate the action on a number of swashbuckling adventure films such as 1953's *Knights of the Round Table* and 1954's *Dark Avenger* with Errol Flynn, while also taking on acting roles in films and TV. "In order to be a stunt coordinator, you must also be a performer," said Diamond to *Starlog* in 1985. "Anybody can tell somebody what to do, but you must bear in mind that things have to be rigged. And unless you've done stunts, and know the dangers and how to eliminate them, you can't advise others."

"In the course of his five-decade career, he generated over 1,200 credits," says Peter Diamond's son, Frazer, when I call him to chat about his father's work. Frazer maintains a website dedicated to Peter's career, often presenting talks on his work at conventions around the world. "You can go back to his days working on the Hammer films in the 1960s; he did at least 18. In *The Brigand of Kandahar* he was in the film 18 to 20 times, it's crazy."

One of the earliest films to feature both Bob Anderson and Peter Diamond was 1958's *The Moonraker*, an adventure film starring George Baker and Sylvia Syms; Anderson took on the role of the film's fencing coach, while Diamond was an uncredited stunt fencer. The pair can also be found working together in films such as *The Princess Bride* (1987), *The Mask of Zorro* (1998), and perhaps most notably, the original *Star Wars* trilogy. Frazer Diamond says, "When people talk about *The Empire Strikes Back*, they'll talk about Bob Anderson playing Darth Vader, but they coordinated this stuff together. They worked together, my father and Bob, not just Bob, the same way it wasn't just my dad."

Frazer Diamond isn't certain about the order that Peter Diamond and Bob Anderson were hired for *Highlander*, noting that the pair called each other "fighting friends" because they'd worked together on so many productions through the years. "What would tend to happen is Bob would get a production and he'd recommend that Dad came on board, or Dad would get a production and say, 'You should get Bob in to swordmaster.' Or they'd swap roles. It might be that Dad couldn't do a production and he'd go, 'I can't do it, but Bob's free.'"

According to Frazer, his father and Anderson had a "very good working relationship. Bob, technically, was an amazing swordmaster. And Dad had the performance skills as well as being a sword fighter, because he'd been to RADA so he knew how actors work. When they worked on a film together, I can always look at a fight and tell which bits Dad did and which bits Bob did. Because you look at the fights and you see the amazing swordplay, you go, 'That's Bob, all the way,' but Dad would always bring in little bits of scenery and have stuff going on with props and stuff. He liked to have the performers roam around sets and engage with them, whereas Bob was always focused on the swordplay and interplay between the two characters."

Peter Diamond was also responsible for bringing Christopher Lambert's stunt double, actor and stunt performer Andy Bradford, onto the picture. Recalling Bradford's work on a Japanese movement show called *Rain Dog*, in which he'd learned to use swords for the part, Diamond phoned him up and asked if he could help train Christopher Lambert to use one.

"He was a nice guy," says Bradford of Lambert. "He didn't want to learn the correct style, which was a bit frustrating, but the producers were happy with the way he fought so I had to adapt. We got on great and suddenly they were looking for a double and the producer says, 'Hey, he's not bad with a wig on; he'd be great for Christopher.' We formed a sort of relationship in the training period, so I became his double through the entire picture, which was lovely."

Moving home

Although much of *Highlander*'s pre-production took place at Twickenham Studios in south-west London, by the spring of 1985 the decision had been made to move everything to Mill Street in Central London, where a former dog biscuit factory on a 3.25 acre plot of land had been transformed into Jacob Street Studios a year earlier.

Part of a historic area known as Shad Thames, Jacob Street Studios offered facilities inside and out. With plenty of undeveloped back streets, abandoned warehouses and quiet alleys nearby, the area could be used for film and TV productions, whether set in London or, as with *Highlander*, the dingy streets of New York. "That film was made just at the right time because all these places were ruins," comments art director Tim Hutchinson, who was designing sets for the film's Scottish locations in an office at Jacob Street. "Shad Thames hadn't been developed at all."

Unfortunately for the crew of *Highlander*, the first production to properly utilise the facility, their new home wasn't perfect. "Jacob Street wasn't really a studio," explained Allan Cameron. "Normally when you go into a film studio it's a big open space and it's soundproofed, but this wasn't properly soundproofed and there were columns down the middle of the stages which I had to incorporate into the design of the scenery."

On Sunday 31 March, Cameron and Hutchinson set off back to Scotland for a further recce, this time with Russell Mulcahy, Gerry Fisher and assistant director David Tringham in tow. Mulcahy finally had a chance to see the locations he'd be filming in, including Eilean Donan Castle which they stopped at on Monday 1 April. Scotland's weather had no respect for its visitors, with Hutchinson explaining that for much of the trip it poured with rain. "Gerry had some light little rain thing on and I had some decent stuff, so he got absolutely soaked at Glen Orchy. That night, every stitch he had was hanging up to dry in the boiler room of the Ballachulish Hotel and he was wearing borrowed clothes."

The small group returned to London on Tuesday 2 April and the next day spent time looking at possible London locations, including Earl's Court Exhibition Centre, specifically its car park. "It's been demolished now and yet more expensive flats built in its place, but the exhibition hall had a car park which is what we used for Madison Square Garden," says Hutchinson.

Hutchinson was back in Scotland on Sunday 14 April, making his way to Fort William and on to the nearby Glen Nevis, where he started marking out what would become the Borders town of Jedburgh. The town would be used for the sequence in which Ramirez tries to convince MacLeod to give up Heather, or forever bear the pain of her loss. Many of the buildings were built in London and transported up to Scotland, though some were created on location.

During this visit, Hutchinson also met a member of the Lochaber Mountain Rescue team, John Grieve, who helped him source some fishing boats for the sequence due to be filmed on Loch Shiel with Sean Connery and Christopher Lambert. A decade later, Hutchinson returned to the area to work on the BBC film *Deacon Brodie* (1997), only to find the same boats rotting on the shore.

Back in the comfort of the Jacob Street production office, Joe Haidar was working closely with Russell Mulcahy to create *Highlander*'s storyboards. The pair would discuss each scene together, the director outlining the shots he wanted to see as Haidar created a quick thumbnail sketch on the spot which he'd finish later on his own. The pair would then review the boards together and Haidar would make any revisions that the director requested. On more than one occasion, Mulcahy made the decision to remove a drawing from the storyboard, putting a cross through it on the spot. To Joe Haidar it made sense to then change the numbering of all the panels, rather than have gaps at odd places.

"What I didn't understand was that all my drawings were being photocopied and handed out to the entire crew, and when I changed the numbers with Russell I didn't inform anyone else. David Tringham was so angry that he came in and yelled at me and took me to the art department and showed me one of the walls from the castle. He said, 'You see that wall? The back of the wall is written 2A and on your storyboard you changed it to 3, but we had planned to shoot 2A on this day and everyone needs to know it was this set.' He was explaining this very basic concept to me that I didn't know at the time. I felt really stupid, but you gotta learn somehow. I thought it was just Russell and I working together, I didn't know that other people were seeing these things."

A cast of characters

Now that his production team was coming together, Russell Mulcahy needed to find his actors. Aware that having a major star attached to the film would help raise the budget and attract other actors, the producers had hoped to attract the world's best-known Scottish actor, Sean Connery, to the role of Ramirez. By 1985, he was still best known to cinema audiences as James Bond, having played the role in seven films between 1962 and 1983, but he hadn't had any major hits for a number of years.

Screenwriters Peter Bellwood and Larry Ferguson worked hard to make the character of Ramirez appealing to the actor, making the character more colourful and giving him some poetic dialogue that no doubt appealed to him. "The script that Larry and I wrote for *Highlander* was the script that made Sean Connery want to be in the movie," says Bellwood. Adds Larry Ferguson: "He was a bankable entity. I went on to make two other films with Sean [*The Presidio*, 1988 and *The Hunt for Red October*, 1990] and we had an opportunity to discuss it. He said he was only interested in it due to the version that Peter and I did."

A memo from Peter Davis to Thorn EMI's finance director, John Reiss, dated 13 February 1985 revealed to the funders that Connery had "stated he definitely wishes to play Ramirez in *Highlander*," going on to note that Davis-Panzer were still in the process of negotiating the deal.

In 2016, Michael Ryan, who had helped raise the money for *Highlander* from Thorn EMI, told *Voice America* that "Sean was always known for his love of money . . . as we say in the UK he's as tight as a nun's knickers," going on to note that the actor felt he wasn't earning enough money at the time and that he was looking to take on projects that would allow him to "just walk through it and get a million dollars. We needed somebody, we knew that he was up for a job and we paid him $500,000 for three days. We managed to stretch those days throughout the film."

According to press notes issued for *Highlander*, Connery was only available for the shoot because another project fell through that he was planning to make with actor Michael Caine and director Alan Parker. Connery's signing meant not only a boost to the film's budget, but also to screenwriter Gregory Widen's bank balance thanks to the deal he'd made when Davis-Panzer bought his script; the higher the budget, the greater his percentage of the profits.

"When I first met him at the Savoy Hotel in London, all I could think was, 'I'm going to meet James Bond!' remembers Russell Mulcahy. "This was an actor I'd idolised and respected for so many years. I knocked on the door and my legs were trembling. Then the door opened and there was 007 and I'm thinking, 'Holy shit.' We sat down and had a cup of tea and sandwiches and got on pretty well. I adore him."

"When I heard it was Russell Mulcahy doing it – and with all his experience with the television videos, I could see he was exactly what the film needed," commented Connery in 1985, referring to Mulcahy's MTV work. "Ramirez is very much a 'live force' character; a Svengali to Christopher Lambert's Highlander. Ramirez is 2,437-years-old and has a wealth of experience and it is possible to draw on anything in terms of what his knowledge would be and his ability . . . and the visual aspects of the film are obviously going to be very important. You couldn't do better than have somebody like Mulcahy doing them."

Connery's casting made the American trade papers in mid-March 1985, with *Screen International* reporting that the film was set to begin shooting on 2 May 1985 in Scotland. Not mentioned in the article was the complicated nature of Connery's tax status in the UK, which meant there were only a limited number of days each year that the actor could spend in the country before being hit with a substantial tax bill from the Inland Revenue. The magazine also claimed that it was believed Scottish comedian Billy Connolly had been set to star in the film, but it's unclear what role he might have played.

While working on the *Highlander* storyboards just along the corridor from Russell Mulcahy's office, Joe Haidar encountered numerous actors arriving to audition for the film. "One day I was working away and this elderly gentleman, in this terribly plain overcoat that looked very unimpressive, popped in and he was looking for Russell. I said he was in a meeting and directed him down the hall. It was only after the echo of his voice in the room started to dissipate that I started to realise, 'Jesus, that was Sean Connery!' At that time he was God to guys like me who had grown up in the 1970s and he was the epitome of everything we wanted to be, then to see him in this very drab coat and to very quietly ask where Russell was."

Despite failing to recognise Connery, Haidar later begged Mulcahy to meet him. "He said, 'OK, but you have to be a pro; they don't like it when people gush,' and I said, 'Absolutely, I will.' Unfortunately I wasn't and I absolutely squealed like a little girl. I had a complete out-of-body experience and had no control over anything that came out of my mouth. To Connery's credit he was a gentleman and came over and looked at my drawings and tried to say some nice things, but I was just giggling and saying things like, 'I'm your biggest fan'; there was no control. I've never had that before or since. It was Sean Connery and he was up there with maybe three actors at the time whom I'd have died to have met. Why they didn't fire me, I don't know."

My own attempts to speak to Connery about his time on the film sadly came to nothing. Although I'd met him briefly at an awards ceremony as part of the Edinburgh International Film Festival in 2009, there had been no time to ask him any questions about his career. An email to his website in 2016 did result in a response from one of his staff, but it wasn't the one I was hoping for: "Sir Sean has retired and asked that I decline all media requests."

With the producers forced to consider British talent first for any role in the film due to the restrictions placed on them by their funding strategy, they had to cast their net wide to find actors who had convincing New York accents. This worked well for some of the smaller American parts, but Bill Panzer struggled to find local actors for roles such as Lieutenant Frank Moran.

"I saw every American living in England who was a member of British Equity: 140 men," noted Panzer, who videotaped each audition, including that of the New York-born, London-based Ed Bishop, an actor perhaps best known in the 1980s for his role as Colonel Straker in the Gerry Anderson TV series *UFO* (1970). "I think he was looking to get the police commissioner role," says Joe Haidar, who met Bishop as he was heading into his audition. "He was in *Diamonds are Forever* and I remember him telling me he'd done a short scene with Sean Connery and he found him to be very generous and not full of himself. I was 24 and totally star-struck."

Unfortunately for Bishop and his 139 fellow auditionees, Bill Panzer decided that none of them sounded or looked enough like a real New York cop. Instead, New York actor Alan North, well known for playing cops and authority figures in TV shows such as *Police Squad!* (1982), was cast in the role of Moran, while Pennsylvania-born actor Jon Polito became Detective Walter Bedsoe. These decisions weren't welcomed by the British actors' union, Equity, which protested to Panzer that his four days spent in a small video studio were "bogus".

In later years, Polito looked back on the shoot fondly, explaining that Russell Mulcahy was "a lot of fun to work with", even if he "didn't quite figure out what the hell was going on . . . I think the film is really a lot of fun to watch as a camp classic. I love the idea [you've got] so many accents. There couldn't be more accents."

One British actor who was allowed to keep his own accent was Hugh Quarshie, who was born in Ghana but moved to England at the age of three. By 1985, Quarshie had appeared in multiple theatre productions and TV series, though his feature film career had been limited to 1980's *The Dogs of War*. Having read the script, Quarshie joined the procession of actors meeting with Russell Mulcahy in London. "I dressed myself up in some African togs, something from Ghana," says Quarshie of the experience. "As I recall he smiled at that and appreciated the effort I was making. It was pretty straightforward; I read and he seemed to like it." Soon after, Quarshie was contacted with the news that he had the job, which would find him filming in both London and New York.

Another early casting decision resulted in Canadian actor Catherine Mary Stewart, fresh from a starring role in the 1984 sci-fi comedy *Night of the Comet*, securing the role of Heather MacLeod. Despite travelling to London to have a lifecast of her body created by special effects make-up co-designer Nick Maley and make-up effects mould designer John Schoonraad, her time on *Highlander* was short-lived. "There was some kind of disparity between her American and English work visas," says Schoonraad, noting she was "a lovely girl".

The role would ultimately go to English actor Beatrice 'Beatie' Edney, whose career was burgeoning in the early 1980s with appearances on British television, having made her acting debut at the age of six in Roman Polanski's *A Day at the Beach* (1970). With Catherine Mary Stewart departing the film late into pre-production, an open casting call was hastily arranged, bringing Edney and a few hundred other hopefuls to meet the producers.

Edney heard she had the part "pretty much the next day", before she was taken to wardrobe and prepared for the role of Heather.

Meanwhile, across the Atlantic, producer Peter Davis was on the hunt for MacLeod's present-day love interest, Brenda Wyatt. While in New York, Davis invited an actor well known on Broadway, television and film to talk to him about the role of the headstrong author and metallurgist who would turn an Immortal's head in 1985 New York. "I think they saw tapes of mine and they offered me the part," reveals actor Roxanne Hart when I ask how she won the role. Having appeared in films such as 1979's *The Bell Jar* and 1982's *The Verdict*, it would have been simple enough for Peter Davis and Bill Panzer to know at least some of the actor's range.

"She was more modern than a lot of female characters in that kind of genre film at the time," continues Hart, recalling the reasons for accepting the sort of "woman in peril" role that can often see female actors sidelined by their male counterparts. "She was a career woman, a smart-ass; I liked that about her. I liked the fact that she was tough and then she had the other side of being vulnerable, getting a crush on [MacLeod] and being smitten with him and the romance of who he was. And she stood her own in the precinct."

Winning the role of Brenda meant that Roxanne Hart had to move to London for a time, something she looks back on with great fondness. "What a beautiful city it was, and I found the people very warm, smart and witty. One of the things that really amazed me was their level of vocabulary. This is going to sound snobby, and I really don't mean it in any kind of a snobby way because I love the crews in New York, but everybody on the crew seemed so educated and literate."

With most of the supporting cast in place, Peter Davis and Bill Panzer still had to fill the shoes of the film's most important characters, two Immortals who were destined to fight down through the centuries in a never-ending battle.

FIVE

CHRISTOPHER AND CLANCY

Christophe Guy Denis Lambert, known professionally as Christopher Lambert, wasn't always the Highlander. For a short time, nobody was, or rather anybody could have been, as the casting process took place at London's Jacob Street Studios.

As he worked on the film's storyboards, Joe Haidar witnessed numerous actors pass through his office on their way to meet Russell Mulcahy. They were auditioning for a diverse roster of roles, from New York cops to Immortals. One of those roles was Connor MacLeod.

One actor spotted by Haidar was Tennessee-born actor David Keith, who had starred in 1982's *An Officer and a Gentleman*. "He'd flown to England and worked with a voice coach for some time to perfect somewhat of a Scottish accent," says Haidar. "He wanted to do this really elaborate audition for Russell." Excited by all aspects of the film-making process, Haidar begged Mulcahy to let him sit in on the audition, successfully persuading his boss to let him watch what he calls "a really cool audition".

Another potential MacLeod was Barry Bostwick, the Californian actor familiar to cult film fans for his role as Brad Majors in 1975's *The Rocky Horror Picture Show*. "Barry popped in as well," adds Haidar. "It was really cool to be sitting in that office doing these drawings and Russell would drop in and make his notes and then I'd keep working."

Keith and Bostwick were just two actors vying for the role, another being Kurt Russell, who had established himself as a versatile actor in films as diverse as *Used Cars* (1980), *Escape from New York* (1981) and *The Thing* (1982). Legend has it that Russell was offered the part by producers Bill Panzer and Peter Davis, though when I ask about casting him Russell Mulcahy only admits his name "was being bandied about". A contemporary report in fantasy magazine *Cinefantastique* stated that Kurt Russell's partner, Goldie Hawn, talked him out of accepting the part.

On the decision to talk to French actor Christopher Lambert, Mulcahy explains that he "was in the Los Angeles office with the producers and I was looking through a magazine and saw a picture of Christophe Lambert from *Greystoke* and I said, 'That's Highlander!' He had the eyes, the brow and this immortal look."

Born in Great Neck, New York on 29 March 1957, Lambert's family left America when he was two thanks to his father's job as a diplomat at the United Nations in Geneva, where he was educated at private boarding schools, away from his parents. His teenage years proved to be turbulent, seeing him kicked out of school five times in six years. On leaving school, he moved to London to train as a stockbroker at the suggestion of his parents, a job he described in 1986 as "interesting for the first three weeks" before it got "boring" and he returned to Paris to continue the training.

When his employers decided they didn't need him, he was accepted into the Conservatoire de Paris as an acting student, leaving after two years because he felt that the school's method of teaching was "highly intellectual and boring". On departing the Conservatoire, Lambert fell into some small roles in films such as 1980's *The Telephone Bar* and 1982's *Légitime Violence*, before director Hugh Hudson chose him for the lead in his 1984 film *Greystoke: The Legend of Tarzan, Lord of the Apes*, a part which saw his star rise internationally.

Due to the intense physical nature of the film, Lambert stated that he had "never worked so hard" in his life, convinced at one point that he couldn't do it. "And then it got better and better and I started thinking, 'I love it.' And then the worst part is you can't stop working. Even when I'm not shooting, I have to work." Mulcahy, Panzer and Davis may have originally been on the hunt for a handsome American actor to play their hero, but a line in the script spoken by MacLeod while in police custody offered them a clever way to widen their search to actors from further afield:

                    GARFIELD
        You talk funny Nash, where you from?

                      NASH
           Lots of different places

"We could open ourselves up to somebody who wasn't American, who had some kind of an accent," explained Bill Panzer. "We saw *Greystoke* and said, 'Well, this guy has an ageless, timeless, placeless quality to him. He could have come from anywhere.'" To convince Thorn EMI and 20th Century Fox, the producers screened a scene from *Greystoke* of Lambert as John Clayton arriving by horse and carriage at Greystoke mansion. According to Panzer, the first question he was asked by an executive was, "Can he speak English?" to which he replied, "Of course he can speak English, he's got an American passport for Christ's sake."

With his latest film, Luc Besson's French language thriller *Subway*, due to open in the spring in France and Lambert attracting attention from other producers, Panzer and Davis quickly arranged to have a copy of the *Highlander* script sent to Lambert. "I liked the story," said the actor in a 1985 interview. "I thought it was great to be an Immortal, and I thought it was great that half the story was happening in Scotland in 1500 [sic] and half in New York, 1986. The contrast was incredible. In fact it's the first script I've read that has everything in it. There are two amazing love stories, a lot of action, great acting scenes: there is a mixture, something for everyone."

On hearing that Lambert was keen to do the film, Panzer and

Davis quickly arranged a contract to be signed, confident they'd made the right choice. Although they hadn't met the actor in person, his on-screen performance spoke for itself and the opportunity to discuss the role came during pre-production in London, when the producers arranged dinner with Lambert and his manager at Le Caprice restaurant in Piccadilly. The first surprise came when they discovered Lambert was five feet ten inches tall rather than the six feet two inches promised by his agent, while the second shock occurred when Lambert opened his mouth to say hello. Said Bill Panzer, "We put our hands out to shake hands to say hello, and he goes [imitates thick French accent], ''Ello, 'ow are you?' . . . this guy doesn't speak English at all."

Despite initial reservations about their decision, Panzer realised that Lambert's background made him perfect for the role. "He is charming, he's engaging, he's intelligent, he's funny," admitted the producer. Events had conspired to bring the producers into contact with one of Europe's most exciting talents who also happened to have a background so diverse that it almost rivalled Connor MacLeod's. An announcement was made to the press in March 1985, the press release quoting Panzer as saying, "We wanted someone to portray the character as a rounded human being – someone who tempers strength with humanity," qualities evident in Lambert's portrayal of Tarzan.

On the phone to Lambert, me in Scotland and him in France, we start by discussing the reasons Lambert was attracted to the film in 1985. "It was a combination of different things," he explains, beginning with the idea of immortality, a concept commonly found in vampire fiction, and the love story at the heart of the narrative. "It always interested me, how do you cope with this immortal life for 500 years? Your friends and lovers are dying and this weight on your shoulders, growing every 50 years. How do you keep on walking with your head up and cope with life? No matter what the action side was, the fighting, the battle between good and evil, I was attracted by the romanticism that immortality brought to the script."

Another reason he accepted the part was due to the involvement of Russell Mulcahy. "I'd seen *Razorback* and most of his videos, but I'd say that the 20-minute video he did for 'The Wild Boys' was incredible: to this day I haven't seen anybody that can visually beat Russell Mulcahy. The guy's got so many ideas."

One aspect of Lambert's performance scrutinised during any discussion of the film is his accent. Producer Bill Panzer's concerns regarding the actor's inability to speak anything other than select English phrases were serious; how could the film keep to a tight shooting schedule if the lead actor had to be fed each line phonetically from off camera?

Joe Haidar recalls Lambert's first day on set at Jacob Street Studios, when the actor stopped to look at the storyboards. "I vaguely remember saying something to him and his accent was so thick that I wasn't sure he fully understood what I said. But he was very nice and he was sitting in front of the storyboards when they were all pinned up. At the time I wasn't thinking the way studios think and I thought it was odd they were picking a French guy who had a really thick French accent to play a Scotsman. But he was a big star at the time, he'd just finished *Greystoke*, and they were probably seeing that side of him, and he was certainly a great actor."

To avoid potential problems, Panzer and Davis hired voice coach Joan Washington. Born and raised in the Scottish city of Aberdeen, Washington was working at London's Actors Centre in the mid-1980s when she was hired to coach Lambert on *Greystoke*. Later, she was approached to work with him again for a three-month period on *Highlander*. "She's an incredible voice coach and a great person," says Lambert of Washington.

In promotional material for the film released to journalists in 1986, Lambert acknowledged the irony of Connery and himself playing characters with unusual accents. "I think so long as you are ready to work as much as possible, anything can be achieved. In *Highlander* it is possible for the Immortals to have a Scottish accent when they are in Scotland and a mid-Atlantic accent when they are in New York. MacLeod is an international character . . . The accent he has for America is unrecognisable and it is not possible to say where he comes from; but it is as close as possible to mid-Atlantic."

Lambert was not only able to learn from Joan Washington, but also from co-star Sean Connery, who Lambert says offered advice on the occasional line reading. "Sean from time to time would say, 'Christopher, you have to say it that way,' so that was helpful too." Today, Russell Mulcahy is quick to gloss over the situation, noting that "he had an English coach and he learned pretty quickly. Christophe is still a dear, dear friend and I love him to bits."

Likewise, screenwriter Peter Bellwood is nonchalant about the decision to cast a Frenchman as a Scot and a Scot as an Egyptian. "I wasn't really all that concerned about it. It was always the case that if Sean Connery had been 30 years younger he'd have been playing MacLeod, but in this movie he's going to play MacLeod's much older tutor."

"I will say that we had fun with that," adds co-writer Larry Ferguson. "There's a scene just before Sean throws Christopher into the water where [Connery] says in a Scottish accent, 'What is that?' and Chris replies in a heavy French accent, 'It's haggis,' and then Sean says, 'What do you do with it?' and Chris says, 'You eat it.'"

In addition to working hard on his accent for 12 weeks, Lambert also spent the time rehearsing the sword fights with Bob Anderson and Andy Bradford. "It's like learning a script; you just learn your lines to get rid of them because it has to be mechanical at the beginning, then you have to forget about it to be somebody else. It's the same with fighting. You have to rehearse the moves hundreds of times so it becomes automatic and you know that when the blow comes from the right, left or above you can protect yourself; you can't think about it."

"[We trained] just to get him familiar with the weapons, [but] he didn't like training," says Andy Bradford. "He was a wonderful character, amazing eyes, but he wasn't like the American actors that you hear now are up at 3 a.m. pumping iron. He was sort of old school, but he knew he had quite an allure on camera. It wasn't difficult stuff, but when he did it he did it with conviction."

When asked in 1995 to name the finest swordsmen of all the actors he'd trained, Bob Anderson listed Lambert alongside David Niven, Mandy Patinkin and Richard Gere as the best he'd worked with, explaining that he found actors pick up the skills well "because they can get the feel of it as they know the emotions a swordsman is supposed to feel".

Going on to explain that he effectively raised himself as a teenager, Lambert looks at the cast and crew of each film he worked on as a kind of surrogate family. "Suddenly I have 150 people on a movie set and I'm happy. When you leave them after four or five months together I'm sad, but then you go onto another movie and you start again. The first day, you're getting to know each other but the second day it's like we've known each other for 20 years."

Creating the Kurgan

In the Hollywood of 1985, any film producer planning their next action film almost certainly had the same few names at the top of their list. Following the release of 1984's *The Terminator*, Arnold Schwarzenegger immediately shot to the top of the list for casting directors, each one determined to hire the physically imposing actor for their next action film.

The producers of *Highlander* were in the same queue as everyone else, keen to fill the rather large boots of their bad guy, the Kurgan, with the feet of the Austrian actor. Producers Peter Davis and Bill Panzer made an approach to Schwarzenegger, but were quickly turned down thanks to his desire to move away from being pigeonholed as a villain, preferring instead to take on roles that were more heroic.

Across the Atlantic at a London party, a chance encounter between Russell Mulcahy and actor/singer Sting led to another name coming up in conversation. Sting had recently starred as the Baron in 1985's *The Bride*, director Franc Roddam's screen adaptation of Mary Shelley's *Frankenstein*, acting alongside the American actor Clancy Brown as Viktor, the monster of the piece. According to Brown, Sting said to Mulcahy, "You should talk to this big American bloke, Clancy Brown, he's a nice fella. He's friggin' huge!"

Brown is explaining to me how he came to be approached by Davis and Panzer for their forthcoming fantasy film. "It was an American company, so they wanted a cheap *Terminator* bad guy. They went to Schwarzenegger to get him to do it, because if they had him they knew they were going to make *Terminator* money, which of course they weren't. They called me and asked me if I would do it. I read it and said, 'Yeah.' It's the first and only time that I haven't had to audition for anything."

Brown was one of the final additions to the cast, with confirmation of the deal only being circulated by Peter Davis in a memo dated Wednesday 10 April 1985 that read: "He should travel today, rest on Thursday and be ready for production needs A.M. Friday".

Was the salary a big issue for Brown at the time? "I talked to Peter Davis and my basic question was, 'How much you gonna pay me?' I thought he was paying me a lot and I found out that I was the least paid of anybody, and he never wanted to pay me again."

In Gregory Widen's first draft of his *Highlander* script, the writer had a clear vision of the character of the Knight. "I envisioned him as a guy who . . . [loses] everything over time and the only thing that he could hold on to, to give him a reason to get up in the morning, is to finish this thing and finish it with our guy. It was really about that more than anything, more than possession of this force . . . nothing is permanent, everything is lost. That made him a much more serious, almost a sympathetic bad guy."

By introducing screenwriters Larry Ferguson and Peter Bellwood to the process, producers Bill Panzer and Peter Davis had made the script more accessible to a wider audience, removing some of the angst felt by the Immortals and introducing the sort of humour that lightened the drama. Said Widen, "The Kurgan in the movie is . . . just a guy who screws with people because he enjoys screwing with people." Although Widen's script had been replaced by Ferguson and Bellwood's by the time Clancy Brown was approached in early 1985, it was his take on the character that seemed to resonate most with Clancy Brown.

With Widen invited onto the set in London to meet the cast and crew and be available for questions, potentially rewriting the occasional line on the spot if required, Brown had an opportunity to hear from the creator of the Kurgan/Knight just what his character could have been like if the original script had made it to the screen. According to Widen, Brown hated what he was being asked to do and would often complain to him about scenes he felt didn't best represent the character, one which the writer felt had become "pretty much like Freddy [Krueger], a cackling psychopath".

Discussing the character with *Starlog* in 1986, Brown had a strong vision for the Kurgan, noting that he disagreed with a line in the script that read "Years of killing have driven the Kurgan insane". Said Brown, "Three thousand years fighting for a prize that's power beyond belief means the guy is *ambitious*, the guy is *going* for it, he *works* at it! Imagine the perspective that 3,000 years would give you – this ridiculous structure, these governments that come and go; *nothing* has any significance to the Kurgan."

When I ask about the changes made to the Kurgan, it's clear Brown still had an affinity with Widen and his view of the *Highlander* universe. "Greg and I, we didn't conspire or anything, but we thought there was a lot more going on here, a lot more comment to be made about history and the trends of ritual. But if it had become that movie, nobody would've cared. The producers bought Greg's script and then hired a couple of Hollywood screenwriters, who were good guys. They wrote a really tight Hollywood script that ignored the real issues that were lying right there under the surface."

Pushed on whether he fought to retain some of the darker sides of the character, Brown shrugs. "You can see me trying to do that in the first part of the movie, then at the end I surrendered to the campness of it. Initially, and especially in your twenties, you want everything to be significant." Did Russell Mulcahy offer guidance on playing the Kurgan? "I wasn't constrained by the script and Russell didn't ever tell me to stop doing anything. I think I was just trying to get him to direct me, but he never bothered!"

Larry Ferguson attributes the decision to lighten the script's tone to his writing partner. "Peter Bellwood introduced me to the idea that when you can get people to laugh and have fun with a villain, they're vulnerable in a way they don't understand. While they're laughing, if he does something really awful, they feel almost responsible for it because maybe they were cheering him on somehow."

"He's an entertaining villain," adds Bellwood. "It's a fairly simple formula: the hero versus the villain. Connor MacLeod isn't a humourless, muscled fellow; he's living his life and he has his own moments of comedy as well as the Kurgan. But it's always much more fun in the movies I've seen where you have a bad guy who, in addition to being horrifying, is also funny." Of Clancy Brown's casting, Bellwood is full of praise. "Clancy was wonderful in that part. He played him so evil and so frightening and in person he's the sweetest, gentlest guy you could ever hope to meet."

I wondered about what it was like to be a 25-year-old American actor working far from home and trying to make sense of a hectic production led by the force of nature that was Russell Mulcahy in his prime. "Russell was a very good choice to direct because he was very at ease with all the conflicting aesthetics and the logic holes didn't bother him. He put together a really stylish and watchable movie and he didn't give a shit that Sean was being Sean and Christophe was being Christophe and that I was being me; all that stuff works for him. We were just having fun and he was real at ease with that and didn't see any reason to justify it."

One person Brown bonded with on the production was swordmaster Bob Anderson, whose work he was impressed by when he happened to catch *The Master of Ballantrae* on TV one evening after filming. When the 25-year-old actor discovered that the then 62-year-old Anderson was staying in a room at a London YMCA while he was living in a small Chelsea flat, he approached him with an offer.

"I said, 'Bob, come and live with me; you're a World War II vet for crying out loud.' So we ended up staying in this flat together and having a great time. He would take me out to nice restaurants and show me how to use silverware, what to drink before and what to drink afterwards. I had a lot of fun and Bob became a great friend. It probably took a lot of time, but it didn't seem like it because it was all just fun at that point, after that friendship started." Anderson would often help Brown choreograph a fight, which the pair would then show to Russell Mulcahy and Christopher Lambert. Says Brown, "Chris would steal all the cool moves that I made for myself, but we'd come up with other stuff."

For Lambert, Brown and the rest of the cast and crew, London was their first destination, the initial stage of a shooting schedule that would take the best part of three months of their lives.

SIX

COMING OUT FIGHTING

By April 1985, things were falling into place for *Highlander* producers Peter Davis and Bill Panzer. Thanks to a knowing script that offered action alongside a memorable love story, they'd secured not only a strong cast of character actors but also a rising European leading man and one of the world's biggest movie stars in what was effectively a glorified cameo.

Although *Highlander*'s $16m budget wasn't insignificant, the decision to film its Scottish and New York exteriors on location did have a major impact on the amount of money available for other aspects of the production. Producers Bill Panzer and Peter Davis were acutely aware of what spend was available at any one time, and soon gained a reputation for reminding the crew of the limitations at regular intervals.

Had Davis-Panzer hired the type of director who planned everything to the nth degree, been satisfied with a couple of takes and generally played it safe, the budget may not have been such an issue for them. Instead they hired Russell Mulcahy, not a man known for his sedate style and budgetary concerns.

"When Russell got hold of something he kind of ran away with it," says Mark Raggett, *Highlander*'s standby art director, who had worked alongside production designer Allan Cameron on *1984* and the recently-completed *Lady Jane*. Initially drawing up sets alongside Cameron at Jacob Street Studios during the pre-production period, Raggett was on set when filming began, liaising with everybody on set to make sure everything was running smoothly and dealing with last-minute changes.

Having worked with Mulcahy on some of his early pop promos, Raggett had an idea of what to expect on the set of *Highlander*. "Russell just doesn't stop; he's on the go the whole time. Every sequence involved some kind of dynamic thing that was going on, or something that he thought of at the last minute and wanted; there was always something happening. He pushed the boundaries and pushed everyone to the limit . . . I seem to remember there were quite a few issues with the budget."

From Mulcahy's perspective, it was a chance to continue doing what he'd done on his music videos, only on a much grander scale and without excessive oversight. "There were very few meetings. I'd done one feature film, but I'd done 400 videos and there was a certain period when people didn't want multiple meetings and I could get away with doing strange images and sequences. These days you'd have to have 20 meetings with the executives and you probably wouldn't get away with it."

One of the first sequences to be put on film at the end of April found the cast and crew leaving their London base and heading north to Brocket Hall, an 18th-century country house in Hertfordshire. In Larry Ferguson and Peter Bellwood's script, MacLeod has offended the wife of Bassett (Ian Reddington), and must fight a duel as the latter's manservant, Hotchkiss (Sion Tudor Owen), assists him. As originally scripted, the scene took place in 1797 on Boston Common, though memos sent by the screenwriters during filming noted that the duel had been relocated to England's Hampstead Heath, explaining the English accents of Bassett and Hotchkiss. Despite Ferguson and Bellwood's request that MacLeod's voiceover be altered to reflect this change, the location is still stated as Boston Common in the film.

Crane operator Adam Samuelson was on set for filming and recalls the crew's initial reaction to their new director. "I remember

Russell turning up in trainers and T-shirt, while everyone was in full weather gear going, 'Who the hell is this guy?'"

When he was approached to audition for the part of Bassett, Ian Reddington was playing the lead in a stage adaptation of Samuel Richardson's novel, *Pamela*, a character he describes as "this sort of posh aristocratic lord. I imagine someone in the [*Highlander*] casting department saw it because they said, 'Will you come in and see us for this film; there's a character very similar in this.' They just wanted me to speak in kind of a posh way, which Bassett ended up being in the film. I literally just said a few lines and they went, 'Great, great, thanks very much.' And that was it."

Rather than simply turning up to do his scenes, Reddington was first required to train with swordmaster Bob Anderson at London's Pineapple Dance Studios. The actor had enjoyed fencing at drama school, winning certificates for his skills, though he'd never needed to use them. "I trained with Bob Anderson for a whole week, which was tiring but fabulous."

When it did come time to start shooting, Reddington was driven to Brocket Hall and had to hide both his excitement and his nerves as it was his first time on a film set. "They had the classic film thing where they've got the chairs, the director's chair with his name on it, then one on the end with no name on, which I presumed was mine. I kind of sneaked into it." According to Reddington, filming turned out to be "crazy and mad; I can only assume [Russell] shot it as if it were a music video . . . he shot it from every conceivable angle and it was an amazing couple of days. Subsequently I've worked with directors who would never shoot that much footage for that size of scene."

When the time came to start rehearsing the duel, the actor had learned his lines and worked hard on his fencing, but he still had some nerves as Russell Mulcahy asked to see what he could do. "I went through all my moves that I'd rehearsed and he said, 'That's great. Now what I want you to do is do that backwards.' I'm thinking, 'Fuck me, this is ridiculous,' so I had to perform the fight in reverse."

With a need to keep expensive special effects to a minimum, the plan was to thread the thin blade of Reddington's sword through Christopher Lambert's costume, with a channel running around his stomach and through the back of his waistcoat. As Mulcahy shouted "Action!" Reddington pulled the sword out of Lambert's clothing and stepped backwards, a shot that was reversed in the final edit to make it look like Bassett was lunging at MacLeod and impaling him.

"This is me on my first film and it's driving me mental," continues Reddington, whose stress continued when he delivered his dialogue to Christopher Lambert. "I started by saying something like, 'My Lord, I challenge you to a duel,' and Christopher goes [mimics incomprehensible mumbling]. The director doesn't say cut, so I say my next line and Christopher goes [mimics more mumbling] and I'm thinking, 'This is ridiculous.'"

In the end, Reddington did the entire scene with Lambert not speaking. "I never heard a word the man said to me, but I knew what his lines were, so I left a pause and then said my line, I left another pause and said another line. Three months later, he dubs it in the dubbing studio. When I went to see it there was one bit where he has a funny line: 'Your wife is a bloated warthog' and my face is entirely expressionless. It gets a laugh, but I didn't know what he'd said to me, otherwise I'd have reacted to it. He was playing drunk anyway, so it kind of works. It was one scene, but people loved it."

Faking Madison Square Garden

The next major set piece to be filmed was part of the opening sequence. Here, Connor MacLeod leaves the wrestling match inside New York's Madison Square Garden and makes his way down to the underground car park to face off against fellow Immortal, Iman Fasil (Peter Diamond) in an explosive sword fight, with MacLeod using an ivory-handled steel katana and Fasil wielding a Toledo Salamanca.

Following the decision to shoot the sequence in the car park of London's Earl's Court Exhibition Centre, planning involved various members of the effects crew, among them special effects make-up co-designer, Nick Maley. Maley had worked with Russell Mulcahy on his 1984 concept concert video, *Arena*, as the film's prosthetic make-up artist, his extensive CV also including films such as *The Man With the Golden Gun* (1974), *Superman* (1978), and the first two *Star Wars* films. Maley's work on 1980's *The Empire Strikes Back* earned him the title "That Yoda Guy" due to his involvement in the creation of the diminutive green alien.

"Russell was a star of directing music videos; that's where his strengths had been up until that time," says Maley today from the film museum he runs in St Maarten in the Caribbean. "His way of filming things was very different to the traditional moviemakers. He would look at it and say, 'Well, we've got ten days, what can we make? How can we do this?' We basically brainstormed and came up with a bunch of different things, all of which ended up in 'The Wild Boys' [video]. When he got *Highlander*, he asked me if I would join and that was part of what was really good about the movie, but also led to some of the things that were not so good, because the other people that I was dealing with were not necessarily as open-minded as he was."

Before Maley committed to the film, he read the script and made Mulcahy aware that he had some questions for the director, starting with what the Quickening was. "It just kept on saying, 'We see the Quickening' and Russell said, 'I don't know, we've got to make it up.' The second thing is we keep on seeing all these people getting their heads cut off. When you've seen the first one, it costs as much to do it the second time, but people have already seen it. Then you do it a third time, a fourth time, a fifth time."

Maley had experienced something similar on Tobe Hooper's 1985 film *Lifeforce*, on which he looked after special make-up effects. Having explained to screenwriter Dan O'Bannon that scenes of people crumbling to dust would quickly get boring, Maley helped O'Bannon rewrite sections of the script, before directing the animatronic sequences for those scenes. Maley was keen to do the same on *Highlander*, for which he created storyboards for the Quickening sequences, ensuring that each time the viewer would be presented with a fresh take on the same event.

"The first time we want to see it without seeing it, so let's see it reflected in the car bonnet. Let's see it from underneath the car, where all you see are feet and something coming up off the floor, the energy breaking the windscreens and maybe running around the wheel hub. You feel like you saw something, but you've got as many questions about what you saw as actually physically seeing it. Then the next time let's see the shadows on the wall. The next time we see it, but the castle gets knocked down, so each time it was something that was different."

"I remember Nick showing me these amazing storyboards he'd done for *Highlander*," says make-up effects mould designer John Schoonraad, who had worked with Maley on *Lifeforce*. "There was even that bit [after the Madison Square Garden fight] where a little bit of glass fell out of the light bulb on the car; that was even drawn at that time. There was a lot of detail put in by other people that was put in the film by Russell. The whole thing was kind of interesting, because it was pretty cutting-edge with those effects."

Though Maley was excited about working with Russell Mulcahy again, his enthusiasm wasn't always appreciated by other members of the crew. "I was having some problems with the producers, who thought I was being impudent when I explained to them that it would take so many weeks to do certain things. We didn't meet eye to eye. And the cinematographer [Gerry Fisher], who was a very old-school guy, could not come to terms with the idea that make-up was going to tell the cameraman how to turn the camera over."

Production designer Allan Cameron and art director Tim Hutchinson had already made a recce to Earl's Court and made the decision early on to black out one end of the car park that was open to the sky and add some extra polystyrene columns alongside the existing cement ones, each painted black with a yellow line around them. Says Hutchinson, "Whenever they whacked a broadsword into a column, that was one of our polystyrene columns so that the sword appeared to bury itself into reinforced concrete."

To convince the viewer that they were now in Madison Square Garden, a sign was strategically placed at one end of the car park that read 'To the Garden', while any British cars had been removed and replaced with a large fleet of locally sourced American cars.

As cinematographer Gerry Fisher set up the lighting required for filming, Russell Mulcahy began to worry that the volume of lights being installed would lead to the car park being overlit. Despite both men's professionalism, tension mounted as the director explained his vision to the cinematographer. "I wanted to be able to pan around and do whatever with the camera," says Mulcahy. "I said, 'Turn these lights off, put the fluoros on and flash them,' and Gerry said, 'Look, this isn't going to work.'" The already uneasy Fisher was further bemused by Mulcahy's next request: "I said, 'Let's have it rain,' and he said, 'What the hell am I doing?'" According to Mulcahy, when Gerry Fisher looked at the rushes he could finally see the effect the former was trying to achieve. "He said, 'Oh my God, it actually works!' So then we became the best of friends."

MacLeod vs Fasil

With the location prepped, it was now time for the cast and stunt performers to make their way to the set, with Christopher Lambert and Peter Diamond required for the sword fight.

According to Frazer Diamond, the decision to cast his father as Fasil came from a suggestion by Bob Anderson to Russell Mulcahy, who pointed out that all the attributes he required from an actor who could use a sword convincingly were present in Peter Diamond. Diamond later commented that "Russell looked at me, put his hand across the top of my forehead, because I've got a bald head, and said, 'Yes, we could put a blond wig on him. Okay, you play the part!'"

With so many scenes needed from one location, the workload had to be shared among four units looking after different aspects of the action. Russell Mulcahy focused on the performances of the principal cast, while assistant director David Tringham attempted to keep the other units synchronised. The second unit focused more on the stunt work, and a third and fourth unit on shots of windshields exploding, car bonnets popping up and other smaller pieces of action missed by the first unit. Stunt director Andy Armstrong, who would play a bigger part on the film when the production moved to New York, also shot some of the fight between Lambert and Diamond.

With the first and second units each filming for over a week, *Highlander*'s editor Peter Honess found himself with plenty of footage to work with. "If you give a second unit director one roll of film, he'll shoot it, if you give him 50 he'll use that as well because they don't know if they've got [the shot] or not." So enthusiastic was Mulcahy, that when the main unit finished a day of filming, he'd remain with the second unit and carry on for another three or four hours.

Having Peter Diamond on set would have been useful to the various directors looking after different units, his background in low-budget productions meaning he was used to working fast and getting the most out of actors. "He absolutely excelled at knowing where the camera should be to cut corners all the time," says Frazer Diamond. "You can point that back to *Star Wars*; effectively that was a low-budget picture. The reason he was hired was because he knew how to get something in the can and move on."

At one point during the fight, Fasil somersaults backwards off the bonnet of a car, before performing a series of backflips through the car park. This addition came late in the day and was another example of Russell Mulcahy's attempts to always keep scenes visually exciting, whether or not there was a logic to them. Rather than encourage Peter Diamond, a man in his late fifties, to perform the backflips, another performer was brought in to double him in the shape of dancer and gymnast, Vincent 'Ginger' Keane.

"I used to train in Hendon, and a guy called Malcolm Wheeler used to come down to the gym," says Keane, whose details have been passed to me by his old friend, stunt performer Andy Bradford. "I got chatting to Malcolm one day and he took my number. Then suddenly he got injured – I think he'd done his shoulder in on a film – so he phoned me up and just asked if I'd like to take over on *Highlander*."

Although he'd had some experience working on music videos, this would be Keane's first time on a film set. Making his way to Earl's Court, Keane met Andy Bradford and Peter Diamond, before being asked to wear padding due to his slight physique. What should have been a straightforward piece of acrobatic work was made more complicated by the decision to slick down the concrete with water. "It was a challenging thing to do, because when you do a backflip your hands can slip on the wet floor, so you have to do them quite high, and when your clothes get wet the fat suit gets heavier. I had to run to get the momentum, and it's fine for the first few attempts, but by the time you get to the last few it's like you've got lead in your shoes."

Keane's initial attempts were carried out to give Russell Mulcahy an idea of where to place the camera for the filming. "They asked if I could slow it down as the camera kept missing me. I think they expected me to take half a day on it, but because I did it on the first take they could move on to something else. But they had booked it in for three or four hours. Russell didn't hang about. He just went, 'OK, when you're ready.' He had all the cameras set up; he knew the angles."

The job was a catalyst for Keane's career, which to date has seen him perform and coordinate stunts in more than 100 films and TV series. "I stayed in touch with Andy and he's helped me out all my career. He's given me loads of jobs; if he couldn't do it, he'd put me in for it. Peter would take the time and explain to you what he was doing. He'd have it all organised so all you'd have to concentrate on was doing the job; you didn't have to worry about anything else."

Keane's day on the set didn't translate to a credit on the film, something he's always assumed was because he was effectively doubling another stuntman. "I didn't ask to be honest; sometimes it happens like that. I don't really tell anyone so nobody knows. Everyone assumes it was Peter Diamond, and that's the way they wanted it, so I think they got their wish."

Andy Armstrong is quick to recall a continuity error that occurred during the fight, when Fasil's mirrored sunglasses fell to the ground. "You see him reflected in the glasses, but then the next time you see the bad guy, he's wearing the glasses. No one ever mentioned it, but it was completely out of sync."

For the death of Fasil, mould designer John Schoonraad and his team created a foam lifecast of Peter Diamond that was hung from a rig and dropped to its knees when the head was sliced off. The body's neck was filled with gelatin, macaroni and fake blood that would spurt out on cue. "We had a fibreglass animatronic head and the mouth would drop open and the eyes would move. It was radio-controlled and quite sophisticated for the time."

Although standby art director Mark Raggett wasn't responsible for sourcing the cars, once they were on set he had to ensure they'd been rigged up by the special effects team to explode on cue, something that took many hours of preparation. "I said to Russell, 'We're going to go carefully with all of these cars, because obviously once they're blown up, they're blown up.' I seem to remember that on the first take he blew the fucking lot up. That was Russell, he was quite a live wire."

Raggett had to quickly coordinate the removal of some damaged cars from the building, while ensuring others were patched up to a decent standard with new bonnets or hubcaps. "[You're trying] to make them look all right again, with Russell going, 'How long do I have before I can shoot again?'"

"There were a lot of things we made up as we went along," adds director Andy Armstrong. "There are people in the cars rocking them to make that energy and I did one of the madder things. There's a scene where the fire hose gets pressurised and goes mad.

We used a real fire hose and we built wooden hides around the camera so they wouldn't get smashed. And when he turned on the fire hose the power was unbelievable and it smashed the hide around the camera. It was like matchwood at the end of it. Blowing all the car windows was a big deal because it's a one-take deal as they were American cars in London, so you couldn't get spare glass for them, all those windows blowing in was a one-take wonder."

Stunt performer Andy Bradford was in the driver's seat for the shot of MacLeod speeding out of the car park, a scene that was later completed in New York at the real Madison Square Garden. Asked by Peter Diamond to slide into the bend without hitting the wall, his control on the car was put in jeopardy when he realised the car park had been hosed down with water. While visually impressive, the water also brought any petrol on the ground to the surface. "When I put the handbrake on the whole car went sideways, it pinged off the wall and sparked. Later on I went out with the girl who was the production secretary and she said there was quite a bill from the guy who owned this beautiful car."

As production began, the film's screenwriters Larry Ferguson and Peter Bellwood spent around a fortnight in London, initially trying to find the fastest way to cross the city, with Ferguson explaining that "being an American, I got an education about how to get a cab to Sloane Square". Adds Peter Bellwood, "We ended up taking the subway, it was much faster." The pair were on set in Earl's Court and were impressed with Mulcahy's take on their script.

Bellwood recalls that the director "would prowl about", rarely interacting with script supervisor Marilyn Clarke, the person responsible for looking after the film's continuity as well as the whereabouts of actors and props in scenes. "He was marching about and the script lady was standing there with everything ready to go, hoping that he'd talk to her. He never said a word to her, all he said was 'Action!' He would talk to the actors but not to her; she was very upset. They became friends later. He was a very interior kind of thinker in terms of the composing of shots, and I think the movie shows a lot of that very effectively."

"The relationship between a writer and a director is pretty much the same as the one between an architect and a builder," states Ferguson. "An architect can sit down and make something make sense, and a builder sometimes doesn't appreciate what an architect has given him and changes stuff, but Peter and I both had an enjoyable experience with Russell. He's one of those deceptive people who looks like he isn't doing anything and all of a sudden he does something and you go, 'Wow, how in the hell did he come up with that?' He brought movement."

In a blink-and-you'll-miss-it moment, after a few seconds of calm, a solitary hubcap rolls across the screen from left to right. "Russell did that," says editor Peter Honess. "Sometimes, just for the fun of it, he'd walk past the camera. If you had a camera facing somebody and somebody blocks it for a few seconds, that's Russell."

For the cost-conscious producers used to more traditional film-making methods, watching the sequence unfold was initially a stressful experience, with Bill Panzer stating that Mulcahy's style was a "different ball game" to the techniques taught by traditional film schools. On Panzer's previous film as a producer, Cold War thriller *The Osterman Weekend*, director Sam Peckinpah was in his late fifties and not in the best of health following years of drug and alcohol abuse, meaning his directorial style was much more sedate than it had been in his younger days on productions such as 1969's *The Wild Bunch*. By the 1980s, the film's producers and financiers knew what they were getting with Peckinpah.

Contrast Peckinpah with the younger Mulcahy and the multiple film units required inside Earl's Court to capture different angles and moments, and for Panzer and Davis the seemingly random footage being captured on each day's shoot was a concern. Peter Honess admits that Mulcahy "stuck the most shots through a camera of anyone I'd worked with, 72 set-ups in one day. Only Russell could shoot that way. He was so fast and I can't recall anything going over eight or ten takes."

If the producers didn't understand exactly what was going on, what would 20th Century Fox and Thorn EMI think? Aware of their nerves, Mulcahy invited his producers into the editing suite to watch a rough cut of the sequence, finally convincing Panzer and Davis that he had things under control. Indeed, Panzer went so far as to admit that Mulcahy "revitalised my whole way of thinking about how you make movies".

The sometimes tense relationship between Mulcahy and Davis-Panzer didn't go unnoticed by other members of the crew, with Mark Raggett explaining that there were a lot of "strong characters . . . people with strong ideas that made [the set] quite lively. It was often quite charged." According to Raggett, the calmest person on set was Christopher Lambert "because he just came out and did it; [he] was really calm and chilled, especially with all this going on."

"[He's] so quick he can shoot in a day what other people would shoot in two days," said Lambert of Mulcahy. "And what is great is that what ends up on screen is fantastic. Talent is something you have, you don't learn it." Of the environment Mulcahy created around him, Lambert noted that "what is amazing is that the crew is all in line with him and everyone is working their arse off for him. That I like. You want to be in the action and to participate, and when you are not it's sad. Sometimes I really want to do something even if I am not shooting – and that's great."

Though Lambert had a stunt double for some of his fight sequences, he also carried out a good number of them himself, something that's all the more impressive given his extreme myopia. "In those days when he took his glasses off he didn't know what end of the sword he had hold of," laughs director Andy Armstrong. "You'd never know looking at the movies. He was utterly brilliant at memorising moves; he could do it like a dance and would be absolutely accurate, so incredibly deft that you'd never know that he was of limited vision. At first I thought it was the worst thing on earth to have someone in that situation do the sword fight, but he never missed the mark."

According to Lambert, his bad eyesight is a plus, forcing him to concentrate on the sword moves and stunts, offering up an experience he had while filming *Subway* as an example. On the first day of filming he was set to drive a car at high speed, though director Luc Besson suggested that nobody would know if it was him or not due to the reflection on the window. In typical Lambert fashion, he decided to do it himself for "fun", though he failed to properly judge the distance between his car and the barrier hiding the cameras.

"I pulled the brakes a little too late, bumped into this metal fence and went through the windshield. That was the first day of a 20-week shoot. I thought I'd killed the director and the director of photography. My tuxedo shirt was covered in blood because my skull was broken, well my skin, and they took out the glass, but it's part of the fun too. You don't feel the pain until the director yells, 'Cut'. You're in a strange bubble, but you're willing to do anything the director says; they've got your back."

Creating the transitions

The unique nature of *Highlander*'s dual timeline was always going to be a challenge for Russell Mulcahy and his team. Gregory Widen's original script matter-of-factly moved the action back and forth from the present to the past with few flourishes, but under Peter Bellwood and Larry Ferguson the decision was made to let scenes merge into each other more naturally.

Page one of their first draft had found MacLeod watching hockey players fighting for the puck as he flashed back to a memory of 16th-century Highlanders battling with broadswords, while on page two MacLeod's yelling at Fasil in the basement of Madison Square Garden cut to cheering villagers in 1536. These transitions worked both ways, with scenes set in the Scottish Highlands also moving back to New York by way of clashing swords in one era being replicated in another.

Though Bellwood and Ferguson had no inkling that Russell Mulcahy would direct *Highlander* when they wrote the script, their highly visual take on the film was a perfect match for Russell

Mulcahy, who seized upon their descriptions as he planned his storyboards. "I've tried to deal with the passage of time, and not make the leap to the 16th century too sharp," announced Mulcahy to *Starlog* magazine in 1985. "I want to lull people back into the period so that they accept it."

In the script, the move from New York to Scotland was written as:

```
In  the  arena  above,  New  York  scores.
The  CROWD  CHEERS.  The  SOUND  DISTORTS,
becoming—

                                    CUT TO:

CHEERING VILLAGERS LINING A ROAD
Loch  Shiel,  Scottish  Highlands,  1536.
Glamis  Castle  towers  over  thatched  huts
by the shore.
```

Mulcahy's idea was to connect the two time periods by raising his camera up through the ceiling of Earl's Court, only to emerge beside Eilean Donan Castle, a challenge that the crew relished.

On inspecting Earl's Court, production designer Allan Cameron and cinematographer Gerry Fisher found that there were large concrete cross beams above them, allowing them to raise the camera high into the air, finishing just before they hit the ceiling. Cameron ensured a false beam was added for the camera to move past, with art director Tim Hutchinson explaining that black velvet was also added to ensure the ceiling was dark enough. "At Eilean Donan we dug a trench and another crane came up through some turf. You crane up and there are all these Highlanders advancing."

Peter Bellwood and Larry Ferguson watched with interest as the shot was set up and executed, the latter noting that Mulcahy was "shooting film in a way that was way beyond his time. He was racing across the floor with a Louma crane and both Peter and I were delighted at that first, wonderful transition. Russell did a lot of really amazing stuff with that material. We wrote the transitions, but there's such a great difference between the written word and a film. He just pounced on it. I still look at that film sometimes and try to figure out what camera he was using to get the effects that he did; it was beautifully directed."

"They're probably some of the most amazing transitions of any film ever," says editor Peter Honess, going on to point out that they all came from the director and that some of them were devised to happen on set, without much camera trickery. "Three of them we did in the cutting room later, but he thought up all the good ones and shot it that way."

As part of the lengthy Earl's Court shoot, all the scenes set in the aftermath of MacLeod and Fasil's fight in the Madison Square Garden car park were shot in the same few days, including the police surrounding the headless body. Although most of the scripted pages made it onto the screen, one moment came under scrutiny from producer Peter Davis.

"I remember when we first got to London, Peter was in a state of euphoria because he felt that he'd just saved an entire day of shooting," says Larry Ferguson, who enquired what he meant. "He said, 'You know when Brenda comes in and she reaches up and gets the sword that MacLeod has stashed there? I cut that, we don't need it.' We said, 'If she doesn't have the sword, what will she be performing the tests on when they're doing the spectrograph?'" After retiring to a local pub to discuss the problem, the duo decided to create a new scene in the police station featuring Brenda and a lab technician (Ian Taylor) who brings her pieces of the sword from Fasil's body to examine, with Ferguson explaining it "was the only way we could save that".

"Producers tend to worry a lot about time," continues the writer. "I understand, you're shooting 60 days, you want to shoot 60 days' worth, but sometimes not having the same relationship with the material as the writers do . . . Peter and I worked hard on that, over and over and over, and he would challenge me and I would challenge him on how things worked. Sometimes producers don't understand the material. I used to think that when you were taking a class in English literature for instance and somebody said, 'What is *Hamlet* about?' there were always one or two fellows at the back of the class who'd say, 'I think it's about the overpopulation of Europe,' and they were the ones who grew up to become producers."

Forging ahead

The next major sequence to be filmed in London was the confrontation between the Kurgan and Ramirez inside MacLeod's forge in the Highlands of Scotland. The interior of the building had been designed months earlier and was due to be built inside Jacob Street, while the exterior was to be shot on location in Glencoe.

The first day of filming this sequence was Sean Connery's first day on the *Highlander* set, kicking off an intensive week of shooting that gave Russell Mulcahy little room for error thanks to the deal arranged for the actor which meant he could only be on set for a total of three days. The plan was to get the London scenes in the can, before the entire crew made their way to Scotland to shoot Connery and Christopher Lambert's scenes together.

Before Connery started filming, *Highlander*'s producers were keen to have him learn to fence alongside swordmaster Bob Anderson, something the film's second assistant director, Michael Stevenson, balked at. "I said, 'If you do your homework you'll see he can swim, he was a lifeguard, a singer in the theatre, and he could have been a great footballer. Sir Matt Busby wanted him to play for Manchester United. He's a very fit man. Fencing? He can do that in his sleep.' I said [to Sean], 'Just tell them you want extra money to come down for the day and spend it in London.' They had to put him up at the Grosvenor House Hotel."

Production designer Allan Cameron had built the forge interior in collaboration with special effects supervisor Martin Gutteridge, designing it so that most of the walls could easily be blown outwards to leave only the staircase which Connery and Brown would fight on. Should a second take be required, it was also important that the wall could be rebuilt. Due to the danger involved in collapsing tons of masonry on expensive actors, the stone blocks were instead crafted from polystyrene by sculptor Keith Short, who also notes that "the collapsing timber staircase, made separately at Jacob Street by the carpenters, was clad in polystyrene stone blocks".

Joe Haidar, *Highlander*'s storyboard artist, had completed work on the film earlier in 1985, and by May he was looking around for new projects, but he couldn't turn down an invitation to visit the set during the epic confrontation between Ramirez and the Kurgan. "They had this beautiful set of the forge with a great mural of the sky in the background, which didn't look very believable to me but obviously worked at the time."

As with Connery, Clancy Brown's first appearance in the scene was also the first footage he filmed for *Highlander*. Was that a memorable experience for the young actor? "Sean said only three words to me the entire show, 'Do you golf?' I said, 'No,' and that was kind of the last time he spoke to me." The Kurgan's dramatic entrance – breaking down the door to the tower, before leaping into the room and bringing his sword down onto the table, breaking it in half – didn't go quite to plan, when his sword snapped and a piece of metal flew off in Connery's direction.

"Clancy had to burst through the door and slice the table in half, with Sean Connery there," says Russell Mulcahy, whose team prepared the shot for the cameras before they rolled. "Clancy burst through the door, [with] wind blowing and lightning, leaps and slices the table the wrong way. The sword breaks, the candelabra flies over the crew's heads, and Sean left the set, taking his costume off. Clancy was in the corner nearly in tears, the poor kid felt so bad. Eventually we all made up. It wasn't that he was irresponsible, [but] he was so nervous about having this big role with Sean Connery that he put everything into it [and] forgot what we rehearsed; he basically blanked out. From then on he became the role, he owned the role and he was the Kurgan. I think he's one of the best actors around. We all make mistakes; I've made many."

"It was one of the most careless things I've done and I have the broken hilt to remind me I shall never do anything like that again," Brown is quoted as saying in the film's production notes. "I think it made an impression." The actor also made an impression on a member of the crew, who found himself being hit on the back of the neck by a candelabra that Brown had dislodged while swinging his sword.

As originally filmed by second unit director Andy Armstrong, after the building collapses on the Kurgan, Brown reached for his sword, brought his head up and looked straight into the camera. To the actor's dismay, in the final edit his look to camera was cut out. "I did part of the bit where Clancy kills Sean Connery on the stairs," reveals Armstrong. "Russell shot 90% of it; I did it with Clancy and a double for Sean, and it was literally the killing moment. The close-ups had already been done by Russell, and we were just picking up a few shots. All the stuff Clancy did with a sword he could really do himself and he looked good doing it. There are certain actors that can do physical stuff and look like they're really doing it. Others, no matter how much instruction they get, they always end up looking like an actor acting. I think he brought a lot to that character."

Recalling his own first encounter with Sean Connery, which had found him gushing in front of the actor, Joe Haidar tried to keep a polite distance this time around, only getting near enough so that he could see him. "I'd told myself I couldn't lose control like that again. I stood for 12 hours of that shoot just watching Connery the whole time." Haidar was impressed by the 54-year-old Connery's energy on set, which put many younger men to shame. "When I met him in the office he seemed like an old man, but when he was in costume he just came back to that youthful Connery. He was so vigorous and he'd climb those 15 feet of stairs with no railing or mattress that I can recall. He actually tripped on one take and I believe he bent the sword he was using, but of course they had a spare."

While on set, Connery never took a break from trying to perfect his performance, working closely with Bob Anderson to prepare for the upcoming sword fight. "They would go off in between takes and rehearse a particular set of choreography with the sword," continues Haidar. "He would never just sit in his chair. I thought, 'This man is fit.' Here he was doing his own stunts and they were risking his life and I thought, 'Wow, isn't this kind of risky?'"

Despite the hectic schedule, Haidar notes that there was still some time for levity on set. "In between takes he always seemed to say the funniest things. Connery and [assistant director] David Tringham had a really nice relationship and were cracking each other up all the time, making everyone else laugh."

As filming of the staircase sword fight began, crew members were strategically positioned behind the walls to ensure that they did indeed collapse on cue, with strikes from the sword of Clancy Brown or Sean Connery often dislodging parts of it. "I storyboarded that scene with the castle and I forgot there were collapsing walls and stairs," says Joe Haidar, who was too busy focusing on Sean Connery's ability to shoot multiple takes and seemingly never get tired. "I was tired just standing there!"

One of those behind the wall was Bill Little, who had originally answered an advert to work as an extra on the film's battle sequences. When it was discovered that he had a martial arts background, the stunt crew asked him to work on some fight scenes in London. Arriving at Jacob Street, he and a handful of other extras were instructed to hold the ends of some string and stand behind the wall as the fight sequence began.

"The extras had string tied to the stone stairs and had to pull it at the right time to make the stairs crumble and fall," says Little, adding that nobody was paid extra because the budget didn't allow for it. "It was all a bit hurried and ramshackle, but that was my first film. TV shoots were better organised." Evidence of the extras' work can be seen in the finished film, with editor Peter Honess adding that "when Clancy's going up the stairs chasing Sean Connery, watch very carefully as he takes a swipe at the wall and you'll see a special effects guy scrambling out of the way. In those days you couldn't get rid of things like that."

"*Highlander* was made before CGI, so it was very theatrical," adds Russell Mulcahy. "We had a paint backdrop of the sky looking like something out of a 1940s movie, and when the stairs collapsed it was like 20 guys below with string and the wind blowing; 'One, two, three go!' It was total theatrics, a bit like Pink Floyd's *The Wall*."

Screenwriters Larry Ferguson and Peter Bellwood also remember being at Jacob Street for the first week of filming, including the day of the fight. "This was the day Ramirez was going to be beheaded at the top of a long flight of stairs," says Davis. "There was talk about whether his head was going to come off or not," adds Ferguson.

Now that Sean Connery's death scene had been shot under the cover of Jacob Street, the rush was on to get the actor and the rest of the production out of London and up to Scotland to continue filming. Any delay would severely impact the budget, putting the rest of the shoot in jeopardy. The pressure was on.

SEVEN

BONDING IN SCOTLAND

Campbell Muirhead had always wanted to be in the movies. Although he'd had some experience acting in amateur theatre productions in his home town of Paisley in Scotland, it wasn't a place well known as a film-making hub.

Muirhead's most recent job as a stagehand for a pantomime version of *Sleeping Beauty* at Glasgow's King's Theatre, a 15-minute train journey from the home he shared with his mother, hadn't led to any offers of moving to London to try for work in the West End. By the spring of 1985, Muirhead was out of work and on the dole, regularly dropping into his local Job Centre to look for new opportunities, and it wasn't unusual for his mother to point out adverts for work that she might have spotted in the newspaper.

One April day, Muirhead's mother noticed an article in the *Daily Record* newspaper that mentioned a new film production was heading to Scotland from London and that they were looking for extras to go to the set in Fort William, 100 miles north of Paisley. Muirhead made his way to the Job Centre and asked a staff member if they knew about the film, aware it wasn't in the area. "He said, 'I'll have a wee look,' and he came back and said, 'Yes, I've got the phone number here. If you phone up the production office they'll arrange an interview.'"

A quick chat on the phone with a member of the production team led to Muirhead giving details of his age, height and build, as it was explained that various scenes requiring extras to be dressed in period clothing would be shot in the area surrounding Fort William. "I was going to go up there for a costume fitting as a warrior in the battle sequence, and about a week before I was due, I think it was a Sunday morning, a production assistant phoned me and said would you like to come up tonight? We've got a special job for you. This was to stand in for this actor, Christopher Lambert, whom I'd never heard of at the time. I didn't know what a stand-in was."

When the assistant explained that Muirhead wouldn't actually be seen in the film, his mood soon soured. "I wanted to be in the film because working as a stagehand, you're backstage and I've got acting training. I'd just be standing there while they set up the cameras, though I would have more days on the film. I thought, 'No, I've got to be in this movie; I'm sick of taking a back seat,' and I turned them down."

Keen to have Muirhead on the team, the assistant offered to call him back later that evening, urging him to think hard about the opportunity. "My mother said she thought I should go for it, but I wasn't really interested. They phoned me back at five o'clock, and the production assistant said, 'The two producers and the director had a meeting and they want you; are you coming?' I wondered how I'd get up there, as it's a four-hour drive from Paisley, and my mother said she'd give me a lift."

When the production offered to put him up in a hotel in Fort William for the night, along with a room for his mother and aunt, Muirhead agreed to take the job of stand-in, heading up on Sunday 12 May. On arrival, he was handed a call sheet which listed all the scenes due to be shot on the Monday and the actors required on set. As he'd never seen one before, he wasn't entirely sure what it was for. "My name was in capitals next to Sean Connery and this geezer Christopher Lambert. I thought I must be quite important. I took it and went to the bar for a few drinks. My mother and aunt went to their room and I went to mine to sleep and then at 2.30 in the morning it suddenly dawned on me this guy I was standing in for was this French guy who just did *Greystoke*, bloody Tarzan! I'm a keep-fit fanatic and thought, *Bring it on!* I never looked back."

Early on Monday 13 May, Muirhead had his breakfast and made his way on foot for around a mile to the base of Ben Nevis, the highest mountain in Britain. "It was seven o'clock, I was a bit nervous and it was cold. I said to the first person I met, 'Listen mate, where's the toilets around here?' and it turned out they hadn't been set up yet. He said [affects American accent], 'Well Campbell, don't worry about it, just go behind a tree,' and then I found out this was the flaming producer, Peter Davis."

As Campbell Muirhead was arriving on set, so was a member of the crew who had worked with Christopher Lambert on *Greystoke* and who had recently found himself in Fort William as *Highlander*'s clapper loader, part of cinematographer Gerry Fisher's team. Paul Kenward was the person in charge of the film stock, the clapperboards and numbering the scenes. "You also work closely with the continuity girl and in between that you have to supply the crew with tea and coffee," says Kenward, who has memories of it being a happy set and of spending time with the likes of camera operator Douglas Milsome, first assistant camera Jamie Harcourt, camera operator Mike Rutter and his assistant, Billy Malone.

Kenward and others in the crew had already worked with Russell Mulcahy on some of his music videos and were happy to be back with him again. "[Working with] Russell made you go to work every day and go, 'Wow, this is incredible.' We stayed in the same hotel as Russell; he was very close to the camera crew. I think he identified a lot with us."

Both Paul Kenward and Campbell Muirhead were preparing to shoot a key scene for Sean Connery's character of Ramirez, as he arrives on horseback to the surprise of MacLeod and his wife, Heather. After the crew had spent hours transporting cameras, film canisters, sound equipment, lights and other paraphernalia into the countryside, the actors were finally able to make their way to the location.

Having met actor Beatie Edney for the first time, Muirhead quickly got to know her better as the pair had to lie on the ground together while the scene was prepared for filming. "I know Beatie quite well now; she was quite lovely then, very voluptuous, and they had me there as she clings on to Connor MacLeod when all of a sudden Sean appears. I'm there with Beatie Edney pressing her bosoms into my back and Sean Connery on a big white charger in front of me thinking, 'This is amazing!'"

After rehearsing the scene with Muirhead, Christopher Lambert was now brought in to lie beside Edney, while Sean Connery mounted his horse once again in preparation for jumping over his fellow actors. The scene was filmed beside the edge of a steep mountain, which made it a difficult stunt due to the slope on one side. As Connery's horse jumped, a golf ball suddenly flew past his head, startling not only the actor but the crew around him.

"One of the drivers was practising his golf where the trucks were parked," says Paul Kenward, noting that the ball hit a rock, came back across the road and flew past Connery, who then jumped off his horse, grabbed the ball and ran to where the golf ball had come from. "There, scuttling into the back of the truck was this driver called Boisey. Connery looks in and goes, 'Boisey?' and Boisey goes, 'Sean, how are you?' They'd worked on about five things apparently, and Connery goes, 'That fucking ball nearly hit me,' [and Boisey] said, 'Sorry, guv, I was practising for Saturday.' Connery says, 'Oh, where are you playing?' and he says, 'Just down in Fort William.' Connery says, 'Oh, I'll join you,' and they ended up playing golf together. Then he came walking back down, smiling, going, 'Oh, it was only Boisey practising for the weekend.' So he got back on the horse and carried on."

"We had great fun," says Beatie Edney of filming in Scotland. "Sean Connery knew my mother [actress] Sylvia Syms, although they've never worked together. He looked after me."

Fort William

The likes of Campbell Muirhead, who worked on *Highlander* for just under three weeks, were placed in hotels or with local families for the duration, where his meals were made for him and his washing done. "You got a call sheet the night before that told you where the location was, but you had somebody to pick you up and I had a place to stay. I didn't have to pay for anything or think about anything, just do the job. They gave me free taxis to get to locations, you just had to phone up the local taxi firm and say, 'Highlander Productions, it's me, give me a lift to the location.' I was living like a king!"

For Paul Kenward, being in the Highlands for a few weeks was something of a blessing, a chance to escape from some relationship problems he was having back in London. "It rained every day we were in Fort William. Every day it would rain, every night we'd have to dry the camera equipment off." Kenward and his team ended up working a large amount of overtime, which led to an argument with the production manager as she questioned them about their timesheets.

"The producers were standing right by me when I was arguing with her and they said, 'The guys are working really hard; let's get on with the film not the timesheets,' and from then on it was like a licence to print money for the camera crew. Panzer and Davis were really nice guys and they were fantastic to work for. *Highlander* was sort of the last old-fashioned production in my eyes, before Maggie Thatcher and the accountants took over the business."

Staying a few miles outside Fort William was the film's official stills photographer, David James, who had been contacted by the producers and asked if he wanted to work on the latest Christopher Lambert film. "I had no idea who Christopher Lambert was, but the project sounded fantastic and right up my street, because I love being out in the open and not stuck in the studio all the time. I'm not one for romantic comedies and one-on-one dialogue pieces. I like action. I like to be out and about. If I've got a suitcase packed and I'm going somewhere on the plane or train, or even a long drive, I'm happy."

With a career stretching back to the 1960s, encompassing such films as *Carry on Cleo* (1964), *Fiddler on the Roof* (1971), and *The Man Who Fell to Earth* (1976), James was used to spending long hours on sets. "Photography is the biggest selling tool for films.

With TV they'll traditionally have maybe a guy in for a couple of days on an episode, but generally on the feature film, especially the sort of feature films I do, you're on set every day and you're on long hours, of anything between 12 to 16 hours a day."

Unaware of Lambert's previous work, James promptly searched out one of his films to get an idea of whom he'd be shooting. "You try to do it so that you are unobserved," he says of his approach to on-set photography. "Some of them find it distracting seeing another lens on the set, some don't. Christophe was no problem. The last thing an actor needs when he's concentrating on lines and his performance is to see somebody jumping around. What was amazing was that after *Highlander* I became pretty much Christophe Lambert's photographer for two or three years; the last film I did with him was Michael Cimino's *The Sicilian*."

Because of Sean Connery's limited time on the film, James had to make sure that everything he did was above average. "It was teamwork; everyone was as important as everybody else. Sean, bless him, was lovely and enjoyed my photographing him. I've worked with him on a couple of things since and we still have fond memories of it."

It was paramount that Connery only spend a week on the film, a requirement that necessitated comprehensive filming from the Fort William base. To ensure the actor was able to get to the set each day without delay, he stayed at Inverlochy Castle Hotel, three miles from the centre of Fort William. From there, he would be flown by helicopter to each location in order to maximise his availability. "They even offered me a shot once as well," says Campbell Muirhead. "This woman with a clipboard said, 'I've just arranged for you to go to Mallaig by chopper, is that OK?' I think they ended up cutting back on the budget and we got a minibus." Muirhead remembers Russell Mulcahy walking around Fort William's yachting club "in bare feet and jeans and fluorescent shirts when it was blazers only. He was a cool dude."

Not used to life on set, it took other members of the crew to guide Muirhead in the ways of being a stand-in, including Sean

Connery's personal stand-in, Roy Everson. "He kind of took me under his wing and told me, 'You've gotta be here all the time, don't go to the loo without telling somebody, watch everything they do and watch their mark.' I used to tell Christopher and Sean where their marks were when they came back from tea or whatever."

Despite Lambert's star status, he tended to keep something of a low profile on set. Says Muirhead, "The first time I was introduced to him he didn't have his wig on and had his hair in curlers, so he looked like [British soap opera character] Hilda Ogden. The runner said, 'You're supposed to go and get him a coffee, hold his cigarette while he's doing his thing; you've got to look after him.' So I started doing that on the first day, and like a toady I kept saying, 'Do you want a coffee, can I get your meal for you?' And he said, 'No, no, I'll get my own.' I kept doing that and he kept saying, 'No, no, don't worry,' and then he just ignored me. So the second day I thought, 'Sod this, I'm just going to ignore him; he can do what he wants and somebody else will get him his lunch.'"

Muirhead also recalls that Lambert's short-sightedness caused some interesting moments during filming of the montage sequence in which Ramirez trains MacLeod. "When he was filming he didn't wear his glasses and he's as blind as a bat. There's a scene in the woods where he's sword fighting with Sean and there are false trees made of polystyrene. He was swinging his sword about and it got stuck in a tree. He's waving about this whole log on the end of his sword saying, 'What is this?' I managed to get in and fence a wee bit with Sean. I said, 'Hey Sean, square go.' I had the claymore and Sean had the samurai sword and we sparred a bit."

In the shot of a tree falling on MacLeod as Ramirez watches, only the back of the latter's head can be seen on camera, a sign that Sean Connery wasn't on set that day. Due to constraints on Connery's time, a number of shots of Ramirez sparring with MacLeod utilised the actor's double. As a general rule, any shot of Ramirez that doesn't clearly feature Connery's face means it was filmed without him. "Sean was a delight to work with," says

Russell Mulcahy. "We'd shoot his close-up over Christophe, then two weeks later we'd shoot Christophe's close-up over a double."

According to *Highlander*'s second assistant director, Michael Stevenson, "Sean is a top professional; he's been in the business a long time. They welcomed him wherever he went up near Fort William. He was never late, couldn't bear anybody else being late, very professional, very friendly but he wanted things to be right. At times he might have had a few differences of opinion with Russell, but most of the film he got on fine with him."

At some point during the week, a problem occurred that saw Sean Connery's contract with the producers work in his favour, as according to Michael Ryan, the man who helped raise the finance for *Highlander*, a technical issue resulted in Connery staying on for two more days of filming. "There was a fault with the camera and the negative was damaged," said Ryan in 2016. "The deal was $500,000 for three days [of Connery's time], $500,000 for every day after that. Because of the technical problems he got another million."

Choppy waters

The sequence that found Ramirez and MacLeod in a small rowing boat required that not only Sean Connery and Christopher Lambert be on set, but also various stand-ins and stunt doubles. Filming took place on Loch Shiel, close to the famous Glenfinnan monument built in 1815, the fictional home of the Clan MacLeod in the film.

"We rehearsed it, just me and Sean in an old Victorian wooden boat," says Campbell Muirhead, who recalls sitting at the stern with his feet up, looking right into Connery's eyes as he rowed the boat. "It was such a heavy boat that I think he pulled a muscle rowing me across. We went back to the dock and there was a make-up girl waiting to get in the boat. She looked over my shoulder with shock on her face. I was getting a bit full of myself; I thought she was looking at me, but Sean was behind and he was waiting for me to give him a hand out of the boat."

That make-up girl was make-up supervisor Lois Burwell, who had already worked on films including Bill Forsyth's *Gregory's Girl* (1980) and Ridley Scott's *Legend* (1985). With the actors wearing wigs and make-up, someone had to take cosmetic supplies onto the loch to fix any problems that might occur between takes, a job that fell to Burwell rather than Connery's make-up artist, Ilona Herman. "My head was trapped under Christophe Lambert's bottom, and my feet were poking out," says Burwell, laughing at the memory of having to lie on the floor of the boat for an extended period of time.

The actors were filming a short scene in which Ramirez tries to prove to MacLeod that the latter can't be killed, rocking the boat so that the young Scotsman falls in and walks along the bottom of the loch. In reality, the two actors remained dry for the scene, with Lambert stopping himself from falling into the water before there's a cutaway to stunt double Andy Bradford toppling into the murky depths.

On their return to the shore, and due to both Connery and Lambert wearing expensive costumes, two prop men were ordered to wade out to the boat to piggyback the actors to dry land, leaving Lois Burwell behind. "I'm five feet one and the water would have come up to my chest; I also had a cold and looked particularly pale. I'm still in the boat going, 'Can somebody come back for me, please?' Then Sean, and I remember this because [costume designer] Jim Acheson blew a gasket, waded into the water and carried me to the shore, but ruined his costume. I have to say, not many people can say they got rescued from a rowing boat by Sean Connery."

Andy Bradford was later rowed out into the loch with Connery to complete the sequence, dropping into the water on cue. Bradford wasn't supplied with a wetsuit, so had to bob about in the freezing water while Connery was returned to the shore in a speedboat ahead of him.

"Filming on the loch went smoothly," recalled Russell Mulcahy, who returned to the loch on a weekend alongside assistant director

Stephen Hopkins and Christopher Lambert to shoot scenes of MacLeod going under the surface. "When he went under, his brain froze and he nearly drowned as there were no divers there. We nearly lost him."

Lambert's version of events is less dramatic than Mulcahy's. "The water was four degrees centigrade, so it was cold," he states, adding that he wore a drysuit under his costume. "We didn't have divers, but we had a couple of safety people. [When the cameras roll] you don't think any more, you're in a bubble between 'Action' and 'Cut', you're somebody else. I just went in the water and the fact it was really cold, and that [MacLeod] can't swim, obviously you go under too many times and at one point you could drown, but I had safety people with me. The danger was much more from the cold because I can swim."

The end of the sequence found MacLeod trying to sneak up on Ramirez as the former exits the water, sword in hand. "I take my hat off to Christopher, he really earned his money walking out of a loch in May," says art director Tim Hutchinson. "We had to build a ramp that was seven foot deep at the lowest end, so he had to walk down it, then he stood and waited for the bubbles and any disturbance to disperse, then he slowly walked to shore and he did it without any shivering. It was really cold."

"The most difficult thing was when I got out of the loch with the two fish in my kilt," adds Lambert. "I had to go under [the water] for the camera and the water had to be still, then I came out, so maybe ten seconds under? After three or four takes the water is too cold for the brain, so we did it four times and had to stop."

The fish had been bought earlier that day by local Clyde Lawson and his brother, who were hired to taxi Sean Connery and Christopher Lambert around various locations by boat. On the day of filming beside Loch Shiel, the Lawsons were asked to find fish somewhere nearby. "I remember we were sent out to the local fish farm, but the guy would only sell us 100 and we had a bin full of salmon," says Lawson. "It took all day to film it and by the time they got around to using them they'd all died." In the end, the shot of fish dropping out of MacLeod's kilt was filmed in Wales using a double for Christopher Lambert's feet, four months after principal photography.

The film's production notes allege that Connery frequently broke into song during filming, most notably while on Loch Shiel. Standing tall in the boat, the actor is said to have shouted 'Farewell, farewell!' as he raised an arm to wave goodbye to the loch, with the crew spontaneously breaking into applause.

Perhaps inspired by the sequence, Beatie Edney remembers that Russell Mulcahy suggested to her that she should swim naked in the loch at the end of the shoot, something she wasn't enthusiastic about. "I would have caught hypothermia! I said I'd go in the water if he would. I never heard another word about that scene."

Glen Nevis

During their February and April recces to Scotland, Allan Cameron and Tim Hutchinson had identified Fort William, specifically the nearby Glen Nevis, as the perfect location for a number of sequences, including the battle sequences, the village of Jedburgh and the exterior of Connor's forge and cottage. "I remember the wind blowing and the rain pouring down and we were actually clinging on to rocks so we didn't get blown over," said Cameron of his initial visit. "Everyone thought we were mad to build it up there, but the aspect was so fantastic that it just had to be built there."

While the interior of the forge had already been built and utilised in Jacob Street Studios for Sean Connery's first day of filming, work on the exterior had started in London many weeks before the unit needed to relocate to Scotland. Early discussions between Cameron and Gerry Fisher resulted in drawings of the Glen Nevis buildings being shared with the relevant departments. "A lot of dressing would have been sourced in London because the infrastructure is quite extensive and you could hire some stuff there," says Tim Hutchinson. "I know we had workshops in Fort

William but some stuff we might have pre-fabbed in London and brought up in a truck and then a smaller crew would have come up to build the forge."

Despite the tough weather conditions, the construction team managed to successfully haul the materials required to an area in Glen Nevis known as The Study. Here, the team had to ensure that the forge was bolted into rocks so that it didn't fly away in the strong winds.

Though the exterior reached more than 50 feet into the air, this was only part of the finished forge, as the decision was made to increase its height with the use of matte painting, a technique that saw buildings or landscapes painted onto glass rather than being built in a real location. Matte painter Ray Caple, who had worked on films such as *Superman* (1978) and *Alien* (1979), was brought to Glen Nevis to add an upper level to the existing building that extended the height by almost a half. "He sat there in a little tent, because it was raining," said producer Bill Panzer. "It was a combination of a very aggressive, modern, stylistic director and that technique, which goes back to the 1930s, in a location that goes back before time."

Campbell Muirhead remembers being at the forge set during filming of the scenes that took place between Sean Connery and Christopher Lambert, when the latter wasn't having a cigarette close by. "Connery's a consummate professional and he was always there in full make-up and wig. He was going over his speech about the Quickening and I interrupted him and said, 'Sean, my arse is all wet,' because I was sitting on the straw on the ground next to him. He said, 'That's why you're sitting there and not me,' and gave me that stare. A local farmer had been watching from afar and he came up to me later and said, 'Campbell, you were in there with James Bond, you're a star!' I had all the locals on my side, anytime Christopher was ill or fell off a horse, they'd say, 'Campbell, now's your chance, you could take over.'"

With the fight inside the forge leading to the building's near complete destruction, Allan Cameron and the construction team had to replicate the aftermath on the exterior, effectively having to dismantle it in Glen Nevis before rebuilding it again as a crumbling heap. Remnants of the staircase were also added to the interior. Connor and Heather's croft was then built further down the slope, with the interior shots once more filmed back in London.

Another sequence to be filmed in Glen Nevis took place in the market town of Jedburgh and featured Ramirez explaining to MacLeod why he must leave Heather or risk being heartbroken when she eventually dies. As well as building a stone courthouse – or at least the shell of one crafted from polystyrene blocks – Allan Cameron's team added depth to the scene by placing stalls around the market selling various goods, including wools, leathers, meats, pottery, poultry, skins, fruit and cloth.

Hundreds of extras were brought in from Fort William and the surrounding area to give life to the bustling market, which proved to be one of Cameron's favourite sets from the film. "I'm always in two minds [about people moving into the set]," explained Cameron at the time. "It's mine until everyone else arrives, then they take over. I always imagine the set with people in it when I design it. I imagine people coming down the steps, standing on the market cross, the horses going through. Then as soon as the camera crew arrives and you see the camera tracks and the lights, it rather destroys the illusion."

On the beach

For the sequence of Ramirez and MacLeod running along the sand, the hunt for a secluded spot took the production team an hour west from Fort William, to a small beach close to the village of Arisaig and the camping site of Camusdarach. Just a few years earlier, another crew had used Camusdarach beach to shoot scenes for Bill Forsyth's 1983 film, *Local Hero*, but for *Highlander* it was decided to move further up the coast to a smaller beach sometimes referred to as Refuge Bay.

I discovered just how secluded the beach was when I took a train to nearby Morar station and walked to Camusdarach, using a photo of art director Tim Hutchinson's original map as reference. It took me an hour to find the campsite and another 20 minutes to clamber over a fence and make my way through long grass and sand to find what appeared to be the beach from *Highlander*. After eating a packed lunch while trying to work out where Christopher Lambert and Sean Connery ran along the sand, I made my way back to Morar station, only to find when I got home that I'd been on the wrong beach and that I should have gone over another set of rocks to find the actual location.

I was able to search again a few months later, this time getting a lift by car to Camusdarach before walking along to the correct beach. Looking down on the glorious white sand, it was obvious why Allan Cameron and his team had chosen this spot for the film, even if they weren't thinking ahead to film fans trying to find the location decades later.

"It was lovely, nice and sunny," says Campbell Muirhead of the day in May 1985 when he and a small army of technicians and actors descended on the beach. "The sea was greeny blue and the sand was like white powder, and of course no footprints whatsoever, because nobody goes up there. So Roy Everson, Sean's stand-in, and I went down to the water's edge, 100 or 200 yards away from the camera crew. There were a few rocks about, it's a wide flat beach, and Sean comes over in his costume and make-up because it's seven in the morning, Christopher is nowhere to be seen. It's a wee bit chilly so Sean rubs his hands together and says, 'Morning, boys, think I'll just go for a piss behind this rock.' He wouldn't use the honeywagon, he would just pee against a tree, and all the local farmers are going, 'Look, there's James Bond; he's pissing against my tree!'"

As the sequence starts, with Ramirez asking MacLeod to feel the blood of a stag coursing through his veins, an actual stag can be seen to the side of the pair just above the beach. Tim Hutchinson recalls that a local gamekeeper was approached to provide a deer for the filming, the plan being to sedate the animal so that the camera operator would be ready for it when it woke up. "The gamekeeper said we had very little time to shoot this as the deer would come round in about 45 seconds, and indeed it did. It struggled to its feet and looked around and made off, so there are shots of it galloping away and they run along beside it."

Of the running sequence, Campbell Muirhead notes that Connery was "a big fella and he was pretty fast. He had a golf club with him and he'd take practice swings between takes saying, 'My God, it's like the Bahamas here.' He was in his element." Russell Mulcahy agrees that the actor appeared to enjoy the scene, explaining that it was over in three takes. "He loved it. He got to ride a great white horse and he loves horses."

After the beach run, Ramirez and MacLeod can be seen running off the edge of a cliff and jumping into the sea. While Sean Connery and Christopher Lambert were able to jump off a small rocky outcrop onto cardboard boxes around 15 feet below, swordmaster Bob Anderson and stunt performer Andy Bradford were led to a much higher rock by mountaineer and explorer Hamish MacInnes. Says Bradford, "He guaranteed it was safe below because he and a number of climbers had climbed it after a number of Scotches. I remember saying to Bob before we jumped, and he wasn't a particularly young guy then, 'Are you okay with this, Bob?' He said, 'Yeah, yeah.' It's very difficult to judge heights when you're looking at sea water, but we estimated it and jumped. I couldn't wear a wetsuit to take out the sting [of the impact]."

"I quite admired his courage, but he was a water expert and it was always dreich and damp," says Campbell Muirhead of Bradford. For his part, Muirhead was doubling Christopher Lambert at the safer outcrop beside Sean Connery. "Connery had his bare feet, so he's running up to the edge and running back again to practise while he's waiting on Christopher. I was standing on the edge in my welly boots. Connery comes to the edge, and because it's a bit slippy he had to grab on to my shoulder to stop himself falling over; he did that four or five times. So me being a wee boy when

James Bond was all the rage, here was Sean Connery leaning on me at the edge of this cliff . . . it was good for me, I don't know what it was like for him. Then Christopher comes along and the both of them jump onto the boxes in one take."

Hamish MacInnes helped the second unit find numerous places to film on Scotland's west coast and on the Isle of Skye, working closely with doubles for Connery and Lambert. A shot of Ramirez and MacLeod beside running water on the edge of an outcrop was filmed in Torridon, while the final shot in the training montage, with the pair standing high on a rock as MacLeod flips Ramirez's sword, took place on Skye's Cioch Buttress.

When I email MacInnes in January 2019 to find out more about his work on the film, he replies that he did indeed set up the Cioch fight, though at 88-years-old and recently recovered from a near-fatal incident that led to his hospitalisation and memory loss, he understandably has little time for interviews. "Though I didn't allow my name in the credits, I did a great deal of work on the film with Lambert and Sean Connery," admits MacInnes, whose remarkable career was detailed in the 2019 documentary, *Final Ascent: The Legend of Hamish MacInnes*.

Wrapping up

Sean Connery's time on *Highlander* had been intense, a week that had seen him ferried around the Highlands of Scotland by helicopter as Russell Mulcahy and his team attempted to get the most from the actor. "We had seven days with Sean, and if we went an hour over it'd be major money," says Mulcahy, a tight schedule that meant the director wouldn't be able to film further shots later if he missed any.

To ensure he got the most out of Connery, Mulcahy spent the last half hour of his last day filming him from various angles. "I got him with the hat on, to turn, to smile, to turn round, with the sword out, laughing, looking shocked . . . I had three cameras on him. I looked at my watch and with one minute left I said, 'You're wrapped!' And he went, 'You bastard!' He was one of the most professional actors I've ever worked with."

Connery had taken some time to relax when not required on set, with photographer David James recalling one particularly wet day when the actor approached him. "Sean said, 'You fancy getting warm and a wee dram?' I said, 'You bet I do,' as we were all miserable and cold." The men headed to a pub that was almost certainly the Clachaig Inn in Glencoe, a regular haunt of one of its neighbours, Hamish MacInnes. "Hamish ran the Scottish mountain rescue teams and he also worked with Sean on a climbing movie prior to *Highlander*. We walked in with Sean and Hamish pointed us to a back room. We sat there with a huge log fire and they brought in locally made single malts. It was quite delightful and I've been a fan of single malt ever since."

"I remember Sean Connery had a wonderful, very attractive, assistant who was his personal make-up lady and she was also a qualified nurse," says costume designer Jim Acheson. "We were working so hard that she'd occasionally invite us to her bedroom, which we were all very excited about, where she would tell us to drop our trousers, which we were even more excited about, and then she'd give us a jab of B12 up the bum to keep us going."

Art director Tim Hutchinson remembers that Connery's last day in Glencoe started like the others, with helicopter pilot Peter Polan flying the actor in from Inverlochy Castle first thing in the morning and collecting him again at 5.30 p.m. "On the last day he said to David Tringham, 'What would you like me to do now, David? Is Peter coming?' and he said, 'We don't need him, you can walk down the hill with the rest of us and get a car back to Inverlochy Castle.'"

Traditionally, the end of a film's production schedule is marked by a wrap party for cast and crew, a chance for the hard work of the preceding months to be celebrated by many of those involved. By mid-May 1985, just over a week of filming had taken place and many more were to come, but the decision was made to hold a 'mini-wrap' party to mark the end of Sean Connery's time on the picture.

"It was my birthday as well," says Campbell Muirhead, who notes that "there was free champagne all night, it was great. At Sean's party he got a cheque for around a million bucks and a wee hip flask that said 'Highlander Productions'. He was drinking whisky and I was drinking champagne, and there was a waitress with a wee hat and pinny filling it up all night. Sean was going around everybody and when he came up to me I said, 'Sean, how did you know?' 'Know what?' 'That it's my birthday; you didn't have to go to all this trouble for me, you're a star!'"

With Connery now gone, the production team could focus on moving on to another section of filming, this time focusing on an iconic Scottish location that would provide the backdrop for Connor MacLeod's home of Glenfinnan.

EIGHT

HOLLYWOOD IN THE HIGHLANDS

The village of Dornie is typical of many in the Scottish Highlands. Composed of a scattering of houses, a hotel, a shop, a post office, a gallery and various bed and breakfasts, the former fishing village is tucked into the coastline on the Road to the Isles at the meeting point of Loch Duich, Loch Alsh and Loch Long.

Taking just a few minutes to drive through, Dornie would normally be just another blip on the map for a tourist in a hurry to make their way to the nearby Isle of Skye. Or it would be if Dornie wasn't home to one of Scotland's most photographed castles, Eilean Donan. Pass through the village at the height of the summer season and it's not unusual to see cars lining the side of the road as visitors stop to take a snap of themselves standing in front of the tourist attraction.

The name Eilean Donan means 'Island of Donan' and likely derives from a sixth-century Irish saint, Bishop Donan. Although a fortified structure was first built on the island in the 13th century, it has altered through the centuries, with the current building dating from as recently as 1932. The compact nature of the castle means it has been an obvious attraction for production crews keen to capture a quintessential piece of Scotland on camera. One of Eilean Donan Castle's earliest on-screen appearances is in 1948's *Bonnie Prince Charlie*, starring David Niven as the titular character, while 1953's *The Master of Ballantrae*, featuring Errol Flynn, makes use of the building's exterior.

In the winter of 1985, Dornie's tourist season was on its annual hiatus, its residents enjoying some respite from the visitors that booked out the rooms in the Loch Duich Hotel and nearby B & Bs. It also meant a lack of work for many locals who relied on visitors to the area, meaning that an advert in the *West Highland Free Press* newspaper calling for paid extras to appear in a feature film that was due to be filmed in Dornie in the spring received a fair bit of attention.

Someone who remembers the arrival of the *Highlander* production team well is Richard MacLennan, a Dornie resident who first became aware of the film in the spring of 1985, when he spotted the newspaper advert. Like many of his peers, MacLennan was between jobs thanks to the lack of tourists, so he replied to the advert and was happy to be contacted soon after by the wardrobe department who were asking local men to present themselves at Dornie Village Hall for a costume fitting. "Everyone who was unemployed or didn't have work was going along to Dornie Village Hall to see what parts they'd give you," explains MacLennan. "It was just stowed out with costumes and tartan and goodness knows what; it was like a closing down sale at a clothes shop."

Someone else who read a call for extras in the newspaper, this time the Aberdeen-based *Press & Journal*, was artist and photographer Richard Easson, who was living 100 miles away in the village of Tain in Easter Ross. The advert read simply "Wanted – Film Extras (preferably with beards, moustaches, long hair or prepared to grow same)". Says Easson, "I had long hair at the time and could easily not shave for a wee while, so I went through to Dornie the next week after phoning them up. I remember going into the hall and there were a couple of girls and lots of stands with various costumes. We went into the room and this girl basically said, 'Right, get your clothes off.' They fitted us with two costumes: one was supposed to be a villager and one more like Highland dress."

Production staff were split into those from the costume department and those from casting, with MacLennan recalling that the latter would decide which roles someone was suitable for before they were handed the relevant outfit. "They'd say, 'I think you could play this, that and the next thing.' If you were a Highlander they'd get some gear off the racks, put it on you to see if it fitted, then they'd ask your name and put all the stuff into a bag and take it away to be freshly laundered for when they came back for filming. They told all the guys not to have haircuts and not to shave; they were looking for an authentic look."

While the wardrobe department was busy fitting the extras for their costumes, the art department was also gearing up for the arrival of the large production team. It was at the end of April 1985 that production designer Allan Cameron and his team began preparing for filming of both Connor MacLeod's crossing of the castle walkway as he marched on to battle, and scenes of MacLeod's banishment from his village. With just over three weeks allotted to the work, Cameron and art director Tim Hutchinson were thankful they didn't have to build a castle for filming, though they did have to construct the village from scratch in the car park next to Eilean Donan Castle.

Richard MacLennan recalls that at the time a modern bungalow stood between the castle and the empty fields, an anachronism that was soon taken care of by the construction of a church which covered the house exterior. Says MacLennan, "The buildings were scaffolded with plastic and thatch; money was no expense. If they needed something they wouldn't wait for it to come from Inverness. There were all sorts of things they needed from the village and they were paying extortionate prices, even for a couple of days' hire, the equivalent of what it would cost to buy it new. They'd employed nightwatchmen to look after it."

Due to Eilean Donan's exterior being completed in the 1930s, time was also spent ensuring chimney pots were covered ahead of filming. "The chimney pots were the modern round ones," explains MacLennan. "To box them off they used plywood and painted them grey. When you cross the bridge there are passing places. They put up wooden gibbets and iron cages on them because I think prisoners used to be put in them to starve to death. They had plastic skeletons hanging over the water. They also put down dirt over the tar."

With cinematographer Gerry Fisher keen to capture the beauty of Eilean Donan and the surrounding area on camera, it was vital that the art department consider what was happening in the distance. This meant scanning the horizon behind the castle for any signs of the modern world. "Over the loch from the castle there's a white house and a jetty," says Richard MacLennan. "There weren't so many houses over the far side of the bridge at Ardelve as there are now, but they went to the modern houses and negotiated to put scaffolding up in front of them. When they were doing the wide shots, they would send members of the crew over to roll down camouflage netting so that the houses wouldn't be seen. That's the way they did it before all this blue screen and whatnot; it was old-style film up there."

Getting kitted out

As the construction of Glenfinnan was nearing completion in late May, down in Glencoe Russell Mulcahy was finishing work on his week of filming with Sean Connery. The plan was to move cast and crew from their Fort William base to Dornie as soon as Connery had departed. Shooting would then take place around Eilean Donan, before the production returned to Glencoe to film the battle scenes. Some of the first crew to head to Dornie were from wardrobe and make-up, with make-up supervisor Lois Burwell recalling that a minibus was hired to take the various team members on the two-hour drive from Fort William after filming finished at 10 p.m. With filming due to recommence at around 4 a.m. the next morning, everyone was keen to get to bed in good time to enjoy a few hours' sleep.

Realising that their numerous hotels and bed and breakfasts were located at the end of winding single-track roads which took a long time to navigate, concern grew among the crew that no sooner would they be dropped off than the minibus would have to return to collect them again. On discovering that she was booked into a hotel situated beside the Skye ferry, Lois Burwell made an executive decision that she and her colleagues would instead stay the night at her hotel.

"We all pitched up at the hotel and there was only one room left," says Burwell. "I said to them, 'We're going to be up and gone before any guests wake up,' and they had a sort of country house hotel thing where there are lots of comfy sofas and a fireplace in reception, so we all bunked down there and I gave my room to someone who was exceptionally tired, one of the older hairstylists. We all used the bathroom in my room, camped out in the hotel foyer and went to work the next day."

Ahead of Mulcahy's arrival, the wardrobe department recalled all of the extras they'd fitted for costumes a few weeks earlier, ensuring that the sleepy village of Dornie was soon filling up with young men with a similar look. "If you'd come up to the area at that time, say the week before filming, it was like going back in time because nobody was shaving and all the men had beards," laughs Richard MacLennan.

Two large marquees had been put up beside the Loch Duich Hotel, and on arrival a member of wardrobe would take names and find a bag with the appropriate costume. "You had to be there for seven o'clock in the morning," continues MacLennan, "then they had a fleet of buses transferring all the extras over to the castle. You'd go there, get changed, and put your gear on. They'd had all the clothing freshly laundered, but as soon as you arrived at Eilean Donan, all these women were there with buckets of mud to cover you with, assuring you that you wouldn't be catching diseases from the 1500s. Then you were filming until seven at night."

Leaving Tain at 3 a.m. to allow for delays on the single-track road caused by sheep, caravans, deer and landslides, Richard Easson arrived at the tented village in Dornie to be faced with rows of kilted warriors and 16th-century villagers. Handed a form to collect his costume by assistant director Jane Studd, he was sent to the changing tent along with half-naked men struggling into their costumes with help from wardrobe assistants.

After a visit to the make-up tent for the application of dirt and long hair as required, Easson was informed that the first work he and his fellow extras would do involved marching to and from the castle, as the Clan MacLeod headed into battle with the Frasers. Actor Christopher Lambert led the march on horseback, alongside his cousins, Angus (James Cosmo) and Dugal (Billy Hartman).

"In the film you'll see smoke going past the castle, like mist on the loch," says Richard MacLennan, going on to explain that the crew placed smoke machines on boats and pushed them out onto the loch, before they discovered there wasn't enough wind for the effect to work properly. "I think that was the only time in the Highlands of Scotland that you had a big company coming up there and being unhappy at not having rain and mist when they were filming. Visitors are always surprised the bridge is really short, but it looks like a really long bridge with all the different angles and shots. When it first started, whatever position you were in you had to stay in that position for the day's filming to help continuity."

After being issued with a shield and axe, Richard Easson was given instructions by the assistant directors, who had split the extras into groups. He would walk round from behind the castle to join the march, speaking briefly to his 'wife' who had come to wave him off into battle, before making his way to the front of the crowd behind the pipers. "We were all full of energy and marched through the castle shouting our heads off, then somebody went mad at the other end because they had black-and-white film in the camera and they forgot to change it. We all had to go back again, I think I counted 17 times we marched across and back again."

While Russell Mulcahy and his crew were busy trying to keep a multi-million pound production moving along smoothly, the arrival of a film crew to a small corner of the Highlands was a chance for locals to both earn some much-needed cash and an excuse to catch up with old friends.

"We'd never seen the likes of Hollywood coming up to the Highlands," says Richard MacLennan. "There were a lot of people that I hadn't seen for years. Plockton is the main secondary school around here, and there were a lot of people you'd maybe recognise and when there was a break in filming you'd all be able to chat away. On the first day we found out when the meal breaks were. When you were in a crowd scene and didn't have to be in any particular place, at lunchtime you would go and make sure you were near the food truck."

MacLennan recalls that the catering trucks served tea and coffee in the morning, a break at 10 a.m. and a cooked meal at lunchtime, followed by tea and a selection of cakes, scones or shortbread. "You'd get in there first, get your meal, and then it was just a short distance to walk into Dornie. The pubs were open, so some of us would go down and get a couple of pints in the village, making sure you were back in time for the filming in the afternoon. There was quite a lot of, shall we say, 'overreaction' going on after the lunchtime meetings. Even though it was May, they had great weather for it; it was sunny and warm. Hence the reason we had to go for extra refreshments."

With the bridge sequence completed at around 4 p.m., the extras now tired and hoarse from shouting all day, the afternoon was spent filming Connor MacLeod, his cousins and his girlfriend, Kate (Celia Imrie), marching through the village on their way to the battle. As the scene begins, the villagers walk past the modern bungalow disguised as a church. "They had to cover the gable end of the bungalow and they put a cross on the top," notes Richard MacLennan. "If you're watching the film, you can see when they're marching through the village that the cross is on fire; that was a way to call the clansmen and not make people wonder what was behind the church outline."

Richard Easson took some walks around the village between takes to see what details Allan Cameron and his team had added to the set, including horses tethered to fake plaster blackhouses with thatched roofs, geese in cages and hens settling down on the mud that had been spread over the car park's tarmac. A row of directors' chairs sat empty beside the cameras and lights, while nearby vans and lorries held the props and equipment required for the day's shoot. He also spotted Christopher Lambert walking around the area in an anorak, glasses and kilt.

With dozens of extras required to make the scene look busy, each one brandishing a sword and cheering, the task of trying to manage them while also concentrating on the main cast led to Russell Mulcahy attempting to split the supporting artistes into manageable groups. Richard MacLennan's memory of Mulcahy is of someone busy "barking orders; nobody wanted to put a foot wrong. The way they worked out [the groups] was by your birthday, so they'd say, 'Anyone born in February, March and April, you can wave your arms and shout, the other ones stay quiet.' Being in the Highlands, that's when the most birthdays are, so he discovered he then had to change the date until he got the ones who were near the camera wailing and bawling and they'd be recording that. Then you'd do another one exactly the same as you did before but you were silent, so they could get the actors' voices."

Thanks to some careful planning back in London, the first part of the transition that took the audience from 1980s Madison Square Garden back to 16th-century Scotland had already been filmed. As the camera was raised up past a false beam placed just below the ceiling in Earl's Court car park, it met a length of black velvet and stopped. When the art department arrived at Eilean Donan Castle, they built a section of wall, placed the camera in a trench, ensured it was as dark as it had been in Earl's Court, and raised the camera up past the edge of the wall.

A shot that hadn't been planned but that added atmosphere to the scene of Connor MacLeod lying on his deathbed, was that of a lone piper playing under an orange sky in front of Eilean Donan. "They hadn't realised it was going to be a nice sunset, so there was a mad rush to get the cameras set up to get the castle with the sunset behind it," says Richard MacLennan. "Some of the sunsets you get up here are pretty cracking. So that was natural rather than your made-up stuff."

Filming of the march through the village lasted until 8.30 p.m., the cast constantly having to move from point A to B and back again as Russell Mulcahy battled bolting horses and technical issues. With the day's work at an end, the extras were asked to return their props before being bussed back over to the tents to change into their own clothes and asked to return for another day of shooting the next morning at 5.30 a.m. On leaving the tent, Richard Easson noticed that the public bar of the local hotel was overflowing with extras, some still in costume, forcing themselves to drink alcohol in order to soothe vocal chords that were strained from shouting all day. "I prescribed myself the same treatment," says Easson.

A yoke's a yoke

The second day of filming saw the newly built village of Glenfinnan become the focal point, as MacLeod's friends and family attack and banish him following his miraculous return from certain death at the hands, or rather sword, of the Kurgan.

Richard Easson had slept overnight in the back of his car, from which he emerged at 5 a.m. to make his way to the costume tents. It was here that he encountered the legendary wardrobe assistant, Dave Whiteing, known for dressing up in his own costumes and providing some entertainment for the cast and crew. The pencil-moustached Londoner was dressed in US Army fatigues and doing impersonations of Elvis Presley, John Wayne and various American generals as the extras donned their kilts. "He was incredible," says clapper loader Paul Kenward. "He used to dress up in an outfit like Hitler, get all the extras in line and talk to them as if he was a German soldier. I remember how old-fashioned the humour was from people like that. He had this little black moustache and looked like the guy out of *Dad's Army*, the spiv."

Easson also spied a cameraman with what may have been a Steadicam "running around, in and out and around us all as we were milling about. There was a crane at the end of the village. The main camera would be up on the crane and they'd have a video camera on there so we could see a take as it happened using replay on the video camera; it was probably quite new in those days."

During the camera rehearsal of the scenes of MacLeod being tied to a wooden yoke and beaten, Christopher Lambert's stand-in, Campbell Muirhead, was once again required on set, travelling up from Fort William for a day's work. "I had the yoke on my back and the stunt guys headbutting me and chucking me in the mud," laughs Muirhead, who reckons he fell over more times than Lambert. "It was great fun. I couldn't believe my luck."

"[Lambert] was lashed to the yoke with leather thongs, which I actually have somewhere as I pinched them at the end," admits Richard Easson. "If you were falling, you had to watch your face because you couldn't use your hands as they were lashed to this thing. Plus, he was being buffeted by what looked like real stones, something a bit heavier than polystyrene that you could throw 20 or 30 feet. We did that quite a few times, as Jimmy Cosmo was trying to stop the crowd burning him."

A well-known face on British television in the 1970s and 1980s, James Cosmo's big-screen career had yet to take off when he was cast in *Highlander*, though in later years he would go on to star in films such as *Braveheart* (1995) and *Troy* (2004), as well as HBO's *Game of Thrones* (2011–19). "It was terrific to be in. I really enjoyed it and it was a lot of fun," says Cosmo. "Its longevity is extraordinary, but then again, it was a groundbreaking film. It used rock music, the camera never stayed still, it was a wonderful mix [of genres] and the ideas were terrific. It really was a seminal piece of work."

"I was quite fortunate that I got two parts," says Richard MacLennan. "I was one of the warriors going off to battle and I was also made a peasant. I'm not saying which one was typecasting. In the village I was a peasant, shouting and bawling and throwing plastic stones. That was where I discovered that you never look at the camera, you always look away. A lot of them were looking down the camera, but if you don't look at the camera you'll end up [in the final film]."

Although MacLennan didn't interact much with Lambert, it was clear that the actor was happy to be on set between takes. "Christopher Lambert wasn't really a name we knew at the time, but he was quite the thing, wandering about, mainly getting into position. He was smoking cigarettes like the rest of us. They were strict that you couldn't wear rings or watches to make it look authentic, but everyone had a wee pouch inside their kilts with a fag packet in it because smoking at that time was a big thing."

According to Christopher Lambert, being a film's lead doesn't mean being aloof during a shoot. "I've always viewed the movie business as a circle, with a lot of people in that circle doing the same job. There's no difference for me between the producers, the director, the actors and the costume designer; we're all together trying to do something good. I never set myself apart from the crew – if there's no crew on the set, there's no movie. It's just a matter of respect, being human; everybody's working for the same thing."

With the yoke sequence completed, it was time for the extras to depart the set, though Richard Easson was stopped from leaving when it was realised that a scene featuring Lambert needed to have a shot of the castle in the background. "We were just heading off home when one of the producers or directors said they needed some people walking out of the castle for the long shot of Lambert up the hill when he was running into the heather with the yoke on. We had to run across to the castle and be walking out of it in the distance so that there was some life down there."

Thanks to the extras imbibing alcohol during their time on set, Richard MacLennan is certain that the art department had more than just hay and wood to remove from beside Eilean Donan when it came time to dismantle the village set. "I think when they took down the houses there were quite a number of cans of beer discovered stashed in there, I think some of the carry-outs we brought back were put in there."

Though the Dornie filming was a short yet memorable experience for MacLennan – "When they came up there, we were just told it was a film about someone who was immortal and living in the Highlands of Scotland. It took them a good while to get it set up and when they stripped it all down we never heard any more" – for Richard Easson it wasn't the end of his time on *Highlander*.

As a professional photographer, he'd been commissioned by an Edinburgh magazine to do some drawings for an article he had written on old Edinburgh buildings. On arrival at the publisher's office, the editor wondered why Easson had long hair and a beard. When he mentioned he'd been filming with Christopher Lambert, "she went weak at the knees. She said I must do an article for them for the magazine, so I left some films with them that I had in my camera and sent more down with a synopsis of my story."

Easson was soon heading back up north to experience his first Highland battle.

NINE

PREPARING FOR BATTLE

With filming now wrapped in Dornie, the cast and crew started their journey back to Fort William on Thursday 23 May, with arrangements having already been put in place for the arrival of hundreds of new extras the following week in Glencoe for the battle sequence that would see the MacLeods fight the Frasers.

For Russell Mulcahy, filming in Scotland proved to be a hugely satisfying experience. "We shot up in Glencoe and the Isle of Skye, with the most extraordinary landscapes everywhere you looked. It rained, the sun came out, you had four climates in a day, but wherever you pointed the camera looked beautiful. For raw landscapes, Glencoe is mind-blowing."

As had happened in Dornie, calls had gone out to newspapers around Scotland asking for extras with long hair and beards to make their way to Glencoe for four days of filming. One of those taking up the call was a familiar face from Dornie, as Richard Easson managed to convince the production team to allow him back for more extra work thanks to the magazine feature he'd been commissioned to write.

Easson arrived in a cold and wet Fort William on the evening of Sunday 26 May, parking his car beside a warehouse housing the production offices and deciding to sleep in his car so that he could be up at 6 a.m. on Monday morning. Upon waking, he then went to pick up a costume, before being bussed out to a boggy moor in the shadow of Buachaille Etive Beag in Glencoe with hundreds of other men. "Some stayed in tents, some in caravans, some were probably local. I think if you wanted to be there you made sure you were there. It's not comfortable but it's a film; you either like it or you don't."

Someone else who'd read in the newspaper that a new Sean Connery film was being shot in Scotland was Fort William resident and film fan, Ian Sutherland. Unemployed at the time, he contacted Fort William Job Centre and asked about being part of the film. "I didn't have a beard, but I was determined to become involved so I started to grow one." After being directed to visit the industrial estate being used by the production unit, Sutherland finally learned more about *Highlander*. "The girl who interviewed me told me the film was about 'the immortal struggle between the Frasers and the MacLeods', which made it sound more like a historical family saga. I was hired as a Fraser foot soldier and told to attend a costume fitting followed by two weeks' work on the film."

For his first week of training, Sutherland would get on a bus each morning with his fellow extras, before they were driven to a remote location to undergo sword training under the supervision of Peter Diamond. "I remember what a thrill it was to see a couple of our stunt coordinators wearing caps with *The Empire Strikes Back* logos. We were each partnered with another extra and given polymer training swords which replicated the weight and feel of a real sword. Our trainer taught us four basic attack moves and corresponding moves designed to block them. These moves soon became second nature and very effective when used randomly."

Although not part of the battle, actor Beatie Edney was well aware of the scale of the sequence. "They cast everyone they could find with long hair to be the supporting artists, so lots of bikers and hippies. On the way to the set every day you'd see hundreds of bikers practising fighting with swords by the side of the road. I went to watch the battle sequence in Glencoe. The guys were having so much fun they didn't stop fighting when the director shouted 'Cut!'"

Another returnee to the *Highlander* set was Clancy Brown, who had been left to his own devices in London for almost a fortnight while initial Scottish filming focused on making the most of Sean Connery's restricted availability. Unlike Connery, Brown wasn't offered a chance to be flown anywhere by private helicopter. "When we first went up to Glencoe to shoot the battle scenes, I wasn't treated like most of the cast and had to take a train up to Glasgow. I got into the station around midnight and there was nobody to pick me up. I thought I'd have to spend the night in the station, until a Glasgow copper told me to move along. I found some place that was open and hung out there for the night and they finally came and collected me."

For the look of the Kurgan, costume designer Jim Acheson looked to the work of the American fantasy artist Frank Frazetta, who "used to do very elaborate and detailed work. I had a wonderful assistant called Gilly Hebden and she was always saying, 'All they need is one image, a big image; go for it.' She came from much more of a theatrical background and her boyfriend, now husband, was I think in the fashion industry, and they understood things much better than I did. I was rather pedantic. I remember doing this crazy drawing of the Kurgan, a very loose pen and ink illustration, and we just kind of built it. We had all these crazy ideas of skulls, fur, rubber, snakeskin and God knows what."

Creating one such costume for shooting in the wilds of Scotland was one thing, but the film's producers had other ideas. "I remember being very close to filming and the producers or Clancy suddenly decided that there had to be a stunt double because Clancy couldn't cope with the rearing horse or whatever," continues Acheson, who at the last moment had to duplicate the original armour in rubber for the stunt double. "Americans of course want everything in triplicate, but the dear old British film industry, certainly the films I'd been working on at that time, didn't understand any of that stuff. The actor just put the stuff on and did it. If it broke we repaired it and did it again. If he broke his leg we strapped it up. So suddenly to be told with 48 hours' notice we'd need a whole set in rubber so that Clancy wouldn't hurt himself, poor love, was a problem."

Brown's first scene in Glencoe was a two-hander between the Kurgan and Chief Murdoch, as they prepared for the arrival of the Clan MacLeod and a battle with the Clan Fraser. The role of Murdoch had gone to London-based Scottish actor, Alistair Findlay, who had been collected from Glasgow Airport and driven to Fort William a few days before he was due to shoot his single scene. "Clancy was a very impressive guy to meet. I was going to be on horseback next to him, and to his credit he suggested we have dinner to talk about the scene, which took about 30 seconds in camera time."

The same night, Findlay was fitted with his costume made from reinforced leather, which was fine when he tried it on while standing up. "It was only the next day that I realised that I could hardly sit. And that I was like a tortoise. It was too late to say, 'Actually, can I have a costume change?' and I realised that on horseback I had very little mobility, which was a cause of some concern to me coming up to the shoot."

Already concerned about his costume, Findlay found that once he was on his horse he had to be careful not to get too close to Clancy Brown. "He was on a huge charger, like a carthorse, I must have been on a mare. There was actually somebody holding its head and keeping it steady because of Clancy's huge black charger. That's why I'm a bit behind them. It should really be a two shot, but if the horse goes up too close, Clancy's horse gets very frisky and the whole thing goes pear-shaped."

"The horse I was on was this beautiful Friesian thoroughbred and it was trained within an inch of its life," recalled Brown. "It would do anything I wanted, it was gorgeous and stopped on a dime; it'd do anything. Then they took it up to the Highlands where the horse would sink into the peat. It actually had its own character, it would put on its own mask and it started to bite all the extras."

Photographer David James was also on set for Clancy's first few scenes, when MacLeod sees the Kurgan for the first time. "The camera is pointing 45 degrees up at the Kurgan on the horse and the camera operator says, 'Look through the viewfinder,' and it was like seeing one of those half underwater shots. Because the matte box was filled with water, you were seeing it half underwater, the horse looked like a fish and the Kurgan was above it and dry; I mean the rain was coming down horizontal." Both the first glimpse of the Kurgan – a close-up of Clancy Brown's face – and a shot of MacLeod looking at him, were filmed later in Wales, while the next shot of the Kurgan's horse rearing up is stunt performer Peter Brace rather than Brown. Lightning was added in post-production using traditional cell animation.

Thanks to Brown's enthusiasm, Brace didn't have much screen time in the film, as Brown explained in 2016 at the Edinburgh International Film Festival. "I was 25 when I was doing that show and he was 52, and I would come to him and say, 'Peter, do you mind if I ride the horse?' And he'd say, 'No son, go right ahead, I'll be here in the tent.' Peter Diamond finally had to go to Brace and say, 'You have to do something,' and he said, 'Clancy's doing a fine job. Let him do that and I'll collect my pay cheque.' Finally Peter Diamond came to me and said, 'Would you stop doing everything; we're going to have to fire Peter if he doesn't do anything.' So he was in the water in the [Silvercup fight]; you can see him as clear as day."

Despite Russell Mulcahy being on set, Alistair Findlay didn't meet him. Instead, he found himself being directed by second assistant director, Michael Stevenson, who recalls that before filming had begun there were problems brewing behind the scenes. "We had a big confrontation, because at the beginning the company wasn't prepared to serve [the extras] hot breakfast in the morning. We had about 500 or 600 of them and I went crazy and said, 'I'm going to go to Sean, because if he hears about this, he'll go absolutely mad. These guys have been up since three in the morning, they're going to be here all day fighting, rehearsing and shooting. They're used to getting wet, they're Scottish, but we're not going to do the English Sassenach thing are we?' The caterers, who were friends of mine, wanted to feed them because it was embarrassing."

With extras threatening to throw their weapons and costumes on the ground and leave, assistant director David Tringham took it upon himself to speak to the producers about the situation. Says Stevenson, "David said, 'The guys have got to be fed or you'll have no battle scene, they'll all go, every one of them.' It was then decided that we'd feed them. In the end it cost more money, because while we were having this debate and talking, the minutes were ticking by and they were ready to film. Clancy came on set, the horses were there, the stunt boys were there, we'd worked out rehearsals, we knew what we were doing with the extras and all of a sudden they were talking about going and they were some of the biggest sequences in the film."

Tensions over the catering situation rumbled on, with Michael Stevenson explaining that the politics of the day found their way onto the battlefield. "The other thing, and I was with them on this, was that they couldn't bear the name of Margaret Thatcher and when she was here she thought Great Britain ended at the Watford Gap. She never gave a thought to the people out of work in Wales, Scotland and Northern Ireland. The boys had made a straw effigy of her and put it up on a great big pole, and set light to it. All the other actors were upset. They're working alongside the stunt people from England, but also alongside the Scottish extras, shoulder to shoulder, fighting with the shields and swords and spears, getting soaking wet, so they felt bad about them not being fed. You can't treat people like that."

"You had 200 or 300 extras that had come up from Glasgow and all over," says Campbell Muirhead, adding that they were sleeping in an old Scout hut with one tap of running water. "There were days when it was pretty wet and they were miserable. They were wearing bearskins and fur, bare shoulders and kilts and wigs and they were all damp. The costumes wouldn't dry, so they were all getting a bit pissed off, to say the least."

War is declared

Michael Stevenson and David Tringham were just two of the assistant directors brought in to help Russell Mulcahy manage the extras, with third assistant director Jane Studd also on set.

Stunt coordinator Peter Diamond was also part of proceedings, having carefully planned how the battle would play out with the aid of a storyboard designed by his 17-year-old son, Frazer. "We sat down at the kitchen table with a big wad of paper and a pencil and he asked me to sketch out what he wanted," says Frazer today. "He was thinking it through and I did very quick sketches for him, around 150 of them. The lovely thing is that even though they're absolutely rubbish, they've got all my father's annotated notes on there, suggesting the cameras and the cuts they should be doing."

Richard Easson recalls that the various first or second assistant directors worked with extras in the background of scenes, including the moment MacLeod is stabbed by the Kurgan. "I was quite near there, and Clancy came charging up on his horse and came off it. It took a few takes because he had a job getting his sword out, as it was too long for the scabbard it was in. Some people laughed, but luckily they didn't see me laughing. Two of them who did get caught were told to go off to the side and they might get back on later."

"The first thing Russell said was, 'Forget about continuity,'" says Lambert. "It's Scotland, so you've got four seasons in one day. What's crazy is that Russell shot the battle sequence in something like four days. Somebody told me there were spirits in Glencoe, but they can be good spirits or evil spirits, and I like that sort of stuff. At one point I was on my horse when he went absolutely crazy and threw me off his back. The sword I was carrying on my side turned around pointing at my stomach, and I had a piece of leather that protected me. I landed on the ground with the sword going into the leather and I hurt my knee. I thought I might have been in an area where there are evil spirits because my horse was very calm, a movie horse, but within half a second he went crazy."

Costume designer Jim Acheson recalls having a difficult time in Glencoe. "It rained so badly that all the extras were wearing boots and I said to the two American producers, 'If we shoot these battle sequences in this weather you're going to have a $50,000 footwear bill, because all these boots are going to be beyond saving.' So they said, 'Well we'd better do something about that,' and I can remember the phrase, 'I'm sure you can pull it out of your ass.'"

Urgent phone calls were made to London and Acheson's assistant went out and bought 200 pairs of Wellington boots and a pile of hessian sacking to wrap around them, ensuring they looked like bound leggings. "Nobody saw them in the mud and the grass anyway. I think it was the first time I'd come across American producers. Having been brought up on the British film industry, it was a bit of a shock. But of course we had this lovely Australian director, Russell, who was a delight. He must have been getting it from all sides but he handled it really well. He was like a little curly-haired cherub running around enthusiastically with these really fancy music video shots."

With a large number of extras ready for battle, the film-makers wanted the fight to look as impressive as possible. This meant dressing Easson and the other extras as MacLeods and ordering them to charge up a hill, before redressing them as members of the Clan Fraser and making them charge the other way. "There was one scene where we charged down a hill and they set up a wire with a stretcher on it. There was a cameraman lying on there, and when we went charging down, they let this thing go and the cameraman went shooting down [beside us]. That looked quite hairy."

For Ian Sutherland, each day of filming began with an early-morning rise in Fort William, where he'd put on his warrior's costume and boots, before plunging his hands into a bucket of mud-like substance provided by the make-up department and rubbing it over his face, arms and legs. "Buses would then take me and the other extras from our Fort William base to the Glencoe location. There we would meet up with our training partners from the previous week, only this time we were given real swords."

Arriving at the location on the first morning of filming, Sutherland had the feeling that he'd gone back in time. "It was a combination of seeing the timeless Glencoe scenery, fake mist coming from the smoke machines, and seeing the rest of the extras in 16th-century dress. We were soon put through our paces by Peter Diamond, who was our main stunt coordinator. For the rest of the week, every time we heard the call 'background action' we had to start fighting around Christopher Lambert, Clancy Brown and the other main actors, remembering the moves we had been taught. Clancy seemed very friendly and approachable during breaks in filming. I remember one time someone asking him, 'How does it feel to be a film star, Clancy?' 'I have no idea,' was his reply."

When I ask Brown if he feels he got his performance right at the time, he's frank in his response: "I didn't know what I was doing. I'm 25. I think I know what I'm doing, but I don't really. When you're 25 you're not smart enough to be afraid, at least I wasn't. I was a little impressed and intimidated by Sean Connery, but that's about it; I didn't give a shit who anybody else was. There was nothing I didn't think I could do. I could get up on that horse and ride it, I could wear this make-up, I could do the sword fights and anything physical, anything they needed me to do I thought I could do, and I'll do whatever you're doing too. You're just not smart enough to be afraid."

While the actors and extras were trying to make sense of the battle, Lois Burwell was trying to deal with their make-up in torrential rain, but the rest of the country was enjoying a heatwave. "It's always like that in Glencoe. It can be 100 degrees everywhere else, but Glencoe is pouring with rain." Burwell had struggled to hire staff for her team due to 1985 being an exceptionally busy year for the British film industry. "At one point in the battle I seemed to have quite a lot of retired people that were coming, which was great because you got people who were tried, tested and true, but on the other hand they're standing outside, up to their hips in mud in inclement weather, so there was a lot of running around and a lot of compromise."

Special effects make-up co-designer Nick Maley's dominant memories of Scotland are "rain, rain and more rain" and he recalls searching for a good place to film on a particularly waterlogged area that required the use of boats to reach. "We were squelching around, but we couldn't really leave without the Aqua Cats because you'd have to go through two feet of water to get out there. Then it just rained on us and I kind of went down with a cold or the flu, and that was the start of me having health problems on that movie."

Art director Tim Hutchinson had worked on 1981's *Excalibur* and was used to extras fighting with swords, explaining to Allan Cameron that they couldn't use real swords "because all of these mad Highlanders had been recruited to be extras for the battle. They used to lay into each other in an alarming fashion. We had to make aluminium and wooden swords coated in resin but they were destroying them and we had to keep making them; they were laying into each other, really amazing stuff."

Richard Easson remembers that some of the swords on set were plastic, but his was stamped 'George III' and had a sharp blade that would have caused some damage if he'd stumbled and fallen while charging the enemy. "Nobody was stabbed as far as I know, but you could have been, as they weren't blunt." Although not sword-related, Ian Sutherland did damage himself while running downhill into battle. "I tripped on a clump of grass, went flying, and landed head first. It could have been worse, but I did have to go home wearing a cervical collar for a few days."

Keeping it real

One of the stunt fighters hired to work in the battle sequence was Bill Little, who had trained in martial arts from a young age and who had already spent some time on *Highlander* during the initial London shoot. "From what I remember the costumes were great, even better than the Scottish plaids you see them wearing on films now. The food was great, but not the accommodation for those who travelled to be extras; they stayed in tents. There was lots of mud and rain and the mosquitos always attacked us, but it was just your typical Scottish weather."

Due to the mix of professional stuntmen and amateur extras, Little felt the fights were "very unsafe", unlike the heavily regulated and well-choreographed sequences that are common in modern films. "The extras went at it for real as they didn't have time to train; I was lucky as I was fighting most of the time with a stuntman. Everything was very quick and erratic and the weapons were always breaking and people getting injured; sometimes there weren't enough weapons, so extras just had a fist fight."

"They did want realism," agrees Richard Easson, "and when you were fighting you quite often started with the same person, take after take, and if he had clouted you on the knuckles in the scene before, you wanted to give him a clout back the next time. There was, I wouldn't say aggro, but there was certainly a tit for tat and seeing who was going to get killed first, because if you didn't get killed it meant you could run on and kill somebody else. Otherwise you had to lie out the rest of the take. We were under orders to make it look real: if something's coming for your head, you put your shield up; that's what they're for."

The unrelenting nature of the battle scenes meant that as the week wore on, the extras became increasingly fatigued. Says Easson, "After a few takes you ended up fairly muddy and tired. Because you might be swinging a sword, there are horses jumping about and running around, and you had to maintain everything through the whole take; you didn't just kill somebody and stand around waiting for a bus. You had to carry on and look for somebody else to kill." By the third day, he became aware of some leaders being appointed by the other extras to approach the production team with demands for cigarettes and whisky, which arrived later on in the day. "They were there on the bus when we were being taken back to Fort William. There were plenty of cigarettes and whisky on the last two days."

According to Campbell Muirhead, the exhausted extras were rewarded with another treat on the third or fourth day, when the producers decided to take them all on buses to the Kingshouse Hotel in Glencoe "to ply them with whisky and whatever they wanted for free at lunchtime. Scotsmen and whisky. They gave them an axe and a sword and they all went absolutely apeshit in the afternoon when they were filming. All these drunken Scotsmen with fighting spirit. One guy put an axe to one of the horses and there were broken knuckles and stuff."

One of the extras enjoying his first day on set was also Muirhead's taxi driver. "There were wooden stakes with tape to cordon off the battle area. This taxi driver managed to get one day in the movie and some guy lifted out one of these stakes and stuck it in his chest. He got taken to hospital. They think it's a movie and you can get away with murder, and that's what they bloody well did."

"After lunch, you could hear people in the background calling 'Nurse! Doctor!' because they'd maybe had a little drink," adds Christopher Lambert.

Although he doesn't deny some of his fellow extras may have partaken of some alcohol, Richard Easson believes there may have been another reason for their exuberance. "It was probably adrenaline, and maybe some people took whisky, but there are specific rules and codes of conduct for extras. You're not meant to talk to stars, you're not meant to get in their way, and you're not meant to drink. You're just meant to make sure you keep your wits about you and do what you're told. If you're not in this scene, you're not in the scene, don't cry to the director. So it's probably more enthusiasm and adrenaline than whisky."

"There was one guy who must have been about six foot four, who looked magnificent in his kilt and his broadsword, a real Scotsman with red hair, big and stocky, even though he was quite tall," explained designer Allan Cameron. "At the end of filming he wandered off singing away with his costume on and his sword. He was last seen walking into the mist and no one dared stop him and ask him for the gear back."

"We all had a great time up there, and the Scots really got into it," laughs make-up effects designer John Schoonraad. "I remember one of them saying to me, 'There'll be a few scores settled out there today!' Some guy went nutty and ran into the hills and the police were up there looking for him. I remember someone dropped a Coke can on the ground and some old Scottish boy turned around and said, 'Keep your country clean, laddie; pick it up and put it in your pocket.'"

"I don't think anyone would have a bad word said about working on it really, other than the weather, and a few arguments about timesheets, but you forget that," adds clapper loader Paul Kenward. "It was a lot of fun and I think people like Russell, who have got great character and like a bit of a laugh, made it a nice atmosphere to work on. Gerry Fisher and Doug Milsome had humour as well. Michael Stevenson is a legend in his own lunchtime."

Ageing Heather

As the battle sequence was being filmed in Glencoe, in nearby Glen Nevis the art department was preparing to shoot Heather and Connor's final days together. It's possible to get an idea of the speed required to shoot these scenes with the help of a call sheet for the day of Wednesday 29 May 1985.

Issued to everyone involved in filming for a particular day, this sheet noted that Beatie Edney was to be picked up from her hotel at 6.15 a.m., to be in make-up for 6.45 a.m. and on set for 8.45 a.m. Christopher Lambert had a 6.45 a.m. pick-up for a 7.15 a.m. make-up stop and was also on set for 8.45 a.m. Stand-ins Campbell Muirhead and Lynn Vescoe were to be picked up for 7.30 a.m. and were due on set for 8 a.m. In addition, geese, chickens, goats, Highland cattle and dogs were to be on set for 8 a.m. to prepare for the Jedburgh market scenes, along with MacLeod's horse.

The call sheet also lists the exterior (EXT.) shots required to be caught on camera on the day, namely:

```
1. EXT. FARM
2. EXT. FARM - HEATHER IN SNOW
3. EXT. JEDBURGH MARKET
4. EXT. HILLTOP
5. EXT. FARM - HEATHER MONTAGE - 1st STAGE
6. EXT. FARM - HEATHER DYING
7. EXT. HILL ABOVE FARM - FARM ON FIRE
8. s/by EXT. ISLAND - SWORD SPINNING IN AIR
```

While most of these scenes were directly related to the location, such as the farm and the market, a couple were required to complete other sequences in the film, perhaps because there hadn't been time to film them on the other days or it was only later realised that insert shots were needed.

One of the most discussed elements of the film comes during the final few minutes of the Glencoe section, when Connor MacLeod finally has to face the fact that his wife is growing old in front of his eyes. In the months leading up to the Scottish shoot, Nick Maley made it clear to the film's producers that he needed time to prepare the materials needed to apply to the actor playing Heather. One of Maley's previous roles had been on 1983's *Krull*, for which he'd created the make-up for the Widow of the Web, a 22-piece prosthetic that took 13 weeks to craft due to each piece needing to be sculpted separately.

For the ageing of Heather, Maley calculated that once again the work would take around 13 weeks, which could have been cut in half had the actors' hands been left out of the process. "It takes time to sculpt each and every piece, then mould each and every piece, and then foam each and every piece, and when you get to the end of the day, if you want to film tomorrow, you've got to have a complete new set of pieces," explains Maley, who anticipated that filming would take one day, but who also wanted to create three sets in case filming was extended to the next day or was postponed.

Maley assumed he would have an actor to work with, but as the 13-week countdown started ticking, nobody had been cast as Heather. "I sent [the producers] a note saying, 'You realise that we're now cutting into this time and we'll have to put the filming back because we don't have an actress,' and they were going on about how I was being impertinent by saying that, but that's like saying if you don't start on time, it's hard to finish on time." Eventually actor Catherine Mary Stewart was cast, but Maley now only had ten weeks in which to work on the prosthetics. "I'm working on those pieces right up until three weeks before we start to film and then they say, 'Oh, she's not going to be there any more, we have this other actress.'"

With Beatie Edney now cast as Heather, Maley only had three weeks to try and salvage the prosthetics he'd created for Catherine Mary Stewart. "I thought [Edney] did a perfectly good job, in fact she was very sweet, but I can't take the pieces from Catherine and glue them all over the next actress. If I sculpt something for one person's face and stick it on someone else's face, it's not going to look the same, their features are in a different place. I'm trying to explain to the producers that this isn't something that you should do, and they're just saying, 'Well, stick those pieces on her,' so I looked at the pieces that might fit and I resculpted pieces that wouldn't fit. This is part of working 96 hours instead of 60; once you go over 60 hours you start to get exhausted."

"The old-age make-up was a bit of a disaster," states Beatie Edney when I ask her about the situation she found herself in during the production. "The poor guy doing the special effects make-up . . . was so overworked. My make-up originally took ten hours. It had many separate pieces of prosthetic and was beautifully created. Every day I would wake up at 3 a.m. and go to the make-up hut. Michael Stevenson was always there to greet me. It was a long and hideous process; you can't drink or eat during it really, and after ten hours I looked like a very old man. This went on for three days. I'd spend ten hours in make-up then everyone would come and look at me and talk about the make-up and we wouldn't shoot. It just wasn't working."

In addition to time pressures, Maley also encountered problems with cinematographer Gerry Fisher, who, as Maley was aware, didn't think he should be directing the second unit. "He wanted to make sure that everybody could see that what I was doing wasn't very good. Prosthetic make-up should be lit from behind. You shouldn't flood rubber make-up, especially if it's been thrown together in three weeks instead of the 13 weeks it was going to take in the first place. They shot a test that they didn't like, which I didn't like either, and then said, 'OK, well let's do it as a two-dimensional make-up; it should look like her,' which I knew was going to be even worse. I don't want to upset the make-up artist who ultimately did that job, as it ended up in the movie, but it was exactly what I didn't want to do."

"Russell didn't like the make-up and Nick didn't like him not liking it," says John Schoonraad, who flew up from London to try and help out. "In hindsight, I think it disguised the face a little bit too much. In those days they used to make make-up so extreme you wouldn't really recognise who they were. Nowadays they make the face more faithful to how they'd naturally age. Nick always pushed the envelope and as a boss he was brilliant, I owe a lot to him."

Although everyone was aware the make-up wasn't perfect, time pressures meant the unit had to move on to other scenes. As filming in Scotland came to an end, cast and crew celebrated in style, with Beatie Edney recalling that the only time she was involved in a drinking session was on the last night in Fort William. "Our hotel had every conceivable whisky. The whole crew and cast and all the producers and their wives had a massive party on the last night. The producers missed their flight the next morning."

Lois Burwell has mixed memories about her time in Scotland. On top of the bad weather and long hours, she remembers one day receiving word from London that her much-loved cat had been run over. "Christophe, who is a very sensitive person, said to me, 'Are you all right?' and I said, 'Oh yeah, I just had a bit of bad news from home,' because you don't want to bring home to work. In fact one of the hairdressers had told him my cat had been run over, so we got back to London and we started to shoot at Greenwich. Christophe turned up and he'd been to Harrods and had bought me a beautiful Burmese cat. She was a wonderful cat. That kind of thoughtfulness and kindness is exceptional."

"I remember buying the cat," says Lambert when I mention the story to him. "Generally I buy presents for every member of the crew at the end. We've spent 16 weeks together. If I've spent two weeks on a movie, maybe you just do a few drinks for the crew, but when you've spent four difficult months together and everybody is happy because they know they're doing well . . ."

The actor has fond memories of Scotland, a country he's returned to multiple times. "I keep going back because I love it. I went back to Glencoe, the Isle of Skye and Fort William. In Edinburgh I stayed four days. It's incredible scenery and I like the people because what you see is what you get. When you're in London or New York you don't have that. Australians, Irish, Scottish people, Belgian people, New Zealanders, South Africans are like that. No bullshit. I like that."

As for Campbell Muirhead, he remembers bonding with actor Billy Hartman at the wrap party in Fort William, before spending a moment with Christopher Lambert, who found him at the bar. "He gave me an envelope with some banknotes inside for me. I've never told anybody how much he gave me and I never will, but on the outside he'd written 'Thank you for being so kind, patient and considerate. All the very best, Christophe'. When they finished all the Scottish scenes they just dumped me and went to New York and had a stand-in there, who's unfortunately passed away now. With the money I made from *Highlander* I went down to London with a suitcase and a furry jacket and I've been here ever since."

TEN

LONDON CALLING

With filming in Scotland completed, the cast and crew returned to London on Sunday 1 June to spend the next month concentrating on shooting many interior and exterior sequences set in New York.

Following earlier filming at Earl's Court as part of the MacLeod/Fasil sword fight, many of the American actors were still in the UK, including Roxanne Hart who was sharing accommodation with actor Jon Polito. "Jon was a very good friend of mine. My husband's aunt's mother had an apartment in London. Jon had a room there and I had a room there, so we hung out a lot." Hart also bonded with Clancy Brown. "We were just getting to know each other then, but we hit it off really well because there was a part of us that was lonely being Americans in London. We just had kind of a giggle, and we rolled our eyes a lot."

Along with actor Alan North, Hart and Polito filmed all of the interior police station scenes in a building on Great Scotland Yard, a street in Westminster. "It was number 223 I think," notes art director Tim Hutchinson. "The interior was great; we just put in partition walls and grilles and doors to make it look like a police station."

The interior of the run-down hotel occupied by the Kurgan was shot at St Olave's Hospital in Bermondsey, a building which had opened in 1875 and had seen better days by the time the *Highlander* crew arrived. Hospital records suggest it had closed down for good just prior to filming.

MacLeod's visit to Brenda's New York apartment was also filmed in London, though the first attempt was not deemed a success by Russell Mulcahy, who stated in the DVD commentary that "the relationship didn't work and neither did the costume". Instead of using what they'd shot, the scene was redone, almost shot for shot, a few weeks later, with the director happy with the second attempt, noting, "It's one of those dreadful things that happen when you get stuck in a location and you basically film yourself into a corner. Every director's nightmare."

For the scenes of the Kurgan encountering MacLeod in a New York church, filming took place inside St Augustine's Kilburn Church on Kilburn Park Road. Clancy Brown was particularly enamoured of the sequence, noting that his favourite line from the film is "Holy ground, Highlander!" Explained Brown, "I do love that line because it just tells you that the Kurgan actually does give a damn about this process, this ritual that they're going through. Even though he's completely blasphemous in that church, he does take the rules of the game seriously."

Discussing the scene in 1985, Brown made it clear that he thought more could have been done to explore his character. "There could have been wonderful dialogue – 'God, this doesn't compare to the Greek Orthodox Church' or 'I liked it better when they did it in Latin', or any type of thing. There's all sorts of twists that could have been done. I like little twists like that because they make the audience *think*. *Highlander* still has its action and everything, but that's really all we went for here, the good guy/bad guy, cops and robbers type of thing."

When I ask Lambert how he and Brown got along during filming, he states that "Clancy was super laid-back, but I don't think he was laid-back with the crew. I was never his enemy, but in the script I was, therefore his way of acting was to put himself apart from me saying, 'I've gotta hate this guy, so I can't be friends with him at all.' That's a different method; I'm not that kind of actor. I never viewed him as someone who wasn't nice, he was just in character, and you have to respect that. I can joke until there's action, then I become the other guy. That's my way of doing things."

A difference of opinion

The look of the Kurgan in 16th-century Scotland may have been iconic, but he also had to be kitted out for the 1980s. Having lived for hundreds of years and survived many battles, costume designer Jim Acheson had discussed with Russell Mulcahy the idea that the warrior would somehow retain elements from his past as part of the costume, with bits of feather and fur attached to his clothes. In one scene, Ramirez's earring can be seen dangling from the Kurgan's leather jacket as he exits the lift in his New York hotel. "Jim Acheson is one of the best costume designers I've ever seen," states Clancy Brown, "but we had a bit of a rough patch on the costume at one point. The original costume was gorgeous; it was the modern-day Kurgan one. He had a very clear vision and I was kind of all over the place. He was right and I was wrong."

Despite spending hours designing, making and fitting the costume, including having it signed off by the producers and director, on the first day of shooting Brown in his new outfit, Mulcahy and Acheson arrived on set to find that the actor had seemingly had a last-minute change of heart. Says Mulcahy, "One day we were filming and I remember him pulling his costume apart saying, 'This is not the Kurgan,' and Jim freaked out."

According to Brown, "At one point [Acheson] wanted to do this punk biker kind of thing and I thought, 'That's kind of typical. What if I was a banker, if I was a shark and a Wall Street dude?' They put that in there with the first guy that Peter Diamond played; they sort of had that businessman thing. There were all these bangles and shit hanging off my costume and I started taking some off."

Brown elaborated on this theory in a 1985 *Starlog* interview. "The Kurgan is in a heavy metal sort of get-up. Now, wouldn't it be interesting if he wore a business suit and a bowler hat – *that's* scary. You expect a heavy metal punker with skulls on his jacket to be a badass. But the really tough, mean and nasty people don't necessarily wear clothes like that and look like that. So, there was a *chance* to make a real statement, but I think the whole idea was to stay away from statements."

"Russell had pretty strong ideas and he wanted him leather-clad and shaven-headed," notes Acheson. "By this time I was getting used to the idea of things being in triplicate. Then I found Clancy on the day of shooting, picking all this stuff that had carefully been applied by teams of staff, pulling it all off. It was the most unprofessional thing I'd ever seen. His behaviour was predicated by him suddenly removing all the texture on a leather jacket; it was crazy."

"I was doing the right thing for the wrong reasons, because [the noise] of that stuff was probably a nightmare for [the sound department]," says Brown today. "Though that's not what I thought, I thought, 'I don't want all this crap hanging off me.' Jim saw me and said, 'What the fuck are you doing? We just made this costume for you; your job is to put it on,' and I was like, 'I was just making it better,' and he was like, 'Don't you touch my stuff.' I felt like shit after that. He was absolutely right and the costume works great."

Unlike his experience with Clancy Brown, Jim Acheson didn't have to worry too much about costumes for Christopher Lambert, although MacLeod does have a distinctive look in the 1985 sequences, namely a trench coat, jeans and trainers. Discussing the planning behind MacLeod's outfit, Acheson recalls that he and his assistant Gilly Hebden trawled London clothes stores with the actor on a shopping spree. "I think it might have been an Armani coat and designer jeans. He was just the sweetest guy. I remember that at the end of filming he took me, my assistants and the voice coach, Joan Washington, and Joan's boyfriend, a shy young man called Richard E. Grant, for dinner."

As well as updating the Kurgan's clothes for a new century, his head and neck also received a redesign courtesy of Nick Maley.

Following the Kurgan's near-defeat at the end of Ramirez's sword, his throat had been slit, meaning he now needed something to cover the scar. Maley decided to give Clancy Brown a neck full of safety pins, neatly tying into the punk stylings of the era, along with a shaved head with a warrior's braid and a tattoo. Unfortunately, Brown's contract didn't stipulate he had to shave his head for the role. "The hard part of that make-up wasn't the slit throat, it was the bald head with a tattoo and the ponytail which had to go on over a full head of hair every day," says Maley. "I would do the make-up with the bald head and there was another make-up artist who would do the throat."

Regarding the make-up, Brown discovered that people soon forget who was really under the latex. "When you do extreme make-up, people tend to regard you that way because we're visually oriented, particularly in the film industry. And so, on *Highlander*, people would stay away from me because I did look pretty scary. I didn't go out of my way to say, 'Hey, it's not me, don't worry about it,' because that helped me out; it helped me maintain my concentration, not break it."

Another interior scene filmed in London found Connor MacLeod in the year 1776, living under the assumed name of Adrian Montagu. As scripted by Larry Ferguson and Peter Bellwood, this is part of a flashback that occurs while MacLeod is being pursued through the Metropolitan Museum by Walter Bedsoe, who is tailing the Highlander around New York. MacLeod spots a painting of Thomas Jefferson, the third president of the United States, sitting atop his horse and recalls a conversation between the pair as Jefferson poses for his portrait. MacLeod/Montagu is an ex-captain of a British gunship now posing as an American merchant.

"Too bad it didn't make it into the movie," says Larry Ferguson of the scene. "MacLeod skids to a stop and there's a portrait of Thomas Jefferson sitting at a table. When he looks at the portrait, there's an instant fade to the fact that he's sitting talking to Jefferson while he's getting his portrait made. MacLeod says to him, 'Do you think that the United States will be able to prevail in this conflict you have with Britain?' and Jefferson says, 'Well England does have a very large Navy.' That was fun. You take two people who understand history and tell them they can go and be wherever they want."

Though viewers never see MacLeod as Montagu, the alias is referenced in the scene between Brenda and the archivist who reveals the similarities between the various signatures MacLeod has used through the centuries.

The Kurgan vs Kastagir

A more ambitious sequence saw the Kurgan fighting MacLeod's old friend, Sunda Kastagir, in a New York alleyway, with the production team settling upon a street in the Shad Thames area close to Tower Bridge. "There was lots of buddleia and weeds growing out of it and it worked really well for New York," says Tim Hutchinson.

"I think it was quite subtle," adds standby art director Mark Raggett when discussing production designer Allan Cameron's efforts to have London stand in for New York. "He was quite a strong designer in that way; I don't think he was one for just putting American signage all over the place. I mean, it's obvious with the accents and what's going on with the cars and everything like that. I think Allan definitely kept all that to a minimum."

Like some of the actors, Raggett hadn't been required for the Scottish section of the shoot, but he returned for the new London scenes. "There were a hell of a lot of late nights, and I suppose one wasn't meant to drink on set but one kind of did because it was so kind of fuelled in that way; it all became sort of a blur really. I remember the nurse giving me a B12 injection round the back because she said I looked so dreadful; I was about to pass out."

Raggett also explains that being part of a Russell Mulcahy production meant needing to take some time to relax after a day on set. "Once you finished people would go clubbing, so it was always a party. Russell quite enjoyed drinking and socialising; [he was] always a very sociable kind of being. With the pop promos, they just went through the night. You were there until you dropped; it was quite incredible the energy he had. You knew you were working on something special because of his energy and his vision, because otherwise it could have been extremely dull."

Adds clapper loader Paul Kenward, "It was hard work because of the conditions we were working in, but I think the art department and what we were filming gave you the adrenaline to carry on and get through it. And then once you'd done a day's work, you felt like you'd done something really well. That summer it poured with rain every night we worked in London. It rained throughout that film; water was a fundamental part of the making of *Highlander*."

With experience in theatre and television, actor Hugh Quarshie was still trying to gain a foothold in the world of film when *Highlander* came his way and he wasn't about to be overly selective when it came to choosing his roles. "You just want the experience of being near a camera, being on set, and learning the discipline and the protocols of film-making. I think you become a bit more discerning with experience."

Quarshie's first film had been the 1980 war movie, *The Dogs of War*, where he'd co-starred alongside Christopher Walken and struggled with the improvisational side of his performance. "My first scene in my first film and Walken was riffing, going off script, but in a very disciplined way. He was matched easily by Colin Blakely and I was thinking, *What the hell is going on?* I was sticking slavishly to the script and wasn't quite sure how to respond. *Highlander* was a different matter, because the culture was so specific and alien to us that you couldn't really improvise."

The young actor was happy to be able to spend some time with Clancy Brown, describing him as "a bit of a scholar. Not long before that I'd played Aaron in the BBC TV production of *Titus Andronicus* and he had seen it. He had played Aaron and we had quite a long discussion about Shakespeare and it turned out he was a bit of a fan of my performance." Like Mark Raggett and Paul Kenward, Quarshie was quick to notice Russell Mulcahy's enthusiasm on set. "I remember the fight between the Kurgan and Kastagir which we filmed in Bermondsey and they dressed it up to look like the Bronx or somewhere and he filmed it from several angles at night."

The Kurgan/Kastagir clash required a number of elements to be prepared in advance, with the sequence requiring gunshots to be fired by vigilante Kirk Matunas (Christopher Malcolm), as he witnessed the pair fighting. "Cold and wet and a night shoot that seemed to go on and on," was Malcolm's abiding memory of filming *Highlander*. "It was fun to do though and being hoisted in the air and held at the end of Clancy Brown's sword was interesting!"

For their battle, Brown and Quarshie spent some time learning a short sequence of around a dozen moves, repeating them multiple times as Mulcahy shot the fight from different angles while the rain fell around them. "He did a little pirouette then twirled around before chopping my head off; that was the one thing he did improvise," notes Quarshie, "but obviously he cleared that with the fight director Peter Diamond and with Russell. It looked balletic. I think it's always appreciated when everybody does their job and does it properly. The crew working at night don't want the actors to start messing around; they want them to know their lines and hit the mark."

Following the death of Kastagir, mould designer John Schoonraad recalls that his team had set up a dummy that was set to drop to the ground once the Immortal's head had been severed. "This dummy had been standing there in the rain to have his head cut off, and I remember Nick [Maley] walking over to the dummy and wringing it because it got so heavy. The fishing line that was holding it in position was beginning to get very tight."

For the resulting explosion, thousands of feet of detonating cord was placed around the windows of the buildings behind Kastagir's corpse and the Kurgan. "When Kastagir stands there, the Kurgan cuts his head off and then all the windows go and the manhole cover goes up in the air; it was just amazing," continues John Schoonraad. "But it was all outside and everyone was going 'Ah!' because the air had turned into powdered glass and we were saying, 'Don't look up!' Luckily the heavens opened up and it just poured down; an unbelievable amount of rain killed all the fragments of powdered glass."

"Russell always wanted the cameras to be closer to the action than they wanted to be," adds Mark Raggett, explaining that it was necessary to build barricades around the cameras and their operators before something exploded beside or above them. "I do remember shedloads of sugar glass being put into windows between takes, which was quite a big job."

Unfortunately for the crew, nobody had informed the police that filming was taking place close to Tower Bridge, with the explosions causing understandable concern among local residents. Says John Schoonraad, "On the other side [of the river] it was dark, then all the lights started coming on and the police turned up and they weren't very happy because they hadn't been told there was going to be an explosion, and the fire brigade hadn't been told. It was two in the morning and there was a massive explosion in London." After enquiring about the explosion, the police also spotted the 'body' of Kastagir lying beside some boxes in the alley. "Nick had to say to the police, 'It's all fake, like this arm,' and he picked it up and took a bite out of it and spat it out, much to the surprise of the police officer."

Under pressure

It was at this point in the production that the physical and mental exhaustion experienced by Nick Maley finally took its toll. While the fight sequence was taking place, Maley was busy in the trailer where various dummies and heads for the decapitations were stored, and at some point that night he collapsed, only discovered when colleagues raised concerns about his whereabouts. "I'd pushed myself beyond the limit," admits Maley today, adding that he'd worked extreme hours on a number of other films but that he was used to a recovery period.

"The problem with *Highlander* was there was no recovery period; it was just one thing after another that required extra time. I can't remember which studio we were going to be in – it might have been Twickenham, which would have taken me 20 minutes to get there in the morning. Do you know what it's like to drive to Tower Bridge from High Wycombe every day? I would leave at quarter past five in the morning, because that would allow me to get there ahead of the traffic. I'm there in the studio before 6 a.m. and I'm working till 11 or 12 at night, and it goes on day, after day, after day."

Compounding the stress caused by the long hours was the fact that Maley was demoralised by the issues that had led to the problems with Beatie Edney's make-up. "When someone – I think it was the accountant – said, 'Oh, people won't really notice,' I said, 'Just remind me who got the Oscar for the Best Budget last year?' Can we put subtitles on the screen to say, 'I know this isn't very good, but they only gave me three weeks?' Our reputation is only as good as our last movie. I think the last straw was that the doctor had said that I had to take ten days out to get back on my feet. The [production team told me] that they'd sue me if I didn't come back the next day. That just made me go, 'What the hell am I killing myself for with these guys?'"

Bob Keen took over as special effects make-up co-designer, while Maley began to reassess his career from the comfort of his home, believing at first that his reputation was big enough that he could easily step out of the industry for two years and come back stronger than ever. As he contemplated his next step, he started looking at his situation from a different angle.

"When we set out on this journey of a career, we start off with high hopes," says Maley. "We're always looking from a distance at this destination that we're heading for, saying, 'Well that looks like a romantic thing to do,' or, 'That looks like a great job to do.' I set out to be the guy who was creating things that people hadn't seen before, and on some movies that's exactly what I did. But that distant place might look green because it's actually a rice paddy field and when you get there you're up to your knees in mud."

Maley's goal had never been to get involved in the minutiae of the film industry, something he grew to despise. "I didn't really anticipate what it was going to be like to have to go to all the production meetings and have someone say, 'Why are we not getting this done?' and have to say, 'Because you keep calling me to production meetings.' I didn't anticipate the politics that would be there. Of course, I knew there were budgets, and I knew that there were schedules and things that we had to work with, but for me the driving force was the work itself, not just a name on the movie. On some of these movies I was spending more time planning things than I was making things."

Ultimately, Maley simply fell out of the film industry, trading in his beloved Ferrari for a boat and sailing the Caribbean for a year, before relocating there permanently with his wife, Gloria. He remains there to this day, working as an artist and running his own non-profit film museum, the Yoda Guy Movie Exhibit, where he's happy to meet fans and tell them stories from his time in the film industry while writing his first novel. "I'm as busy now as I ever was, but doing stuff I want to do and at the pace I want to do it, and I don't have to worry about some other person making some stupid decision that saves them $10,000."

Recreating Silvercup

Having secured permission to shoot at Silvercup in New York for the final Kurgan/MacLeod battle, it was decided to film as much as possible in London, mainly due to the need to demolish the famous Silvercup sign, which would require sections to be rebuilt on a smaller scale.

"The plan was to go to New York to shoot the exteriors, but we were building a set of that rooftop in London at Greenwich in an extraordinary fertiliser factory which I understand isn't there any more," says Tim Hutchinson. "What's extraordinary is that it was like an extended Nissen hut with a semicircle with no columns to get in the way. We built a three-quarter-size rooftop and sign, so when you look at that fight sequence you cut between Long Island and Greenwich."

Before Nick Maley had left the film, he had worked with Russell Mulcahy on ideas for the sequence, attempting to design a more dramatic climax than another straightforward sword fight. "Discussions with Russell led to the electric sign on the roof, which wasn't originally mentioned in the script. Then I said, 'Oh, electricity and water. What if we had a water tank on the roof as well?', so in the fight, the water comes down and then you've got a flooded roof. The way that it was originally planned doesn't really come over 100% in the final cut, but the principle was that they were going to electrocute the girl because they've got the water and they've got the electricity and that's why he breaks the glass skylight so they get sucked down and have to fight down below as well. So all of that was to try and produce something more than just another beheading."

Sculptor Keith Short, who had earlier helped to build the interior of Connor MacLeod's forge, was tasked with creating the replica Silvercup sign. "I had to draw and cut out each letter on a lightweight metal sheet. An electrician then made a fluorescent strip around each letter and wired it all to light up. I and a couple of others then hauled them into place onto the scaffold on the Silvercup rooftop set. The idea was to tie each letter in place and get ourselves onto a gantry above the set, which was some 70 feet high. Each letter was given a number, so on the director's request, individual letters would fall. In the finale, the whole structure collapses in the water. This was a one-shot attempt, as the set could not have been rebuilt, and it worked perfectly. Much celebration took place in the pub that evening!"

"It's a bit obvious when we go from the set to the real location, particularly when the crane driver drops the water tower," reckons

The MacLeods make their way into battle. © *David James/STUDIOCANAL*

Supporting artists gather in the newly-built Jedburgh. © *David James/STUDIOCANAL*

Christopher Lambert and Sean Connery between takes. © *Staff/MIRRORPIX*

Glenfinnan is constructed at Eilean Donan Castle. © *Tim Hutchinson*

Director Russell Mulcahy prepares to shoot. © *David James/STUDIOCANAL*

Bob Anderson waits while Sean Connery, Christopher Lambert
and Russell Mulcahy discuss a scene. © *David James/STUDIOCANAL*

Russell Mulcahy and Christopher Lambert pause
during the Glencoe battle sequence. © *David James/STUDIOCANAL*

Cast and crew gather for a photo as Clancy Brown
watches on horseback. © *David James/STUDIOCANAL*

The Kurgan (Clancy Brown) observes the clashing clans. © *David James/STUDIOCANAL*

Sean Connery poses in full Spanish peacock garb. © *David James/STUDIOCANAL*

MacLeod (Christopher Lambert) says farewell to Heather. © *David James/STUDIOCANAL*

Producers Peter Davis and Bill Panzer observe filming. © *David James/STUDIOCANAL*

Christopher Lambert on the beach. © *John Hancock*

A candid moment between Christopher Lambert
and Beatie Edney. © *David James/STUDIOCANAL*

Clancy Brown resplendent in his armour. © *David James/STUDIOCANAL*

Christopher Lambert is carried to the
shore of Loch Shiel. © *David James/STUDIOCANAL*

And you thought Queens was just a traffic jam between you and J.F.K.? Next weekend, train your binoculars across the river o
the roof? So we can see you! The skyline of Manhattan co-stars with Sean Connery and "Greystoke's" Christopher Lambert. Le

Beatie Edney takes her position in Glencoe. © *John Hancock*

Hugh Quarshie, Jon Polito and Christopher Lambert
film inside the Dugout. © *David James/STUDIOCANAL*

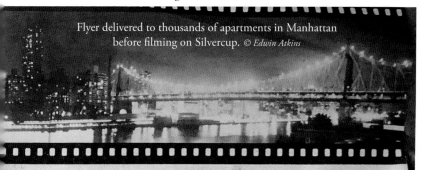

Flyer delivered to thousands of apartments in Manhattan
before filming on Silvercup. © *Edwin Atkins*

Studios where we will be staging the climactic battle sequence of "Highlander", a major movie from 20th Century Fox. Why on
your windows face the river, please leave a light on till dawn, July 12th and 13th. Join in this spectacular portrait of Manhattan.

Bedsoe (Jon Polito) visits Nash (Christopher Lambert)
at his store in a deleted scene. © *David James/STUDIOCANAL*

Lt. Moran (Alan North) visits Rachel (Sheila Gish) as
Nash's store burns in a deleted scene. © *David James/STUDIOCANAL*

The Kurgan (Clancy Brown) prepares to behead Yung
Dol Kim in a deleted scene. © *David James/STUDIOCANAL*

Christopher Lambert and Roxanne Hart pose
for a portrait session. © *Georges De Keerle/Getty Images*

One of animator and storyboard artist Ravi Swami's early
sketches of MacLeod for the final sequence. *Ravi Swami*

Early concept poster art for Highlander's UK
release created by artist Mike Bell in 1986.

Nick Maley's original vision for the Kurgan at
the end of *Highlander: Lost Kurgan.* © *Nick Maley*

Clancy Brown returns to Scotland for the 4K Highlander premiere at Edinburgh International Film Festival, 18 June 2016. © *Jonathan Melville*

Christopher Lambert and Clancy Brown reunited at a 30th anniversary screening of Highlander at London's Prince Charles Cinema, 26 June 2016. © *Dave J Hogan/Getty Images*

art director Tim Hutchinson. "The tower was built of thin angle iron and had gallons of water in it, but it was held up by a crane and the driver just out of shot. He had to release it because it was hinged at the back. There was steel scaffolding at one side and then it was hinged down and dropped and all the water would spill out on cue."

"We did a lot of stuff where we were in water inside a studio called The Bunker that was in Docklands," adds clapper loader Paul Kenward. "That's where all the scenes were shot when the sign collapses in some water. When we did the first effect we had a day off as the whole place was electrified because some electrical system had fallen in the water. We had an old nine-millimetre lens that was smashed: it sheared off the front of the camera, but I think they still got shots on it. We had days off because of the set being electrified."

Stunt performer Andy Bradford was doubling for Christopher Lambert in the fight, while Peter Brace took over for Clancy Brown. The scaffolding surrounding them was part metal and part plastic, with Bradford admitting, "It would still hurt if it hit you, but it certainly wouldn't do major damage." Bradford remembers seeing Brace standing up at one point as a large section of the real scaffolding started to fall towards him. Running at Brace, Bradford pulled him out of the way, only for Brace to swear at him, unaware of what had just happened. "Suddenly the scaffolding crashed down very near to us and the whole studio went quiet. I probably saved his life."

Make-up supervisor Lois Burwell recalls lengthy filming days in Greenwich, with at least one falling on the longest day of the year, Saturday 21 June. "We shot an 18-hour night shoot, interiors and exteriors, battling traffic on the way there and the way back with a four-hour turnaround. It was insane. But we all turned up, we all did it." Working closely with Burwell throughout the shoot was make-up artist Graham Freeborn. "Graham was at my side all the time and we had a laugh; we used to do things to brighten and jolly the day. That was his last film, because he had cancer and passed away."

One night, after preparing a double for Clancy Brown in replica Kurgan make-up, Burwell and Freeborn were soon presented with yet another unexpected double for Clancy Brown, who had arrived to have his own make-up applied. When a bald cap didn't fit him, the pair had to improvise. "We found something more like a swimming cap, it was the only thing that would fit on his head, and we couldn't cut it around the ears without it sliding straight back. You needed ears because you can't have a head without ears, so we cut up a powder puff and glued them to his head."

Neither make-up artist had a copy of the tattoo that was pre-painted onto the 'official' bald cap. "We didn't have the stencil for the tattoo, so it was freehand. Graham, God love him, had a wicked sense of humour. He drew on it and I said, 'What the hell is that?' and he'd drawn Hitler's head but in dragon form. It was perfectly right when you looked at the detail, but you couldn't because the bloke had powder puff ears. He got sent out and began filming."

"The parapets were like the side of a swimming pool and they were fighting in all this water before they went through the skylight and dropped down," explains Tim Hutchinson. "Then they come down on wires inside a warehouse at King George V Dock, which is not there anymore because it's now London City Airport: the runway is where the glass wall section that shatters was built."

For the final fight inside the warehouse, Nick Maley had spoken to Russell Mulcahy about how the battle from the rooftop would be continued, still determined that the death of the Kurgan wouldn't be another "tumbling beheading . . . but that the sword goes across [his neck] and there's a moment where you think, 'Hang on, what's going on?' and then his head just kind of slowly comes off." Maley's idea was based on what he calls the Lost Kurgan, whereby the spirit of the Kurgan would come out of his body and resemble the armour that he'd worn at the start of the film. "[MacLeod] had to fight and behead that as well: it was made of snakes and worms and nasty wriggly things and the parasite that was the crest on the front of his helmet."

Maley had been influenced by suggestions from Russell Mulcahy to use snakes and worms, and the work carried out by James Acheson and the wardrobe department. "I always try to look at something else that's in the movie and try to echo it, because it gives the whole thing a more designer-like feel than a whole bunch of different effects or different story parts that go off in different directions."

"I remember Nick Maley wanted to make some incredible designs for the Kurgan to be revealed as a Medusa-type monster, but the producers wouldn't go for it," recalls make-up effects mould designer John Schoonraad. "I was at a party that night with [creature effects creator] Rick Baker, and I told him Nick had just had his main creature design turned down. He said, 'It happens to everybody.'"

With the decision made not to proceed with a practical effect representing the Kurgan's spirit, Russell Mulcahy and the producers would have to find an alternative way to depict the massive burst of energy that would lead to the film's climactic ending, but this would have to wait until later in the year.

Before then, and with the UK portion of the filming completed, Mulcahy was getting ready to move production across the Atlantic as *Highlander* went stateside.

ELEVEN

NEW YORK STATE OF MIND

A crack cocaine epidemic. A soaring crime rate that made the subway a no-go area. A rise in homelessness. A racially divisive mayor. The early 1980s was a difficult period for New York, a city that was emerging from a decade of financial woes just as gentrification was starting to turn run-down neighbourhoods into trendy middle-class destinations.

Anyone picking up a copy of the *New York Post* in the first half of the decade would have read about the shooting of ex-Beatle John Lennon on the Upper West Side, the murder of two women and eight children in Brooklyn in what would become known as the Palm Sunday Massacre, the shooting of four unarmed black men on the subway by a white man who claimed he was being robbed, and dozens of lower profile, yet equally shocking, reports involving murders, drugs and violence.

It's debatable whether or not New Yorkers would have been surprised to see a headline that screamed "HEADHUNTER – 3, COPS – ZERO" on the cover of the *Post* on Tuesday 2 April 1985, a reference to the gruesome decapitations being carried out by an unknown assassin that saw officers from the New York Police Department branded "baffled" and "incompetent" by their critics.

Thankfully, this story only appeared on the front of the copy of the paper being held by actor Damien Leake, who was playing hotdog vendor Tony, the character taunting Lieutenant Moran and

Detective Bedsoe as they filmed outside the St Regis Hotel on the corner of 55th Street and Fifth Avenue on 8 July. This was the first day of filming for *Highlander* in New York, the production team having arrived in the city a week earlier after leaving the UK behind on Sunday 30 June.

A new city also meant some new faces joining the existing cast and crew for the next three weeks, including Tony Mitchell, the cinematographer who would replace Gerry Fisher on the film when the latter didn't make the trip to America. Mitchell's story of how he was brought aboard *Highlander*, related to me via Skype from his home in Hamburg, proved to be the most unusual I heard while researching the history of the film.

"I was in New York, shooting a video in the middle of the night in a warehouse, where a train went through it to bring goods. These guys were standing there with trench coats and hats on. I looked at my key grip and said, 'Who are those guys?' He said, 'I don't know, but they're asking for you.' I said, 'Tell 'em I'm not here,' and I ran off down the train tracks; they looked like IRS or police or government officials or something. It turned out they were from London and they'd come to ask me if I'd be interested in shooting *Highlander* with Russell Mulcahy as director."

Starting his career shooting documentary footage in Vietnam in 1966, Mitchell next headed to New York to work non-stop on commercials for the next 12 years "making tons of fucking money", before attempting to take his own life due to the intense pressure of the job. Giving up his career, he bought a boat and sailed around his native Florida and the Caribbean as the 1970s tipped into the 1980s. Mitchell's life of tranquillity was interrupted when a young New York director tracked him down to a small bay on the west coast of Florida and introduced him to the world of the music video. "He said, 'This is like a three- or four-minute film. You can do any fucking thing you want to, you just have to be cool and different.' We talked, but I didn't go back; I kept living on my boat."

The younger director didn't give up, this time tracking Mitchell down in Miami and offering him a music video shoot, even though he hadn't shot anything in two years. "I had a pair of shorts, one T-shirt and a pair of sandals. I bought some clothes, went to the studio, shot this music video and fell in love. It was the right thing for me. Two months later, I had a friend from Key West who lost his boat in the storm. I took him out sailing one day, handed him the papers for my boat and said, 'It's your boat. You have to take me back in now, I have to catch a plane to New York.'"

Upon arriving in New York, Mitchell rented an apartment and watched MTV for three months solid. "I said, 'No matter what I see on MTV, I'm not going to fucking do it. I don't care if I'm wrong. I'm gonna be me." Mitchell's subsequent work included videos with the likes of David Bowie and Billy Idol, leading to multiple award nominations. "That's how I met Russell [Mulcahy]. We worked with each other shooting music videos for fucking ever. I don't remember what music video we met on, but it was like end of fucking story. Didn't have to say a fucking word. It was just meant to be."

Prior to Mitchell being confronted by two men offering him a job with Mulcahy, he had already been considered for the position as *Highlander*'s cinematographer by his old friend, something the film's producers put an end to when they hired Gerry Fisher. When the film re-entered his life, he was already booked on a flight to London to shoot a music video with Tina Turner, a job he and his focus puller interrupted to attend a screening of *Highlander* footage already shot in London and Scotland. "There were things that were good, there were things that were not so good. My assistant and I were sitting there and the producers were listening to what we were saying. They didn't talk to me."

Mitchell always felt that the producers didn't like him, initially because of his lack of experience on feature films and later because they had no control over him, while Russell Mulcahy did. "I'm the kind of guy that does not like to be told what to do, which has been a problem for me all my life. For me, it's not what you say, it's how you say it. Many times people are telling you what to do and they don't think about what they're saying, and I say, 'Go fuck yourself, I'm not going to do it even if I'm wrong. Talk to me that way and I ain't fucking doing it.' But I don't think the producers really cared for me. Nobody explained what the film was about."

Mitchell goes on to note that he was surprised by the lack of interaction between himself and other members of the crew, expecting he'd have a chance to communicate with Gerry Fisher, whom he calls "an incredibly talented man". As it turned out, nobody introduced the two men to each other and they never discussed the film, its style or its unique look.

"I've thought about it many times and the only thing I can come up with is that Russell knew me," says Mitchell, going on to state that Mulcahy "trusted me, 1,000%, not 100%, 1,000%. I'd never shot a movie before, so it wasn't a script, it wasn't a story, everything was a scene for me. So that's how we made it. It was supposed to be dangerous and dark and this and that. So I just took that as my lead. I felt that Russell wanted me to be Tony Mitchell; crazy, out there, fuck it, do it. At that point in my career, that's the only thing I would do anyway. I did it like I was shooting a music video, except it was a 180-man crew."

Soon after joining the film, Mitchell was invited to scout New York locations with Mulcahy, with a memo dated Wednesday 3 July noting that the pair were due to visit locations including Central Park, Prospect Park Zoo, Madison Square Garden garage and Silvercup Studios' roof on Friday 5 July. They would be joined by Peter Davis, Bill Panzer, Allan Cameron, David Tringham and others involved in the New York shoot.

Tony Mitchell admits that for his first film experience, *Highlander* was a daunting prospect. "All of a sudden they rocked up in New York. It was like an explosion, like a bomb went off. A massive crew. I'm walking down the street on the first day and I'm looking at all these fucking trucks. I can't believe what I'm looking at. There were two or three kilometres of equipment trucks. Anything I can possibly imagine was there. I didn't even order equipment. They brought everything."

Just as Russell Mulcahy wanted to work with people he knew he could trust, so Tony Mitchell wanted to surround himself with a crew that he'd worked with on his music videos. "I tell everybody, 'I'm not going to tell you what to do. I want to tell you what I want. And then you go fucking do it. And if I say no, it means no discussion. I say change that, change it. Period.' Very few people understand the way I work with my crews, and especially on this movie, where all of that embracing and trusting and picking my crew slowly over the years came together. I would say five words and they would do 100 things."

One of the team members that Mitchell had been working with for a number of years was Jimmy Crispi, a head electrician who looked after the lighting on his music videos. "Jimmy Crispi was a big guy. He's not a cameraman, he'd never shot anything, but he was so intense with the light and the mood that I made him the second cameraman on that film. I said, 'Jim, come here. You're shooting the second camera.' He almost exploded, I almost had to call the ambulance. I did that to a few people."

Filming in New York

Central Park was the main location for the first day of filming on 8 July, primarily the scene on Bow Bridge featuring MacLeod and Kastagir meeting for the first time, perhaps better known as the 'boom boom' scene. "Bow Bridge was no big deal as we had great cooperation with the Parks Department and New York City Film Office," explains Edwin 'Itsi' Atkins, production coordinator for the New York shoot. Atkins had worked on several productions with *Highlander*'s associate producer, John Starke, and his knowledge of working in the city proved vital on their latest collaboration. "We did need to have a camera in a boat to get the long shots of them on the bridge."

In the finished film, Kastagir and MacLeod only talk briefly before there's a flashback to the latter fighting Bassett on Boston Common. In the script, and as filmed, Detective Bedsoe is following MacLeod and loitering in the bushes nearby when the latter meets

Kastagir. Bedsoe then follows the Immortals to a nightclub called The Dugout, described in the script as "a steel-and-neon Village hang-out" with sawdust on the floor.

"There was a scene in a kind of nightclub with an exotic dancer," recalls Quarshie. "It was a real dive that they'd dressed up to look like a New York nightclub. Christopher and I did a pincer movement on Jon Polito, who was the copper shadowing MacLeod, we came from two sides and forced him to sit between us and drink the boom boom. Of course he gets drunk and ends up on the floor dancing with the semi-naked go-go dancer." Dialogue in the nightclub scene originally led into the Boston Common flashback, but its removal meant that Lambert and Quarshie had to dub similar dialogue onto the end of the Central Park sequence.

According to Quarshie, "Christopher was very easy to work with. I speak a little French and he was kind enough to say, 'Oh, you speak very good French,' which I don't. I liked him a lot, he was an easy-going guy and not at all starry; neither was Clancy. I've since met American actors who are really quite intense, and they're not easy to hang around with afterwards. Jon Polito was a bit serious, but he wasn't a diva."

Another moment between MacLeod and Kastagir was also filmed in Central Park, before being cut in the editing room. "MacLeod and Kastagir discuss joining forces to defeat the Kurgan," says Quarshie. "Kastagir, although he and MacLeod go back and are friends, says it wouldn't work because there can be only one. MacLeod takes his leave and Kastagir is left sitting on the bench and looking up. Suddenly a flock of birds shoots up. There were a couple of interesting scenes, but I guess they weren't critical to the story. I'm just gratified that the stuff that did remain has become part of cinema legend."

Quarshie's short spell on *Highlander* may have ended, but he remained in New York for a short time, enjoying the sights of the city and seeing the newly released *Back to the Future* at the cinema. Aware that a friend of his was working on Steven Spielberg's *The Color Purple* in North Carolina, Quarshie flew down to Raleigh and spent some time with her, Whoopi Goldberg and Oprah Winfrey.

"Oprah had just got the news that her programme had been syndicated. She was into her book club at the time and was appalled that I had never read *Uncle Tom's Cabin* or *The Grapes of Wrath*. She bought them for me and I think I still have her signed copy of *Uncle Tom's Cabin*, which I have read now. That was the year of Live Aid, and on the day off, cast and crew gathered in the hotel we were staying in to watch the broadcast. I found myself sitting behind Spielberg, who was saying, 'I just want to see Bob' – that was Bob Dylan."

As well as Moran and Bedsoe eating hotdogs beside Tony's stand, a shot of a newspaper vendor (Louis Guss) on the south-east corner of 53rd Street and Seventh Avenue was filmed on 8 July. Elsewhere, the exterior of MacLeod's antiques store and apartment, supposedly Hudson Street, was filmed at 71 Greene Street in SoHo, with the art department's Tim Hutchinson applying the lettering, Russell Nash Antiques, to the windows.

"Most of it was shot downtown, below 23rd Street," notes Tony Mitchell. "It was SoHo before it was called SoHo; it was a bit funky back then." Mitchell also lived in the SoHo/Lower Manhattan area at the time, taking advantage of the artist-in-residence zoning law which saw 200 lofts converted to residential use, on the condition that each one contained a resident artist. "I could rent a loft space in a factory building on the third floor. An elevator came up to my loft and I could put my car in it. In the other corner [there was a] little elevator for people. It was $125 a month for 3,500 square feet."

Tuesday 9 July found Christopher Lambert, Roxanne Hart and Clancy Brown required for filming at Prospect Park Zoo, with the production notes revealing that costume supervisor Helen Butler twisted her ankle at 2 p.m. while coming down some steps to the concession stand. That night, Lambert and Hart were taken to Peter McManus Cafe at 152 Seventh Avenue to film the interior bar scenes of MacLeod and Brenda meeting for the first time.

Filming began after an 8 p.m. dinner for the actors, and although Lambert and Hart were the focus of the scene, actor Anthony Fusco also found himself working alongside the pair on the day as Phil the bartender.

"It was one of my very earliest experiences on a film set and I was quite nervous," admits Fusco, adding that the bar's owner was present to watch the shoot. "He told me I used my wet rag just like a real bartender would, which I found reassuring. I remember Christopher Lambert using the bar's pinball machine, or maybe it was a video game machine, a lot between takes, and that he had a very intense way about him. I was very excited to be working with Roxanne Hart. I was a recent graduate of Juilliard and admired her greatly for her New York theatre successes; she was making quite a splash then."

Despite the scene taking place at night, cinematographer Tony Mitchell decided to take some liberties with his lighting set-up. "We're shooting in the bar and these two people are talking, so I lit it like a music video, with streams of light coming through the window. Everybody in the crew was snorting cocaine and doing their thing, like we normally do on a music video. Russell was totally behind it."

Another contributor to the look of the scene was stills photographer David James, who was required to photograph Christopher Lambert at the bar. "They had a really good cinematographer on all of the London stuff, but for some reason they didn't take him to New York. They had a guy who was a friend of Russell's to shoot the New York part, he was on another planet. [Christopher] is sitting there and the camera's behind the bar, but you can't see Christopher's face because he hasn't been lit. I grabbed a little flashlight, switched it on and shone it in Christopher's face, and the director said, 'Oh, that's awesome, let's shoot it again with that.'"

Anthony Fusco's time on the set wasn't his last contribution to the bar scene, as he was called back to re-record his dialogue sometime after filming. "Due to the aforementioned nervousness, my voice had gone rather high and breathy and they wanted me to sound more masculine and 'New York'. Also they wanted to add the brand name Glenmorangie into the scene. Of course I had no idea I was working on a film that would become so iconic."

Adventures with the second unit

With Russell Mulcahy busy directing the first unit in New York, elsewhere in the city a second unit was preparing to cause mayhem under the watchful eye of director Andy Armstrong. Born in England, Armstrong entered the film industry as a vehicle stunt performer before working his way up to becoming a second assistant director on films such as *The Spy Who Loved Me* (1977) and *Krull*. "I was very lucky, because the only things in life I was interested in were high-performance vehicles and movies," says Armstrong, who became one of the youngest assistant directors in the world by the age of just 24.

Armstrong had worked on some of the initial London filming in the underground car park sequence, and was next due to fly to New York to shoot some scenes leading up to the final battle. "Originally I was only going to go and shoot the scene where the Kurgan picks up Brenda and takes her on a drive through New York. Literally that was just two lines in the script. The Kurgan arrives at her place, forces his way in, kidnaps her and takes her on a ride in New York. It was going to be a Ford Bronco four-wheel drive, but I suggested they change it to a Cadillac so there was something more retro, an iconically big American car that you'd normally see old people in."

The director also suggested to the producers that the sequence was expanded to make it a more terrifying drive through the city, something they agreed to. After talking to the American crew by phone from London, Armstrong discovered that his stunt coordinator would be Vic Magnotta, before he requested two stuntmen, Shane Dixon and Greg Barnett, from Los Angeles to carry out the driving sequences. "It was a pivotal movie for me because a lot of these long-distance, long-term friendships were established on it. Greg and I are friends to this day. Shane unfortunately got cancer and died not many years after *Highlander*. We were friends till the end. Vic was killed performing on a movie soon after that."

Despite the importance of the car sequence to the film, Russell Mulcahy and Andy Armstrong didn't spend too much time discussing its intricacies. "I always had the idea of two narrow trucks going by and knocking a motorcyclist off. That motorcyclist was [stunt performer] Brian Smrz. A lot of that stuff we just made up a day or two before. I wanted it to be like a sort of force of nature blasting through New York."

Armstrong was determined to try and match Mulcahy's signature visual style on his sections of the film, keen to avoid the problem he'd witnessed on other productions when a different director took over for action sequences. "The second unit director should emulate the style of the main director; it's his or her movie." Emulating Mulcahy meant using long lenses rather than mid-range lenses in the car sequence. "If you look at all the imagery in the film, it's either shot with a very wide, almost a fisheye, lens or on very long telephoto lenses, and that was the style he was shooting the picture in. There are lots of people that shoot like that now and kind of claim it as their style, but Russell was doing it 30 years ago."

Before the sequence started, Russell Mulcahy and cinematographer Tony Mitchell were on hand to help light the interior of the car, with Mitchell deciding to place a small light in the back of the Cadillac that shone on Clancy Brown. "Russell said, 'It's terrible,' and I said, 'Yeah, I know it looks fucking terrible, I'm not finished.' I took a piece of black wrap and cut little slices in it and put it in front of the lights. Then I put this little light in front of him, so it's just barely a glow, with a little glue on his face. And everybody freaked the fuck out. That's how I lit it, two of the smallest lights. It was all innovative because that's the way we shot music videos."

One of the New York stunt performers working on the film was Tim Gallin, who had begun his career at the age of 21 in the hope of making his name in Los Angeles. Arriving in California in 1980, Gallin was politely told to go back to New York until he had more experience. "When I started in the business there were maybe 30 guys competing for work in New York. Today there's well over 300, maybe well over 350, and not all of them are what I would call A-class young guys. In those days we really got the crumbs. When I went out to California, and I was told to come back, I finally realised that I might as well just stay in New York and be a bigger fish in a smaller pond. I was fortunate to get on *Highlander*; primarily it was on the car chase with Clancy Brown."

The third day of first unit filming took place on Wednesday 10 July, and saw the crew heading to the exterior of Madison Square Garden to film MacLeod's car being apprehended by Garfield (Edward Wiley) and other cops. Filming then moved to 126 East 36th Street, the exterior of Walter Bedsoe's house. In the script, following the burning down of Nash/MacLeod's shop and apartment by Rachel as the Immortal left his old life behind, three delivery men bring MacLeod's aquarium to Bedsoe's apartment for him to look after.

The same day saw the second unit begin filming in the city, setting up on First Avenue to shoot scenes of the Kurgan driving the wrong way down the street against the traffic. Production manager Itsi Atkins explains that to facilitate filming on New York's busiest streets, he employed a well-known industry system. "Every location man in New York City has 'street grease', which is a wad of $50 bills. I remember needing to stop traffic, which was accomplished with a tractor that pulled into the intersection and stalled creating a backlog and 'grease' was needed." The production report for 10 July notes that due to a water shortage in the city, an out-of-state water truck had to be brought in to slick down the roads. "Russell wanted everything covered in rain," explained Atkins to the *Highlander Rewatched* podcast. "You might be looking at one scene, but he'll want rain to the left, to the right, behind you, everywhere."

Due to the film's relatively tight budget, Andy Armstrong had taken his personal camera mounts from England, hiring two Cadillacs for the first scene, with one of the cars being a back-up in case of accidents. "We were trying to shoot a lot of it with available light. If I'd have had to light every junction I could have never done that sequence. I went around at night looking for streets that were very well lit for the one sequence where he's going against traffic."

With Armstrong keen to have as much light as possible in the background, he ended up swapping the flow of traffic around. While it appeared the Kurgan was driving the wrong way, in fact his was the only car going the right way, with all the oncoming traffic heading in the wrong direction. "They were all our drivers and they were the ones actually going in the wrong direction and we only had a few good stunt people; the rest were sort of extras in cars at the back," continues Armstrong. Other stunt performers noted on the day's production report include Jerry Hewitt, Edgard Mourino, Harry Madsen, Deborah Watkins and Paul Lee.

Feeling the first take was too tame, Armstrong went for a second and third, with the latter causing a head-on collision between stunt performers Shane Dixon, driving the Cadillac and accompanied by stuntwoman Lisa Cain standing in for Roxanne Hart, plus Greg Barnett. "Somebody in the pack had confused whether they went to the right or left and it had a whole knock-on effect down the line. I was right down the road shooting with a long lens and the crash is in the movie."

In the film, the Cadillac can clearly be seen hitting a car, which in turn hits another car which bounces into a fourth. Says Armstrong, "It caused mayhem because it was the first night shooting of the whole sequence . . . it destroyed a car that was parked and which was owned by the chief of police, who was stopping traffic." After checking that nobody was hurt, Armstrong discovered that the most noise was coming from the irate police officer whose car had been destroyed. "I thought he was going to have a heart attack, he turned purple and was screaming and shouting. I think if he could have got away with it he'd have shot me. I was hiding for the rest of the night."

Filming of the car chase continued for over a week, during which time Andy Armstrong and his team had more than a few encounters with the NYPD. At one point, Armstrong was threatened with arrest when he jumped off the camera car towing the Kurgan's Cadillac. "While I was rolling the second and third cameras, Clancy did a funny little thing that was not scripted where he was singing 'New York, New York' while he was waiting for the cameras to get up to speed. Meanwhile I was getting severely reprimanded by a New York police officer who said if I got off the camera car again, he'd arrest me."

"New York at the time was not a great place to be; it was kind of seedy and dangerous," recalls Clancy Brown. "The cops were not friendly, they mouthed off to Andy, or maybe Andy mouthed off to them, and I was just singing it ironically, trying to have a good time that night."

Tim Gallin speaks fondly of the opportunities stunt performers had in the 1980s to make sequences look real. "Today, with the advent of terrorism and the militarisation of the police forces, there's a feeling you can't get away with much or Big Brother's watching. They're very conservative, and they supposedly won't let you go over about 30 miles an hour. That's why there's so much cutting going on, because they can only do small pieces at a time and then they have to cobble it together. Back in those days it was more of a Wild West feel. We were able to get away with more and live a little more on the edge. It was fun."

The stunt performers may have been used to living on the edge for a living, but for the actors it was a different story, with tensions occasionally rising as complex set pieces were created around them. According to Andy Armstrong, Roxanne Hart was less enthusiastic about speeding the wrong way down busy roads than co-star Clancy Brown. In one shot, the Kurgan's car had to play chicken with three trucks which looked like they might collide with him, only to part ways at the last moment to let the Cadillac through. On the first take, Armstrong felt he needed more emotion from his leading lady. "She reluctantly got in the car and did it again, but the next time I told the guys in the trucks to go closer and part much later."

As instructed, when the truck drivers got close to the car they hit their air horns, with the shocked look on Roxanne Hart's face in the film a genuine response to the sight of three huge vehicles bearing down on her. "It's a tremendous reaction," says Armstrong, "but when she came back she slapped me around the face because she was really scared. She laughed about it later."

When I ask Hart about the scene she pauses for a moment, before replying carefully. "The shoots were difficult for the actors, like the stuff on Silvercup and the night shoots that Clancy and I did through the tunnel. I mean, that was really long. It was long for the actors and almost twice as long for the director, because he's there at the beginning [right to] the end."

Russell Mulcahy included a surprise for keen-eyed viewers of the car sequence, which takes place when the Kurgan's vehicle is seen mounting a pavement and speeding along it. "Two people get hit on the sidewalk: one is Russell and one is his boyfriend," explains editor Peter Honess. "There's a quick cut of people being hit. I'm very proud of it." The director can also be seen for a split second on the right-hand side of the screen as the camera tracks through New York library, a scene filmed back in London at the National Liberal Club. "I don't do it for ego, I just do it for fun," says Mulcahy of his cameos.

Mulcahy's next major task was to match up the sequences he had overseen in London on top of a replica of Long Island's Silvercup building, though this time it would be the real thing.

TWELVE

IMMORTAL COMBAT

By the end of the first week of New York filming, the first unit was finally able to return to work on the Silvercup sequence they'd begun filming in London a few weeks earlier, with Friday 12 and Saturday 13 July scheduled to complete the scenes.

Despite the impressive scale of the fight sequence, the production team had realised in the run-up to filming that there could be an issue. "They wanted all the lights on in the skyline of New York City," recalls second assistant director Ian Woolf. "From the Lower East Side all the way to the Upper West Side [there are] like 200,000 apartments that face Silvercup Studios. They wanted everybody to keep the lights on because we were shooting all night. The location department literally flyered 200,000 apartments to say, 'Hey, guys, we're shooting this movie *Highlander*. We're going to be on Silvercup Studios, the Manhattan skyline is in the background, and we need you to keep your lights on all night.'"

"I had a group of production assistants cover each building on the river and work with the residents to keep their lights on," says production manager Itsi Atkins, who had thousands of flyers printed out and handed to locals. "We also had to keep all major buildings lit as they go out during the night. This was a big challenge to keep all buildings from 34th Street to 64th Street on."

Says Ian Woolf, "If you watch that sequence, early at eight or nine p.m. it's just beautiful. But then as we got to two, three and four, people were starting to get tired or just forgot about the lights. Slowly seeing the lights of the skyline [go out], that's one of the main things that sticks out in my mind." Photographer David James vividly remembers filming at Silvercup and the stunning Manhattan backdrop it offered the film-makers. "They did it on Friday night, and at that time New York was in a big energy-saving mode. So of course, most of the office lights went out and as we're shooting you can't see Manhattan anymore. I thought that was hilarious."

One way the crew kept in touch was by utilising the latest technology available to them. "Before *Highlander*, as a second assistant director you'd run around New York City with a roll of ten-cent pieces in your pocket because you had to call the office, report the first shot, all that stuff," explains Ian Woolf. "On *Highlander* we had the very first cell phone, which came in a 40-pound briefcase. You'd open this thing up, and it was like this giant phone mounted into this case with the old style handset."

In preparing the roof for filming, Itsi Atkins knew it was important to protect it from the heavy equipment that would be placed onto it by the crew. His solution was to lay lengths of plywood across the top, though when he inspected it a few days before the shoot he realised that the roof no longer resembled a regular roof. "[I said] 'It's got to look like a roof; it's got to look like shingles.' I had to get every painter I could get all night long, two nights before we showed up, to make all that plywood look like shingles."

Just as rain had hampered filming in London and Scotland, so it did on the Friday in New York, with weather warnings suggesting a stormy night ahead. The cast arrived in make-up early in the evening, with Clancy Brown the first at 6 p.m., followed by Christopher Lambert at 7.30 p.m. and Roxanne Hart at 8.30 p.m., with the actors due on set for 9.30 p.m. Also returning from the London Silvercup shoot were stunt performers Peter Brace and Andy Bradford, who had flown into New York the previous day, while swordmaster Bob Anderson was on hand along with second assistant director François Moullin, hired by Itsi Atkins because he could speak French and converse with Lambert more easily.

Cinematographer Tony Mitchell recalls the crew clambering up the side of Silvercup to film, and that the Louma crane was also present and correct to capture shots from various angles. "All of a sudden, these black clouds came in and lightning was striking all over New York City. I had a crane sitting up in the air and the producers said, 'We have to keep shooting,' and the crew just ran off the roof and lightning struck." The production report shows that rain and lightning began at 10.55 p.m. and ended at 11.30 p.m., beginning again at 12.15 a.m. and going on until 2.50 a.m. As a result, shooting was halted for three hours for safety reasons.

"I remember Silvercup vividly," says make-up supervisor Lois Burwell, "as we shot there when a massive lightning storm came and we ended up all wearing bin liners, a trick we first used when shooting in Glencoe to keep our feet dry. It was a very exciting location, with the most fabulous view of the Manhattan skyline."

Also recorded on the production report is the fact that Roxanne Hart suffered a minor mishap with a sword during the last shot, but that she declined medical attention. In addition, the report notes that "Christopher Lambert jumped into the airbag and accidently put a 12-inch cut into the 20 x 20 covering of the bag with his sword", something Ian Woolf vividly recalls.

"When they were doing the fight sequence on top of that sign we had a giant airbag below it for [the actors] for safety reasons," explains Woolf. "When we broke for lunch, there was a whole staircase system to come down from. Christopher Lambert, with his sword in his hand said, 'The hell with walking down all those stairs to get down to the roof to take the elevator,' and he jumped off the platform. It was probably 40 or 50 feet up, it punctured the airbag and cost the company $15,000. He just jumped and it was like, 'Holy shit, he could have killed himself.'"

Lambert denies that sequence of events, noting that he'd done a huge amount of mattress work on *Greystoke* and was used to them. "When I saw the inflatable mattress being put on the Silvercup building I thought, 'They've got the inflatable mattress, I'm going to jump,' and while I was in the air I heard the stunt guy say 'No!' The mattress wasn't ready, but it was inflated just enough, otherwise I'd have crashed on the ground. The sword didn't touch the mattress, it was just the stunt guy saying, 'You're crazy, the mattress isn't ready,' so I said, 'Sorry!'"

Though the production report doesn't state that the mattress had to be replaced, the report from the following night's filming notes there were two punctures resulting from swords being dropped, along with burn holes resulting from miniature explosives. Also on 13 July, gaffer Denver Collins hit his chin on the suspended steam pipes and cut his lip, while the head of the Louma crane was dropped with minor damages to the mechanics. "The equipment demands on the roof were major," says Itsi Atkins. "Even though we didn't hurt the roof, the owners tried to get paid for damages. We worked it out after the shoot."

Ian Woolf enjoyed his time on *Highlander*, noting that "Christophe was a nice guy. My wife came to visit me on the set one evening; we were shooting somewhere on the East Side. I gave her a director's chair and Christophe was sitting next to her. She came over and said, 'Where's Christopher Lambert?' I said, 'Patricia, he's sitting right next to you.' She didn't recognise him because in person he wasn't that big of a guy. He had his glasses on and they were thick like Coke bottles."

As for Russell Mulcahy, Woolf had little interaction with him other than handing him the occasional cup of tea or coffee, explaining that the director is only approached if there's a reason to do so. "I remember that he had an entourage that surrounded him and that he was very Hollywood at the time, with the scarf around his neck. Russell spent most of his time with Tony Mitchell, who was pretty flamboyant in his own right."

Roxanne Hart adds that Mulcahy "had his whole coterie of people around him. [He was] really kind of driven, he was a really hard rock and roller. He worked us hard, worked me hard. He was relentless."

Filming of the Silvercup scenes in London and New York aren't a happy memory for Hart. Having to hang from scaffolding and avoid falling metal while being pummelled by water clearly took its toll, and today she isn't keen on discussing the sequence in detail. "Silvercup, that was pretty bad. It was a very late night of shooting. It was the eighties [and safety was] not really of the utmost concern. It was a little scary. I possibly wasn't equipped to . . . I wasn't a gymnast, let's put it that way. I did have stunt people, but it was difficult."

Madison Square Garden

Monday 15 July was important for the *Highlander* production team, marking the final day of first unit filming in New York, while the second unit would continue for another few days. The production report shows that a number of scenes were due to be shot that day, starting with a visit to Madison Square Garden for the scripted opening scenes of MacLeod watching a wrestling match, before he disappears into the crowd to fight Fasil in the car park.

Just as the car park scenes had been shot in London, the interior of Madison Square Garden also had to be shot somewhere other than the actual Madison Square Garden. "We worked hard to get the local hockey team and venue to shoot the opening shot," says Itsi Atkins. "We quickly moved from Madison Square Garden to the Meadowlands Arena for the wrestling. It was a big loss but we made it work."

The match filmed involved Greg Gagne, Jim Brunzell and the Tonga Kid versus The Fabulous Freebirds, Michael P.S. Hayes, Terry Gordy and Buddy Roberts. Due to Russell Mulcahy's desire to keep the camera moving at all times, he decided he wanted to 'swoop' in on Connor MacLeod as he watched the wrestling match. The system chosen to do this was a relatively new piece of equipment called Skycam, a network of pulleys and wires that were hung over the arena and that allowed the operator to move a camera remotely via computer.

Invented by Garrett Brown, who had also invented the Steadicam, the system was first used in an NFL game in 1984, and was perfect for Russell Mulcahy's requirements. "Inventing Skycam was difficult in that computationally primitive era, so my 'Skyworks' company was nearly on the ropes in 1985 when Russell Mulcahy booked us to shoot his spectacular opening shot," explains Brown today. "We had pioneered a film version with an ultralight Panavision camera, and we agreed to $15,000 for the entire job."

J.D. Freedman had been working as a grip on a music video for musicians Hall and Oates in Virginia when he first met the Skycam team. "The Skycam guys liked me because I work hard," notes Freedman, who was then invited to work on more jobs as chief motorman, including the Live Aid concert in Philadelphia and *Highlander* in New York. "I got my friend Bobby Gorelick on the job as an assistant cameraman, and Tass Michos as the camera operator."

Although not mentioned in the production report, Freedman recalls that the Skycam team set up the day before shooting was due to take place. "The shoot was at night during an actual WWF wrestling match, and the camera floated close over the ring, sometimes right over the wrestlers' shoulders. We shot a lot more than they ever would use. I worked closely with a guy who was on staff with them; he was a steel walker. He walked out unsupported across the beams on the top of the arena to set the four pulleys for the Skycam's wires. As I recall the fans didn't make too big a deal about the camera."

Garrett Brown was also present at the arena, delighted that his team had delivered what he calls "Russell's unique and textbook perfect shot. [It was] brilliant both for the film and for our reel, flying supernaturally down from the rafters, swooping over the ring and soaring up to find Chris Lambert glowering from the high bleachers. We nailed it in a few takes and Russell was thrilled."

According to production designer Allan Cameron, he and Russell Mulcahy had to improvise to ensure the zoom effect from the arena ceiling onto Christopher Lambert was going to work. Mulcahy wanted to go from a wide shot of the crowds watching the match, to a close-up of Lambert. The solution was to use the flashes from the cameras of the audience to mask the switch from a wide angle lens to a regular lens. When the Skycam reached a certain point, the shot was edited with another of the closer lenses and the result was an almost seamless zoom in on Christopher Lambert.

Cameron and Mulcahy's solution didn't sit well with producer Peter Davis, who called Garrett Brown a few days later. "He refused to pay us, saying, 'That's not the shot I wanted,' because he said we had not flown right up to Chris, who was inaccessibly seated a dozen rows back from the balcony edge. I spluttered, 'You weren't there, we worked to Russell's direction and he loved the shot!' Russell had simply pulled the old 'flashbulb switcheroo' to a tripod shot zooming into Lambert's close-up, but Davis was brutal and said, 'I'm not paying, sue me.' I was stunned."

According to Brown, his associate at Technicolor, Jocy Vee, "was furious and held the *Highlander* negative on our behalf, but a New York judge released it since they were an English company and suggested we sue them in London, which we expensively did. Of course we won, so they eventually had to pay up. That's the only time in my long career anyone had simply refused to pay for our work. I was, and remain, profoundly shocked by such sociopathy. In fact I daydreamed that if I happened to come across Panzer or Davis at a Hollywood party, I might go berserk and invert one or both in the punchbowl, but the occasion never arose."

Brown is still stung by the experience, keen to tell others who might encounter similar situations to follow his lead. "I can only advise not accepting, not giving up, not turning away . . . go straight at it and do all you can to achieve justice, even if locally expensive. Incidentally, a belated Oscar for Skycam cited the four motion pictures we shot on film, including *Highlander*!"

The same day also saw a helicopter hired to film various shots, including MacLeod and Brenda on the Silvercup sign and the Kurgan driving through New York. However, the production report shows that approximately three hours of filming were lost due to heavy rain causing the helicopter pilot to refuse to fly. It's possible that the Silvercup scene was sacrificed on the night, as there's no evidence of an aerial shot in the finished film.

Enter (and exit) Yung Dol Kim

Though the first unit had completed filming on the Monday, Tuesday 16 July saw Andy Armstrong's second unit continue filming the car sequence featuring Clancy Brown and Roxanne Hart. On Wednesday 17 July more of the car stunt was filmed, along with filming inside an office building at 77 Water Street, part of New York's Wall Street financial district, close to the East River.

In their *Highlander* script, Larry Ferguson and Peter Bellwood had crafted a fight sequence between the Immortals Yung Dol Kim and the Kurgan in an empty office. Mistaking a mannequin for his enemy, Kim smashes it to pieces with his sword, before the Kurgan appears and pushes Kim into a computer room where the pair fight. Without warning, Kim drops his sword and allows the Kurgan to take his head, explaining that after 400 years he's tired and wants peace, before the Kurgan slices off his head. The resulting explosion sucks Kim's body out of the window and down 40 storeys to the pavement below.

What makes this sequence particularly interesting is that it didn't end up in the finished film, with no mention of Yung Dol Kim in any other scenes. According to *Highlander* lore, the footage was lost in a fire, though photos of the Kurgan and Kim fighting do exist online.

According to Frazer Diamond, son of stunt coordinator Peter Diamond, there's evidence that his father planned the fight while back in the UK. "I've got the storyboards and breakdowns for the fight between Kim and the Kurgan. Looking through the storyboards and then looking at the photos that exist online, I have to say absolutely categorically that is a 'Dad fight'. There is no doubt that he coordinated all of that, because it almost mirrors the exact same fight he put together for Oliver Reed in *The Brigand of Kandahar*, in which he gave him two swords to fight against Ronald Lewis."

Although the production reports for 17 July have no reference to Russell Mulcahy filming that day, Andy Armstrong is certain that the director shot in the building before him, stating that he "can remember all the blown-up computers and debris when I got there to shoot the body". Armstrong arrived to find that the special effects team had constructed a large cannon with a dummy placed inside it, the plan being to use air pressure to fire Yung Dol Kim's headless torso through the window and onto Wall Street, noting that "you'd never get permission to do that nowadays, it's madness". The panes of glass had already been removed by the cleaners who regularly washed the skyscraper's windows.

"The special effects guys were saying, 'Where do you want it to land?' and I thought it'd be nice if it went down and landed in the street," explains Armstrong. "The guys doing the glass went, 'No, no, whatever you do, however hard it's thrown out, no matter the speed it's doing, it'll land right back where the kerb meets the road.' Convinced that the workers knew what they were talking about, Armstrong heeded their advice, keen to ensure the body went a decent distance as "it seemed a bit underwhelming if it just went down to the kerb". Despite asking the effects coordinator to increase the pressure, the window cleaners were still convinced it wouldn't work. "They said, 'It doesn't matter what pressure you put on it, it'll just go to that spot.'"

Undeterred, Armstrong's team blew the cannon, the dummy flew out of the window, cleared Wall Street and landed in the middle of a building site across the road. "I said to the guy cleaning the window, 'What the fuck?' and he said, 'Wow, I've never seen that before.' Had there been a building there, it'd have landed in someone else's office. Within seconds we started getting phone calls from the boats on the river that someone had committed suicide. I remember talking to a police officer and saying, 'Look, if it was a suicide then this guy was really determined – he cleared six lanes and he had no head at the time.'"

"There was a scene in an office that I think they abandoned while shooting," agrees editor Peter Honess when I mention its disappearance to him. "I put together this break-in scene in an office and I cut what I could with what I had, but the producers pulled the plug on it because they weren't happy with it. It could never have been in the film because it was never complete. Russell wanted to complete it at some other time, but it was quite dreadful."

The actor playing Yung Dol Kim is unknown, though make-up effects mould designer John Schoonraad is convinced that the British actor David Yip, best known for his BBC TV series *The Chinese Detective* (1981–82) was originally cast in the role. Says Schoonraad, "I had a nickname at the time, 'The Chinese Detective', because I looked a bit like David Yip, and when we met we did think there was a resemblance. We did a lifecast. The David Yip scene took place in an office and there was an explosion. They cut the David Yip scene right out, but he filmed it."

Intrigued by the mention of Yip, I contacted his representatives to try and arrange an interview with the actor, only to be met with a one-sentence reply: "Thank you for your email, David didn't actually film any scenes so doesn't have anything to contribute." This didn't contradict John Schoonraad's memory that the actor had a cast of his body made, but it didn't help solve the mystery of why he left the production.

If Yip was hired in London and a cast of his body was created there, was his scene filmed in London, later abandoned, then reshot in New York with a new actor? Or perhaps the actor was due to fly to New York to film the sequence, only to pull out and be replaced? It's a mystery that may never be solved.

When filming finally ended in New York, the *Highlander* production team left just as quickly as they'd arrived. For assistant director Andy Armstrong, the film was an experience like no other, with his abiding memory being of the energy Russell Mulcahy brought to the film. "The interesting thing about *Highlander* is that there are all these mad things going on, but it's in an environment that you recognise, it's a New York that's not out of this world. I don't think Russell will ever be given enough credit for the stylised look he gave that movie. A lot of what people respond to is this very dynamic look that came from those very wide and very long lenses, and his fantastic cuts and wipes. That stuff was years ahead of its time."

Cinematographer Tony Mitchell soon returned to a globetrotting life of shooting music videos for the likes of Tom Petty, Ozzy Osbourne and Cyndi Lauper, and he looks back fondly on his time spent with Russell Mulcahy in the 1980s and 1990s. The pair never spoke of *Highlander* again, with Mitchell explaining that life was such a blur of travel, film sets and strange cities that he barely remembered being part of the production. "At that time I was never home. LA, New York and London. Tina Turner, Elton John and Freddie Mercury. It just went on, and on, and on. For me it was just a job. It didn't dawn on me until years later that I shot the New York part of *Highlander*; it never occurred to me."

Additional photography

On their return from New York, the production team began taking stock of the footage they had accumulated during filming. Thanks to the general unease surrounding the make-up applied to Beatie Edney in her old-age scenes in Scotland, the decision was made to take her and Christopher Lambert to Wales to restage the sequence, with Connor and Heather's cottage rebuilt in the countryside. Other shots were filmed back at London's Jacob Street Studios.

"We shot the scene way after principal photography was finished," says Beatie Edney, who at one point suggested that her mother, actor Sylvia Syms, should be cast as the older Heather. "I was doing a TV series called *Lost Empires* by then and had a couple of days of reshoots. There was a racket in the street when they were filming Heather's death scene and we had to keep stopping; it wasn't a proper sound stage. We also did some montage shots of me carrying a lamb and looking old. I remember the lamb pissing all over me the whole time, poor little thing."

"The lamb was basically freaking out," laughs Lambert when I ask about his memories of the Wales shoot and the death scene. "The dialogue and her on the bed was fine; it's just when she was outside, she turns to me and we see that she's aged. The camera had to stay on her for no more than three seconds."

The film's ending, featuring MacLeod and Brenda sitting on a Scottish hillside while planning their next move, was also shot in Wales, with Roxanne Hart recalling that the countryside was "just extraordinary". Other shots filmed in Wales included MacLeod being struck by lightning during the opening battle; long-distance shots of the Kurgan on horseback; and fish falling out of MacLeod's kilt.

A major scripted sequence that had been deemed unnecessary during the principal photography period was the World War II flashback that introduced the character of Rachel. With a rough assembly of the footage available to the director and producers, it became clear that it was an important sequence that needed to be in the film, forcing Mulcahy to hastily put together a team to shoot the sequence in London.

Christopher Lambert and child actor Nicola Ramsey were ferried to some waste ground in the city, along with an actor playing the Nazi soldier who, according to Mulcahy, "stormed off", leaving assistant director Waldo Roeg to don the uniform. In the DVD commentary, Mulcahy notes that the gunfire and explosions took place where cyanide had been buried, with the cast and crew advised "they'd only get mildly sick" by breathing in the fumes.

With principal photography now complete, it was left to Russell Mulcahy to join editor Peter Honess and begin crafting a cut of the film that could be screened for studio executives. At the same time, Mulcahy and producers Peter Davis and Bill Panzer were actively searching for a band that could provide a soundtrack for *Highlander*, though finding one that could somehow match the rock-and-roll vision that the film's director had brought to the film wouldn't be an easy task.

THIRTEEN

SETTLING THE SCORE

On the evening of 13 July 1985, the New York cast and crew of *Highlander* would have been forgiven for thinking that their work filming a major fight sequence between Connor MacLeod and the Kurgan on top of the Silvercup building was the most important event going on in the world.

For some of them, it probably was.

With tens of thousands of dollars resting on the sequence's successful completion, it was a relief for everyone when the long night finally came to an end and they could return to the comfort of their assorted apartments and hotels. While it's likely that many of them went straight to bed after yet another exhausting day on set, it's equally likely that some tuned their television into a music extravaganza taking place in London and Philadelphia.

"I remember coming back, switching on the telly in the hotel room and seeing various huge bands at Wembley Stadium," says stunt performer Andy Bradford, who was one of an estimated 1.9 billion viewers around the globe watching Live Aid for some of its 16-hour run time.

The event had been conceived by musicians Bob Geldof and Midge Ure in response to the ongoing Ethiopian famine, a follow-up to the previous year's charity single, 'Do They Know It's Christmas?', which raised in the region of £8 million for the appeal. Dozens of acts made their way to both London's Wembley

Stadium and Philadelphia's John F. Kennedy Stadium, including David Bowie, U2, Paul McCartney, Bob Dylan and Neil Young.

One of the bands who graced the Wembley stage was British rock act Queen, who had recently finished an exhausting tour to accompany the release of their 11th studio album, 1984's *The Works*. Composed of lead singer Freddie Mercury, guitarist Brian May, drummer Roger Taylor and bassist John Deacon, Queen was founded in 1970, and 15 years on still commanded the devotion of millions of fans, despite disappointing US sales of the previous year's album. Whatever the status of Queen before they were introduced by comedians Mel Smith and Griff Rhys Jones in front of the 72,000-strong crowd and a billion or so TV viewers, by the end of their 20-minute set they were on their way to becoming the biggest British live act of the 1980s.

"Queen were absolutely the best band of the day," Bob Geldof later stated, "they just went and smashed one hit after another." Sales of *The Works* and their three-year-old *Greatest Hits* album skyrocketed after the performance, with official Queen biographer Jim Jenkins recalling that a friend of his who worked in a record shop told him that on the Monday morning after Live Aid "every person in the queue had a Queen album in their hand, and if it wasn't Queen it was U2."

Says Jenkins, "[Live Aid] took them to another level, even though they'd been touring for quite a while. They were still in the public eye, but the 20 minutes they did was pure magic. Queen were always innovative with lights and spectacular stage shows, but they went on stage to the world with no gimmicks, it was just them and the music. It was a very powerful performance and they won people over." By August, it had been decided that the band would capitalise on their resurgence in popularity by repackaging their back catalogue in a new box set, and by September the foursome made their way to Munich to record some new songs at Musicland Studios.

Around the same period, Russell Mulcahy and his editor Peter Honess were beginning to assemble some finished sequences from the previous few months of filming in their London editing suite, allowing the film's music supervisor, Derek Power, to start considering the type of soundtrack the film would have. Power was a talent manager and film producer who had been friends with *Highlander* producers Peter Davis and Bill Panzer since the early 1970s, during which time he had both sold films for them and raised money for productions.

After casting actor and musician Sting in 1982's *Brimstone and Treacle*, Power became partners with his Police bandmate, Stewart Copeland, their manager Miles Copeland and their booking agent, Ian Copeland. "I had been in business with the Copeland brothers from 1982 and I'd made Stewart's deal on *Rumble Fish*, the film he did for Francis Ford Coppola. I was deeply into the pop music soundtrack business as a consequence of my relationship with the three brothers, and with Miles particularly, because he also owned a record label, IRS Records."

Agreeing to work on *Highlander*, Power notes that he was determined to put together what he calls the "perfect soundtrack, which involved rock and roll on the one hand, and more classical film scoring on the other", stating that he "worked very, very, very hard to make that whole thing happen". A key influence on Power's approach to the *Highlander* soundtrack was Tom Waits' score for Francis Ford Coppola's 1981 romantic drama, *One from the Heart*, which also featured singer Crystal Gayle. "It was kind of a 'call and response' score by two different country artists. I had a very clear vision about *Highlander* using one artist or group who could write a bunch of different songs, at the same time seamlessly integrating the score."

Power knew of New York-born composer Michael Kamen thanks to his score for an early Davis and Panzer film, *The Death Collector* (1976). Trained at Juilliard in the 1960s, Kamen had formed the New York Rock and Roll Ensemble, which fused rock and classical music, the style that would come to be associated with the composer as he went on to collaborate with acts such as Pink Floyd and Roger Waters. In later years he went on to score for films including John Waters' *Polyester* (1981) and David Cronenberg's

The Dead Zone (1983). Says Power, "He was the perfect person to work with an artist or artists on a score. I had this vision of a score where the songs, as best as we could make work, would help move the storyline along, not just act as hit singles."

Of Kamen, Power recalls that "he was a lovely, very expansive, talented composer. My original idea was to do it just with a guitar, I actually looked at hiring [Pink Floyd's guitarist and co-lead vocalist] David Gilmour. I'm not sure that he wasn't the very first idea that I had because of Pink Floyd, in fact [I would have] hired them had they been playing as Pink Floyd at the time."

Although the members of Pink Floyd were never approached to work on the soundtrack, Jim Jenkins notes that David Bowie and Sting were at one point linked to the film, while British rock band Marillion turned down an offer to write the soundtrack due to their commitment to a world tour they were on at the time. "That was a really stupid thing for us to turn down," ruminated guitarist Steve Rothery in 2014, "as always in those sorts of cases you don't get offered it again." The band's lead singer, Fish, reportedly accepted a part in the film, before turning it down due to scheduling conflicts.

Russell Mulcahy may have worked with dozens of music artists by the time he came to *Highlander*, but he'd never directed Queen, despite being a fan of both them and of 1980's science fiction spectacle, *Flash Gordon*, for which the band had written the soundtrack album. By September 1985, Mulcahy and Peter Honess had edited together 20 minutes of footage that they were happy with, leading to a decision between Mulcahy, Derek Power, Peter Davis and Bill Panzer that they screen it for Queen and their manager Jim Beach, with the intention of inviting them to write and perform a song for the film.

"We brought Queen in and the whole band turned up," says Mulcahy. "We showed them different scenes and they came back and said they each wanted to do a song. Freddie loved operatic music and Michael [Kamen] had a rock-and-roll history, so the marriage of the music was wonderful. The music is one of the best things about the film."

"They were smart enough to know they needed good music," adds screenwriter Larry Ferguson. "I remember Bill [Panzer] coming to us at one point and he'd announced the fact he was going to go and get them and that Freddie Mercury had told him, 'This is the best script I've ever read in my life.'"

"I know the idea had been already put out there that we might do some music [for *Highlander*]," says Brian May, speaking to me from his London home during a rare enforced break from touring caused by 2020's Covid-19 pandemic. "We saw the script, liked it and thought this would be a nice project. So we went in and saw some rough edits of certain pieces of the movie."

"The film wasn't totally finished," adds Roger Taylor from his home, going on to explain that the band "sort of knew" Russell Mulcahy through their work with music video director David Mallet, one of the co-founders of MGMM alongside Russell Mulcahy. Mallet had directed the band in a number of videos, including 1984's 'Radio Ga Ga' and 'I Want to Break Free'. "[Russell] was a very good director, visually excellent, and he asked us if we wanted to have a look at some of the footage. We loved it, especially the way he was editing scenes into the next scene and going backwards in time. We thought it was a great-looking film and it sort of caught our imagination, so we said, 'Yeah, we'd be interested in doing some of the music to the film.'"

"Music in a movie is probably the second most important thing," states Christopher Lambert when we touch on the contribution of Queen to *Highlander*'s success. "You can have a great scene with bad music and it becomes a good scene. A good scene with bad music becomes a bad scene. So the music is highly important. Queen were meant to do the opening credit song, 'Princes of the Universe', and that was it, then they watched the movie, went back to the producers and said they were going to do the whole movie."

Returning to London from Munich, Queen began recording music for *Highlander* at Townhouse Studios in Shepherd's Bush from Sunday 10 November until Friday 13 December 1985.

Roger Taylor explains that Queen's first work on the film was a joint effort on 'Princes of the Universe', the song ultimately credited to Freddie Mercury which was used over the film's opening titles and some of the wrestling match in Madison Square Garden. "It was a song really made of bits, sort of, 'Let's make up the next bit . . . now we need another bit, let's make up another bit." Adds Brian May, "Nobody knew quite what to do with it, but it ended up over the fight sequence at the beginning. We just threw things at it really, and then tried to mould it all together."

One of the first sequences that had been screened for the band was the montage depicting Connor and Heather's time together as she grows older and eventually dies in his arms, with the scenes hitting Brian May particularly hard. "I found that incredibly moving. I was going through very difficult stuff in my own life at the time and I think a whole lot got triggered in me. My manager, Jim Beach, drove me home after we'd seen the clips and I could hear this song called 'Who Wants to Live Forever'. In those days I used to carry a little tape recorder around with me, and in the car I sang into it the way I heard the song in my head. It was almost complete."

Rarely being in the situation where words and music came to him almost fully formed, May made a demo of the song when he arrived home. On his return to the recording studio, May attempted to fit the song to the montage he'd watched a few days earlier. "Every single piece matched up to the mood of what we were watching; it was the most uncanny thing. It doesn't happen very often in your life, but really nothing needed changing, except obviously we polished what the track actually sounded like. But every sequence of the song, and the whole outro end section where he goes up and puts her on the funeral pyre, everything fitted. It was the most incredible thing. We were all kind of shocked."

Just as May had been inspired from a sequence in the film, so Roger Taylor was struck by the World War II flashback scene in which MacLeod saves young Rachel from being killed by Nazi gunfire. "Christophe gets up and I think the kid is looking at him and he says, 'It's a kind of magic.' I thought that was a lovely phrase, which turned into a song which tried to encapsulate the story in a way. "There can be only one', 'This race that lasts a thousand years', and so on."

While the lyrics for 'Who Wants to Live Forever' came to Brian May in a car, for Taylor the 'A Kind of Magic' lyrics had originally come to him while he was in bed at the Queen's Hotel in Cheltenham. "I woke up in the middle of the night and suddenly jotted down a whole bunch of words," recalls Taylor, noting that Martin Luther King Jr.'s iconic 1963 'I Have a Dream' speech almost certainly had an influence on his thinking. "The basis of the words was all about one vision, one hope, one whatever, that was the thrust. Those lyrics ended up as the sort of lyrical skeleton of 'A Kind of Magic' and 'One Vision', they were both kind of on the same theme, and they both came from that one piece of paper."

The version of 'A Kind of Magic' used for *Highlander*'s end titles was the band's original recording. Says Taylor, "We later worked on the song to turn it into a single to make it more commercially viable. Freddie and I worked on it quite a lot to turn it into the riff-driven 'A Kind of Magic' which was obviously a big hit."

Taylor also composed 'Don't Lose Your Head', which was used on the New York car sequence. "I remember I got Joan Armatrading to do the spoken vocal of that," says Taylor, explaining that the singer was recording along the corridor from Queen while they were at Townhouse Studios. Taylor's abiding memory of the sound equipment at Townhouse during that period was that their studio housed a computer which he dubbed "the world's most expensive coffee machine . . . terrible things they were, it ended up being pretty useless. We just used it as a coffee table in the end."

Other songs composed by the band included May's 'Gimme the Prize (The Kurgan's Theme)' and 'One Year of Love', credited to John Deacon and Freddie Mercury. The latter song included a line paraphrased from an early draft of Peter Bellwood and Larry Ferguson's *Highlander* script, with "Just one year of love, though it ends in death, is better than a painful eternity alone" becoming "Just one year of love / is better than a lifetime alone". Although the original idea for the song may have been Deacon's, as with many of the group's songs the finished piece was something of a joint effort. "Freddie worked on that a lot with John trying to whip that into shape," notes Taylor. "One person would have an idea regarding a particular part of the film, then we would all work on that idea, and that was kind of the way it worked."

According to Russell Mulcahy, John Deacon wasn't happy with 'One Year of Love' being played on the radio in the New York bar sequence, the suggestion being that there was a lack of confidence in the track. "It's the worst place you can stick a song, because you know it'll be played low," explained the director.

Working with Michael Kamen

With Queen's music completed, Michael Kamen was now able to begin work on his score. Unusually for a feature film of *Highlander*'s scale, Russell Mulcahy cut to the music rather than the other way around, with Derek Power explaining that "Michael wrote the score to the picture we had cut."

As the process began, Power discovered that the composer was having some trouble finding the right tone for his music. "His first passes at the score were very dark and depressed. I remember him telling me, 'I guess I've just done too many Roger Waters albums.' Even though he was a very sunny personality himself, his music often took a dark turn. I had to sell what he wrote in a demo version to Peter [Davis] and Bill [Panzer]. I think all of us had some reservations about it, particularly Russell because he was a very cheerful sort. We had romantic moments and we had a lot of humour in the film, so it just needed to be right for those moments. He rewrote everything and we loved it."

Although he was aware of Kamen's work, Brian May didn't know him personally before *Highlander*. "We spent some great time collaborating and experimenting," says May. "He was one of those people who's very instinctive, classically trained but also very instinctive and a good improviser. So he would generally have a few puffs of whatever he had in his pipe at the time, and sit down at the keyboard, watching the film and play away to do his demos. We became very good friends."

Having heard Queen's version of 'Who Wants to Live Forever', Kamen set to work finding elements that could be expanded upon, teasing out chords and weaving them into his score. "Weaving's a good expression for it," agrees May. "We worked together on an arrangement to make it very big and orchestral. But it was all based on that original demo; we actually used it as the backing track. It was quite old-school in those days. You just watched the film and played along. It was all analogue and it wasn't done to digital clicks. In those days you would work offline looking at the film, but you would also work online, working to wipes on the film's rough cuts. We had a great time finishing it off; I remember that was quite amazing."

As Kamen started work recording at London's Abbey Road Studios, the composer requiring the 60-piece National Philharmonic Orchestra to fully realise his score, time was spent with Queen trying to weave each sides' music into the other's. "We incorporated [Kamen's] music around the songs," says Power. "Not all of the score by any means, as he obviously [wrote] a lot that was not dependent on their songs. I worked very hard with Brian May, particularly on the integration of the songs in a way that would not get in the way of the film. The whole point of doing this was to make it so that it was a seamless whole."

One of May's happiest memories from working with Kamen was at Abbey Road with the orchestra, the recording of which took place in Studio A on 22, 23, 27 November and 6, 10 and 12 December, though the musician admits he was initially slightly worried about the set-up. "I was a bit shy of orchestras in those days, and probably I still am. I tend to go in there quite humble knowing that I can't do what they do. But it's great to see an arrangement that you've worked on come to life in the hands of these wonderful professionals. He did a wonderful job, and ['Who Wants to Live Forever' is] one of the very few Queen songs which has an orchestra on it, but there's a very good reason in this case. It really makes it very expanded and cosmic."

"Brian really wanted to have a real orchestra, and obviously Michael Kamen was a very accomplished orchestrator and conductor," adds Roger Taylor. "I didn't really have a lot to do with that. It's a wonderful song, [though] I thought it ended up being over-arranged."

Just as Kamen complemented Brian May's music, so May worked with Kamen on enhancing parts of the composer's score. "One of his demos was what he called the 'Highlander Theme'," notes May, referring to the music that plays under various sections of the film, most notably just after MacLeod is banished from his village. "I had fun working on guitar versions of that with him which crop up in the film. I've actually quoted it in versions that I've done of 'Who Wants to Live Forever' since then, so Michael kind of lives on with me." A clip of the 'Highlander Theme' was also appropriated by New Line Cinema to accompany the logo at the start of their films.

"There are certain parts of the film that simply won't work with just Queen," states composer and broadcaster Neil Brand when I ask for his thoughts on what Michael Kamen's process might have been for *Highlander*. "There is some sense with the Queen music that it's commenting on what it's underscoring, rather than growing from inside the scene out. What a composer like Kamen will do is sit right in the centre of a scene and try and bring out of that the music that he feels fits. That sense of a timeless romance was much more in Kamen's music, for me anyway, than in the Queen element of it. For me, what Queen made work was this idea of bridging the gap between the Highlands and New York."

When we speak, Brand has recently spent time dissecting Queen's *Flash Gordon* soundtrack for BBC Radio Four's *Film Programme*, a picture he describes as "an out-and-out comic book film, which never really moves outside of a comic book world. Under those circumstances, guitar-driven rock will actually work for pretty much the whole thing. *Highlander*, for all the fact that it's got comic book elements to it, actually lodges itself in what you might call a historical epic world. It's a world that you can recognise, both in terms of the New York stuff, but particularly obviously the beginnings, and the beginnings are entirely tied up with Sean Connery."

Going on to reference shots of Connery and Lambert training on clifftops and in forests, Brand's main takeaway from *Highlander* is that "Sean Connery doesn't work with Queen. You either have one or the other. If you're going to have Sean Connery, and his whole *mise en scène* is going to work, it has to be that big, epic adventure style of music, which lends itself to shots like galloping along the beach. Whereas the Kurgan is Queen, he's hard rock, he's leather, he's punk, he's got safety pins holding his neck together. The main reason for the orchestral music is that the heart of the film has to lie in his love for his wife, in his learning from Sean Connery, in being spurned from the village, all those things which Queen's music simply won't work with, because Queen cannot go back to the 16th century and make us believe it."

Another of Brand's observations is that for him *Highlander* might be "the first openly gay rock adventure film . . . though obviously *Flash Gordon*'s out there. In terms of coming out of a *Mad Max* world of leather-clad violence, knowing something about Mulcahy, it did feel like it came from a gay sensibility in which there was much more of a sense of immediate heightened emotional change, which had less to do with the plot and more to do with imagery. The imagery was so strong, so much of it is about sparking light, either electrical power or flashing light, that it just felt that a couple of more degrees on, a few more substances, a bit more pace and it would be right-on underground film-making. It feels really close at times to the gay underground film-making in the 1980s and 1990s."

Following Kamen's work on *Highlander*, his career went from strength to strength, his next score being for Neil Jordan's 1986 crime drama, *Mona Lisa*. "Although he had done a couple of big movies before, I personally felt that *Highlander* was the breakthrough," says Derek Power. "Because of *Highlander* they were able to sell him as the guy you could put a rock act with. He then scored *Lethal Weapon* with Eric Clapton, and a couple of other movies with Eric."

Michael Kamen's music continued to impress film-makers and audiences well into the late 1990s on projects as diverse as the James Bond film, *Licence to Kill* (1989), *Robin Hood: Prince of Thieves* (1991) and *Mr Holland's Opus* (1995), the latter leading to Kamen creating The Mr Holland's Opus Foundation, providing musical instruments to those who would otherwise go without them. In 1997, Kamen was diagnosed with the degenerative disease, multiple sclerosis, which affected his mobility but didn't stop him composing for films such as 1999's *The Iron Giant* and 2000's *Memento*.

Kamen also collaborated with Brian May again in 2002 as part of the 'Party at the Palace' celebration of Queen Elizabeth II's Golden Jubilee. As part of the event, May played 'God Save the Queen' standing atop Buckingham Palace, while Kamen conducted the house band, the Royal Academy of Music Symphony Orchestra. "That's the last time we worked together," says May, referencing the fact that Kamen died from a heart attack on 18 November 2003, at the age of just 55. "Michael could hardly stand by that time, but he conducted the orchestra, which is a great memory of mine. Mostly when people play ['Who Wants to Live Forever'] these days in concert they use the arrangement that Michael contributed to, with that lovely throbbing string section. It's become a big favourite of mine and I very much miss Michael."

Releasing the album

With work on recording the music completed, *Highlander* editor Peter Honess recalls attempting to mix it into the film at De Lane Lea Studios in Soho, but that Brian May and Roger Taylor weren't happy with the initial result. "We moved the mix to the main recording stage at 20th Century Fox Studios in LA. Brian and

Roger were there most days and had a big say in how their music was mixed. Don Bassman, the legendary mixer, ran the mix and took no prisoners. I remember Brian being really impressed with the quality of the sound, so much so that he enquired if future Queen albums could be recorded there, however he was taken aback by the cost of hiring the sound stage so nothing came of it."

"We sat there for two or three weeks with the movie sound guys," says Taylor of the experience in Los Angeles. "They had an enormous SSL sound desk; it was about 30-feet long."

Now the soundtrack mix was complete, the various parties went their separate ways, with Derek Power describing the experience as "incredibly rewarding, it just all worked". Following the successful collaboration, Power was hopeful that a *Highlander* soundtrack album could be released featuring the music of both Queen and Michael Kamen, but he explains that the discussion was "probably the stickiest point of the negotiation" between *Highlander*'s producers and Queen's manager, Jim Beach. "We wanted the soundtrack to include Michael's music and his version of 'Who Wants to Live Forever', which was an absolute keynote track, but the band decided they didn't want to."

"It was a major discussion: do we do the soundtrack for the film?" says Brian May today. "It was sort of a bone of contention really. I think probably myself and maybe Freddie would have liked to deliver the soundtrack album complete, but I think Roger was very keen that it should not be done that way and we should incorporate what we'd contributed to the film into the next Queen album. And that's what we ended up doing."

"It developed a life of its own," says Taylor on the subject. "We had a massive tour coming up in 1986, and we really needed an album. 'A Kind of Magic' wasn't really in the first movie, apart from a line of narrative and a different version used over the end credits. In the meantime we released that as a single and it was a big international hit. It just seemed like sense to build the album around that. It's not a pure soundtrack album, it's a Queen album with some stuff that we put in a movie."

Taylor's memories of recording the album are positive, noting that he, May, John Deacon and Freddie Mercury were "a very good team, and I never really had a cross word with Freddie, ever. We got on like a house on fire. He put a lot of work into the album just like everybody. He wasn't writing as much as he had written before, he was leaving it more to the rest of us really. But in the studio he was full-on."

Russell Mulcahy may have missed out on shooting a Queen video prior to *Highlander*, but with the decision made to release both 'Princes of the Universe' and 'A Kind of Magic' as singles to accompany the film, he finally had an opportunity to direct the band. It was on Friday 14 February 1986 that Queen and Mulcahy made their way to London's Elstree Studios to film the video for 'Princes of the Universe'. Also in attendance was Phil Howard-Jones, Head of Creative Services at Thorn EMI, the company bankrolling *Highlander*.

"We didn't have anything to do with the music," says Phil Howard-Jones. "Queen were breaking new ground with MTV promos, but we as Thorn EMI Screen Entertainment didn't really have any power over them to say, 'We've got to have a promo, you've got to do this or go to that.' When we heard that Queen were making promos we got excited, because we thought if we could get the timing right and get those singles out ahead of *Highlander*'s theatrical release, it would have been an enormous boost to the publicity."

The concept for the video involved the band performing the song while standing on a replica of the Silvercup rooftop set, three of the band – Brian May, Roger Taylor and John Deacon – wearing replicas of MacLeod's trench coat, while Freddie Mercury sports jeans and a grey waistcoat. Behind the stage is another replica set from the film, this time a crumbling version of the exterior of MacLeod's Scottish forge.

As the band play, the camera rushes past them and lands on the kneeling figure of Christopher Lambert, who then joins Freddie Mercury on stage and "clashes swords" with the singer, or rather

Lambert raises his sword to Mercury's famous 'stick' microphone stand. As the wind whips up and the Silvercup sign starts to collapse, Brian May can be seen playing guitar on the steps of the forge as it begins to fall apart around him, all of which is interspersed with clips from the film.

As well as attending the video shoot in person, Howard-Jones also took along a camera to film some of the production, footage of which survives to this day. An enthusiastic Russell Mulcahy, dressed in a red sweater and jeans, can be seen directing the band as a camera moves left and right in front of the Silvercup set. Lambert, Mulcahy and Mercury then spend time working out the best moment for the actor to walk on stage and engage in a mock sword fight with the singer.

When the pair do finally clash their sword and mic stand, the end of Lambert's sword flies out and hits Brian May on the arm, much to the amusement of Mulcahy. "I told you, this one wins!" shouts Mercury as he waves his stand in the air and they go for another take. The footage also shows more of Lambert crouching on the ground near the stage, with the actor standing up and running behind the Silvercup set, something not seen in the finished video. "We had a private Queen concert for about 15 people for 48 hours as the crew was very small," says Christopher Lambert today. "It was incredible."

"That was quite an enjoyable video," admits Roger Taylor. "I remember Russell put water all over the floor, which was a very good effect, and then Freddie and Christophe had a mock duel, which was intercut with pieces of the film. Christophe gave me the raincoat that he wears in the film, and I still have it actually. It's an Armani, slightly ripped and rather worn. I thought it was a very cool raincoat, and he made a gesture and gave it to me, but I think he regretted it afterwards!"

The video for 'A Kind of Magic' was shot in March at London's derelict Playhouse Theatre, and featured the band as hobos who are magically transformed into Queen by Freddie Mercury, while animated dancing girls interact with them.

'Princes of the Universe' was the first single to be released in the US on 12 March 1986, but it failed to chart there and was never released in the UK, while 'A Kind of Magic' was released in the UK on 17 March and went to number three in the singles chart. The decision was made not to feature Christopher Lambert in the 'A Kind of Magic' video, meaning there were no visual clues that it was connected to a forthcoming film release. Perhaps the theory was that viewers would have been confused by clips from a film that they had no way of seeing for another five months.

For some lucky Queen fans there would be a chance to see the film four months ahead of its cinema release. The first Queen Fan Club convention took place in Great Yarmouth over the weekend of 25 April 1986, and a one-off screening of *Highlander* was held for fans on the Saturday. "I remember we were all outside the cinema singing 'We Will Rock You', and we blocked the street off, 700 people waving Queen scarves," laughs fan club member and Queen biographer Jim Jenkins. "The album wasn't out, so people got to hear songs in the film that they didn't even have yet. We were given a cassette with messages from the band on one side, and when you turned it over there were clips from the film."

On its release on 2 June 1986, the *A Kind of Magic* album went straight to the top of the UK album charts and remained there for 63 weeks, selling more than 100,000 copies in its first week.

For many Queen fans, *Highlander* remains a firm favourite, with some going on pilgrimages to the locations used in the film. Jim Jenkins gives an example of the scene in the bar when 'One Year of Love' is played. "When MacLeod goes into the bar in New York and orders a Glenmorangie, Queen fans go to that bar and if they tell the barman that's why they're there, he'll play it for them. The music pulled the fans to the film, and it pulls them to New York."

FOURTEEN

MAKING THE CUT

If it wasn't nerves that Peter Honess felt as he waited in the 20th Century Fox lobby in the heart of Los Angeles on an autumn morning in 1985, it was probably jetlag.

The Englishman had made the 12-hour flight from London many times, but adjusting from the cold British weather to LA's heat was never easy. Added to that was an eight-hour time difference. Not that he was a stranger to the city. Honess had moved to LA in 1971 to work as a film editor, working on titles such as Larry Cohen's *Hell Up in Harlem* (1973) and *It's Alive!* (1974), before returning to Britain in 1976 so that his American-born daughters could have an English education.

Today, Honess was a man on a mission, screening what he was confident would be the final cut of a film he'd been editing for the best part of six months in both London and the States alongside Russell Mulcahy, minus the special effects required for the final sequence.

For this screening, Honess had been sent on his own to Los Angeles to meet the Fox executives who were preparing to release *Highlander* in US cinemas the following year. Though the film had been fully funded by the UK's Thorn EMI Screen Entertainment, producers Davis and Panzer had secured theatrical distribution in the USA through Fox. The film's editor was the man chosen to present the newly struck 70mm film print to Fox executives while Russell Mulcahy remained in London.

As he made his way through the winding corridors of Fox, Honess was cautiously optimistic about what was to come. Although there had been some unhappiness with early edits of the film, resulting in tension between the pairings of Davis & Panzer and Mulcahy & Honess, with changes debated and compromises made, today was a chance for the editor to show the executives what he knew was a strong version of the picture.

On arriving at the small screening theatre, Honess checked with the projectionist that the reels had arrived in one piece, before introducing himself to six Fox executives who were deep in conversation. Sitting himself near the volume controls just before the titles began to roll on the film, Honess waited for the men behind him to stop talking and enjoy the film.

At. Any. Moment.

Lights barely dimmed, no sooner had the film's music started playing than one of the men stopped talking to his colleagues, stood up, moved over to Honess, and said simply:

"You'll need to turn it down, man."

Though he hadn't thought the sound was offensively loud, Honess did as instructed and turned the volume down a notch. Settling back into his seat, he was immediately interrupted by the same executive.

"No man, I said turn it down."

Once again, the editor moved the dial, worrying that if he turned it down much further the dialogue would be barely audible. Still not happy, the executive reached over himself and turned the dial down to the bare minimum, resuming his discussion with colleagues behind Honess. His work was reduced to background noise by a group of men who seemingly had no interest in his film.

The same men who would go on to orchestrate the release of *Highlander* in the United States just a few months later.

***

Over the previous six months, Peter Honess had avoided cold mornings in London alleyways, the boggy glens of Scotland and late nights in New York, but the editor was as involved in the film's production as any other member of the crew.

Joining the film on the first day of production, Honess quickly began to get a feel for Russell Mulcahy's style, excited by his enthusiasm and unique approach to film-making. "We had a great time," states Honess, explaining that because the director came from another world than he was from, "he had a much keener sense of things and was very energetic and enthusiastic. I loved the zaniness of the stuff he did and we had a good relationship."

Working out of a small studio in the heart of London, Honess soon found that with multiple units filming on *Highlander*, he had more material to work with than on many films. "There were four units and I used to get tons of film. The second unit shot an awful lot of material and there was a third unit doing something else. I'd get a lot of film, not just from Russell."

Due to the speed of filming and the amount of footage, Honess initially had to put up with various members of the production team entering his cutting room to look at the different sequences for reference purposes. In the days before digital, if someone needed to see how a scene looked, they'd ask Honess if they could take a photo of a frame or sequence. "I used to work at night because I couldn't work during the day – there were so many people coming into my cutting room I couldn't get any work done. I reverted my whole working week to nights, so my assistants during the day would look after all these questions from people in need of references. They'd come in, see it, take a 10 x 8 of it – it was much more intense in some ways."

Honess recalls that Russell Mulcahy was always very open to playing with the footage he'd shot. "I'd have loved to have cut *Highlander* on a computer. Now you can do lots of things, but back then you didn't have those choices because you only had one piece of film for a shot and you couldn't use it again in another version. You could use another take, but that's not the same thing.

You'd film something then discuss maybe going a little bit crazy, then I'd do it and he'd have to come back some other time and see it. You didn't have the luxury of saying, 'Hey man, this is really weird, shall we use it?' and then go yes or no; you had to think about it, then do it. Now it's very different."

One aspect of *Highlander* that had been present from the start were the transitions between scenes. The screenwriters may have written them into their script, but it was Mulcahy who took the idea and ran with it. Says Honess, "The one we struggled with was the close-up of Chris Lambert, when he's lying on the battlefield after he's been killed by the Kurgan and we went into his face, if I remember, and we came out on the speeding car."

Despite advances in technology, the low quality of the shot still stands out in copies of the film today, including in a new 4K restoration created in 2016 for the 30th anniversary. "We made that transition in the cutting room and we struggled like hell. If you look at it carefully, it's very bad quality. In those days there was nothing digital – you had to shoot it on film, send it to a lab and the only way we could do that was that we went to an editing house Russell had used for his videos. We gave them the film and they made that transition on their equipment, then we had to transfer it back again to film. They shot it in their optical cameras and couldn't make it, so they did it on their TV and transferred it to film."

Another transition that was added in post-production saw MacLeod's face cut to that of a mural on the side of a New York building, with Honess noting that close inspection reveals "it's not very well aligned, it has some rough edges to it. Again we did that one in the cutting room. The ones that look good and clever, he devised those in camera; the ones that look a bit hokey, we did those in the cutting room."

Despite the impressive nature of Mulcahy's vision, I wonder if Honess ever thought it was too much, that a hot MTV director was trying too hard to make his mark on the film. "I never thought it was too much for the movie, and I never thought Russell was too much, though some people did because of where he came from.

I was always terribly impressed by the ideas he'd come up with and he was absolutely brilliant. The wonderful scene of the Kurgan when the hooker comes to the door, that little montage of him clipping the sword together, that was all him."

Honess' time with Russell Mulcahy may have been a rewarding one, but he doesn't have such fond memories of working with the film's producers. "I was there during a lot of fights with Davis and Panzer; they were quite difficult. I remember threatening one over Steenbeck; he was on one side and I was on the other, and I would have gone for him if he was on my side."

The issue had started during the shooting of extra footage in Wales. With Mulcahy out of phone reach, Honess received a call from one of the producers who had called to say they'd talked to the director about taking a shot out of the film that had to then have fake snow added later. "They said they didn't want to spend the money and Russell had insisted it was in the film. One of them had gone to Wales and said they'd just spoken to Russell and to take the shot out. When Russell came back a few weeks later, I said, 'Why did you take that shot out?' and he said, 'I didn't take it out, where is it?' I said, 'They told me to take it out and that they'd spoken to you.'"

When all four men were gathered in the same room, tensions finally erupted. "It was an enormous battle, shouting and fighting. I was a fairly young editor and it taught me a few lessons: never believe anybody unless it comes from the mouth of the director. We put the shot back and it's in the movie; I think Russell paid for it himself. It was a matte painting; they painted in the snow and it was a big job in those days. Russell would often pay for things himself."

The editing of the scene of MacLeod and Ramirez running along a beach together elicited some nervousness from Davis-Panzer about the footage captured in Scotland. "They got twitchy about the stag. They thought it was hokey because we didn't have a very good stag cutaway; we had a pretty lousy shot. We tried other things like library shots and other animals imitating stags.

The one in there's not that strong, but they wanted that out which would have meant cutting down that sequence." Despite toying with inserting stock footage from *National Geographic*, Honess and Mulcahy convinced the producers that the stag should remain in the scene.

Another sequence that led to heated discussions involved the Kurgan's licking of a priest's hand during a confrontation with MacLeod. "We got some shit for that; there was a great deal of hoo-ha. The producers didn't want that; they thought it was insulting and we fought like cat and dog. It's actually quite short, as there was a much longer lick. The church who rented it to us had no idea they'd be filming that sort of stuff in there, I'm not sure they'd have allowed that if they'd known."

One of Russell Mulcahy's abiding memories of the editing is that at one point he was informed that the final edit was running eight minutes too long. "One of the producers had counted how many shots were in the movie and said, 'If you cut one frame out of the beginning and end of every shot, you'll save eight minutes,' and Peter threw him out of the room and slammed the door! I was an editor, and you cut to a frame, you're frame accurate. To come back and say 'take a frame out of every shot', I was like 'Oh my God!'"

Perhaps Peter Honess' least favourite moment in the finished film comes at the end of the final battle between the Kurgan and MacLeod, when MacLeod slices his enemy's throat with his sword. The scene was filmed quickly, mainly due to the need to keep down costs. "We wanted it far more dynamic than that. We cut his head off completely, then that was too much, so we came back to his head being half cut off, which was pretty cool, then the version that's in there now was just a little cut and you just begin to see his head going back. You could have extended that shot, but we weren't allowed to use it. I think they did a pretty good job for the time they were given, but it was a bit disappointing, along with the scene up on the hill at the end. I don't think Russell likes that."

A post-production schedule from the time reveals that Peter Honess' rough cut was due to be delivered to the producers on

Monday 22 July 1985, at which point Russell Mulcahy was set to commence work on his director's cut, which was due to be completed by Friday 13 September, followed by a public screening on Saturday 14 September.

Mulcahy would be given another shot at the edit for delivery on Friday 27 September ahead of a public screening on Saturday 28 September. It's not possible to say whether all these deadlines were met, but Peter Honess does confirm that it was in the autumn of 1985 that he took the print of Mulcahy's cut to executives at 20th Century Fox in Los Angeles.

Both Honess and Mulcahy were happy that they had a high-quality product, but the resulting screening in front of six executives left the editor reeling. "They turned the sound down so much that it ruined the film, but they didn't care. It was heartbreaking," explains Honess, going on to note that he didn't phone Mulcahy in London afterwards as he "didn't want to depress him".

Although nobody at Fox gave Honess a reason for the tepid reaction to *Highlander*, it later dawned on him that it might have been related to something he'd been told earlier in the year. While driving to the studio one day during the editing process, Honess had learned that *Highlander*'s producers were involved in legal wranglings with Fox over the six-picture deal that included *Highlander*. Contemporary production notes for *Highlander* state that Peter Davis and Bill Panzer had two productions lined up to work on, *Cat Chaser*, an adaptation of Elmore Leonard's 1982 novel due to be directed by John Mackenzie (*The Long Good Friday*, 1980), and *King of The Wind*.

"[The producer] mentioned that he was suing Fox because they had reneged on a deal with him [on *Cat Chaser*]," says Honess. "I asked, 'How can you be suing Fox when they haven't even opened *Highlander*; surely this will make a difference to how they promote the film?' He replied, 'You don't understand how Hollywood works. Me suing Fox over another movie will not affect how they support *Highlander*.'" Whatever the reason for the initial disagreement, Davis-Panzer retained rights to the novel and finally put *Cat Chaser* in front of the camera in November 1988 under the direction of Abel Ferrara (*The Driller Killer*, 1979), resulting in a notoriously troubled production that was never shown in cinemas and made its debut on VHS in 1991. *King of the Wind* wouldn't arrive in cinemas until 1990.

Making adjustments

Despite the negative reaction to *Highlander* in Los Angeles, back in the UK work continued on making adjustments to the film when the answer print, an almost-complete version of the film, was struck. This period was a chance for screenwriters Peter Bellwood and Larry Ferguson to try and make more sense of some of the film's more confusing moments.

"In the editing room we did a whole lot of changing of lines when the camera was on someone's back and they were speaking," explains Ferguson. "We had four, five or 13 seconds where the camera was on the back of the person speaking and we could rewrite additional dialogue that an actor could come in and do ADR [Additional Dialogue Recording] on. We'd add dialogue to try to make it a little clearer as to what the hell was happening and what the Prize was."

While changes were being made to dialogue, work was also beginning on a trailer for the film, details of which I discovered while sifting through files devoted to the film in the offices of the British Board of Film Classification (BBFC) in London's Soho Square. Established in 1912, the BBFC is the independent regulator responsible for classifying films for UK cinema release, and a cut of the *Highlander* trailer was submitted to them at some point in November, resulting in feedback from a BBFC examiner on 4 December 1985.

Notes reveal that some edits were requested, including the decapitation of Fasil in the underground garage; a shot of MacLeod under a car; a sword thrust into a body [presumably MacLeod's] during the battle sequence; a shot of a man with blood on his face seen in lightning flash; and a close shot of an eye and following explosion. The request was that the trailer be resubmitted, though this wouldn't happen until January 1986.

As 1985 came to a close, Peter Honess was still working on the final edit while Russell Mulcahy was busy trying to complete the visuals for the Silvercup fight sequence. Before special effects make-up co-designer Nick Maley had departed the film, he'd suggested that the death of the Kurgan would result in an explosion of spirits leaving the Kurgan and entering MacLeod, with Maley planning to build a physical creature for MacLeod to fight.

Although Maley had left and been replaced by Bob Keen, John Schoonraad was still on board as make-up effects mould designer. His recollection is that more money was made available for visual effects thanks to an insurance payment resulting from Nick Maley's sudden departure. "We started doing a load of stuff with Bob Keen about spirits flying around and all kinds of weird stuff."

While Schoonraad would go on to experiment with effects for the sequence, the decision was made to use an external company to complete the work, though details of who they were remain elusive today. What is known is that at some point Russell Mulcahy realised things weren't going quite to plan.

FIFTEEN

GETTING ANIMATED

Working in music videos and commercials had proved to be lucrative for Russell Mulcahy in many ways, providing him not only with a steady income and a chance to flex his creative muscles on a variety of projects, but also bringing him into contact with a number of professionals from other areas whom he'd come to rely on in later years.

One early big-budget commercial for the American corn chip snack Doritos found Mulcahy working with an old MGMM collaborator, director Matt Forrest, and a small team of animators at Elstree Studios. Not long after, when Mulcahy realised he required the help of a trusted group to help bring the final special effects-heavy finale of *Highlander* to life, he once again approached Forrest. "Russell was pissed off with the people who were doing the effects," says Forrest. "He came to me and said, 'Can you help me, I need you to do some stuff on this film?' And I said, 'All right, what is it?' And he said, 'Everything!'"

Forrest's company, Snapper Studios, which he'd set up with animator Nina Robbins, was charged with producing all the animation for the end sequence, requiring him to pull together a team of animators at short notice, including many of those who had worked on Mulcahy's Doritos commercial. Mulcahy continued the connection between *Highlander* and Doritos when he had Jon

Polito's Detective Bedsoe eating from a packet during the car park sequence at the start of the film.

One of Forrest's animators on the Doritos project was Ravi Swami, who went on to design effects for Russell Mulcahy's 'The Wild Boys' video that were ultimately not used, before going on a well-earned holiday. On Swami's return, he says "Matt Forrest sort of roped me into working on *Highlander*. I was pretty much the first person pulled in on it, because it needed a storyboard of the final effects sequence. Matt set up the animation department really quickly. Once I finished the storyboard I was pretty much the only person in the studio and he said, 'Find me animators,' so I basically went around Soho, knocking on doors trying to find people to work on it."

Also approached to work on the sequence was animator Mike Smith, whom Matt Forrest encouraged to bring as many of his friends and acquaintances on board. Smith admits that he and some of his team weren't accustomed to working on live action productions, noting that they "were animators, not special effects people. And a lot of effects were done on film, with optics and things like that. So that was another thing we didn't know much about."

In 1985, Smith was still relatively fresh to the animation industry, explaining that London was "buzzing" with talent from around the globe, including a number of Canadian animators such as Joe Haidar, who had worked on *Highlander*'s storyboard, and Roger Chiasson, a veteran of cartoons such as 1978's *Challenge of the Superfriends* and 1984's *The New Scooby-Doo Mysteries*. Chiasson divided his year between Asia and Europe, supervising animated television series for different studios because it paid well, before returning to London to work on commercials. "I was afraid I'd lose my edge, because when you're supervising a series, you don't really do much drawing."

It was in London that he met Matt Forrest, Nina Robbins and Mike Smith, who were working on small music video projects at weekends which Chiasson notes didn't pay particularly well but which were extremely creative. "Before *Highlander*, Matt would call up me and Mike and say, 'I've got this video for Grace Jones,' and they'd have this stable of directors shooting videos that always wanted to use animation as filler. You'd only get three days sometimes, basically the weekend, and we would animate, clean up, paint and shoot our own stuff. By Monday they would have it on a three-quarter-inch broadcast quality tape that we'd shot."

Aware that he had to move fast, Smith secured a basement at the six-storey MGMM offices co-owned by Russell Mulcahy in Golden Square for his team of animators, including Roger Chiasson and his brother Claude, Don Spencer, Chuck Gammage, Peter Chiang, Colin Hughes and Tim Walton. Ravi Swami only worked on the storyboard, though there was talk of him perhaps animating some of the sequence. Others, such as Keith Ingham and Robert Stevenhagen, went uncredited on the final film.

The animators rubbed shoulders with the writers, technicians and producers who worked on live action pop promos and commercials, a very different discipline to Smith's team. "Animation people [are] always saying, 'How much have you got? Let me see if I can do something with it,' and you kind of work for virtually nothing," says Smith. "Whereas live action guys, especially those at MGMM, were working with big name pop or rock stars. When you see some of the videos it's the same thing over and over again, art directors going, 'Throw more water on the girls!' and 'More smoke, more smoke!' I think everyone there wanted to be a major film-maker."

With his team settling down at MGMM, Smith and Chiasson had a chance to review the sequence shot by Russell Mulcahy, which the director handed over as black-and-white rushes in their fully edited form. Says Smith, "Russell said, 'I've done the cut, there you go,' and I [tried to] go through it with him, but he didn't have any idea about why he cut from what to what. Also, there were wires everywhere and we didn't have computers to paint them out. We were stuck with this cut that meant nothing." Roger Chiasson also recalls seeing the raw footage, noting that "it was basically Christopher Lambert spinning around, up and down, and going into contortions with these huge wires holding him up and we're going, 'Holy shit, what are we going to do?'"

The decision was made to print out each frame of the sequence onto paper and pin them to the wall, allowing the animators to see how it flowed. "I just went through and made up ideas: 'On that shot, this happens and on that shot this happens.' We added the visual effect ideas after the cut and we tried to make sense out of it," explains Mike Smith. At the same time, Ravi Swami was trying to build up a storyboard for the team to work from, noting that "it was a ridiculously short amount of time to do things. The actual details of what those things flying around were, were pretty vague."

The main reason for the creation of the "things flying around" was to help sell the idea that Connor MacLeod was levitating as a result of the Quickening. When Mike Smith had asked Russell Mulcahy why it was happening, the director's response was simply that that's what he wanted to shoot. "At one point Christopher Lambert actually does a somersault and hits the wire and wobbles; it's just awful," says Smith. "I had no choice but to have lightning coming down where the wires were and it's just a bit ridiculous, but we had to move very fast. I had a ghostly thing kind of hit him so that it hides the wobble. It's really a manufactured thing more than anything else. He spits out lots of demons and things. I don't really get the rules of the world of *Highlander*; it seems like they made it up [as they went along]."

"I had all these fancy ideas right at the beginning that these flying things are supposed to be all these people that the Kurgan has killed in his many lifetimes," says Ravi Swami. "I thought about how many lifetimes he'd had, maybe going back to prehistoric times, and maybe some of these things flying around are prehistoric things. I tried to approach it from quite a logical angle, but when it came down to it the animators went to town; they just wanted loads of stuff flying around."

Before Bob Keen and his team were sidelined on creating practical effects for the sequence, his colleague John Schoonraad had been asked to step in to play an Immortal alongside other crew during effects tests. "[The idea was] when MacLeod kills the Kurgan, all the Immortals that had gone before, and who were in the Kurgan, all flood into him and he gets all the power," reveals Schoonraad. "There was a strobe effect with hundreds of Immortals standing there with gowns on, [and we were] on our knees putting our hands out, with a fan blowing our hair about. For the scene where he goes up on wires and you see his head blow up, I made a wax head that blows up and there's a strobing effect with the Immortals in there, but it's very fast."

Due to the time needed to create just a single frame of animation, Chiasson and his fellow animators spent a lot of time in the basement of MGMM. "We would work until we dropped and slept under our desk as much as we could. [We'd get] a couple of hours' sleep, then get back [up and start working again] because we realised there was no time. It was not a normal day; some of us were up for 90 hours working. We were young and energetic and stupid. And it was wonderful."

Chiasson explains that the animation process began with the artists first drawing straight onto paper, before it was handed over to a team of renderers, a "stable of ink and paint girls who worked at all the major studios. They would transfer it to a frosted cell [using] a black china marker, as black as we could get it, and then we backlit and reversed the exposure so that everything black is white. We were trying to give a ghostly look to it and it kind of worked; we were satisfied with the look of it but it's just that it became a huge burden to ink on the cells. There's a scene that Rob [Stevenhagen] worked on. [MacLeod's] got all these skulls inside his body and he pulls his jaw open and all these skulls come out, and every drawing took at least an hour and a half to do."

When it came to putting the artwork onto frosted cells, Roger Chiasson notes that the core *Highlander* team was helped by "pretty much everybody in London" at some point during the five-week period, with staff from many larger studios dropping in after their day job to work four or five hours in the evening. "They didn't mind it, they just loved working on it because it was very interesting."

Getting it on film

When it came time to put the work prepared by Matt Forrest's team onto film, he approached John Swinnerton who ran the rostrum camera department at Geoff Axtell Associates in London. "John was a brilliant cameraman," says Forrest, who had previously worked with him on the Doritos commercial at Elstree. "There were some great animators, but he was key to getting those optical effects done so fast."

"I think I was asked to do the work at a fairly late stage in the production," says Swinnerton, going on to note that Axtell's was one of the top film optical houses in London. One of the sequences requiring completion involved the Kurgan's neck being sliced open and consisted of four shots. "The only brief was to make it look exciting but not too gory," adds Swinnerton, explaining that he next had to remove his head. "I set about rotoscoping his head and arms to create mattes. This was done by loading a negative perforation print into the rostrum camera, projecting down onto the table top and hand-drawing the shapes onto paper." These shapes were then coloured in with black felt pen and rephotographed onto Agfa 553 to create the mattes on film.

"The next stage was to film all the plasma and ghostly stuff. For the centre, Matt had some animation done as a base layer to follow the neck track, so that was stage one. Stage two included all the other layers that surround the Kurgan, and it was important to me that this felt like it was moving in perspective and had some solid form to it and not be hand-drawn. So to do this I needed six things: a 35mm camera, a moy head, an anamorphic lens, a separate stepper motor, a computer to control the motors and a big bag of cotton wool."

Swinnerton's plan was to shoot layers of different spinning shapes of cotton wool with controlled amounts of motion blur and add them together in the optical. With the camera set at the correct angle he could then give a sense of looking up, into and through the layers. "I did shoot lots of small bits, as if flying in the centre to create a vortex. Some were shot in coloured red and yellow light and looked like red hot embers from hell. I did a comp to show these but Roy Field [at OFE] thought it was a bit 'too Disney'. I did manage to sneak one big one in at the very end when the Kurgan drops out of frame. I probably spent a week of nights shooting that."

According to Matt Forrest, one of John Swinnerton's experimental ideas for the Kurgan's decapitation which didn't make it into the film involved a pane of glass borrowed from Snapper Studios. "John said, 'Take out the toilet window,' which was rippled glass. He put orange and red gels under the rostrum and panned the camera across, then panned the piece of glass the other way to get a ripple burning effect for the Kurgan's throat."

With Christmas fast approaching and work still ongoing, Swinnerton was busy on other projects at Axtell's, meaning that in order to work on the aerial image camera he had to spend time on it in the evenings as well as during the day. "Right up until Christmas Eve I was shooting wedge tests for the opticals. I picked them up at 6 a.m., dropped them off at work and went and had a beer. I didn't bother going home, so I stayed in the rostrum room, got up the next morning, Christmas Day, and started shooting the opticals. I spent the next four days shooting."

Despite giving up Christmas 1985 for *Highlander*, John Swinnerton is happy to have been a part of the project. "When I saw the film, I thought it all worked quite well. Looking at it now, I have fond memories of being given the freedom to create something with hardly any interference from anybody."

After so many hours spent drawing and rendering the creatures and lightning effects in the basement of MGMM, Mike Smith feels that when many of the animators and renderers saw the finished film they were disappointed that their work ended up looking fuzzy and blown out. "We were aiming too high. We should have tried to design something that worked with the medium and what it was doing, because would it have mattered if it was simpler? Maybe the mistake I made was that I was trying to do something that would look very real, which of course we would never be able to achieve drawing it. But we were young, and we aimed at something like that. I've since learned that there are ways in which you can put things together and be a little more creative with it, and simpler in terms of design, and it can actually work better."

On completion of the project, Claude Chiasson was asked by Matt Forrest to arrange a Christmas party for everyone who had worked on the animated sequence. "We had everybody from London at that party, it was amazing," says Roger Chiasson. "Claude went and bought this huge three-foot bottle of champagne and Brian May was there. I couldn't believe it. It's like everybody knew what we were doing and it became pretty big, so that was pretty cool."

After his work on *Highlander*, Roger Chiasson was approached by Matt Forrest to help with the animation on the video for 'A Kind of Magic' along with Mike Smith and Chuck Gammage, and to design the cover for the *A Kind of Magic* album. "Mike did the three girls that are dancing and then Chuck did the guys. I animated those girls and the guys once they had the drawings. There was no time to submit it to anybody, we kind of did it ourselves. That's why on the *A Kind of Magic* album cover I put in top hats and frogs and rabbits, anything magical that I could think of."

Finishing the edit

With the animated effects now completed and added to the film, a cut of the film was screened on Monday 13 January 1986 for the producers, screenwriters and other members of the crew. It didn't take writer Peter Bellwood long to compile his thoughts on what he'd just watched for Peter Davis and Bill Panzer, in a letter dated 24 January.

Bellwood kicked off by stating that the "wrestling, battles and sword fights are great" and that "Lambert and Connery are fine . . . Hart is pretty" before going on to outline his "major concerns particularly regarding the love story" between MacLeod and Brenda, which he felt had been reduced to little more than a "one-night stand" thanks to trims to the sequence that followed MacLeod forcing Brenda to plunge a dagger into his heart. As scripted, the dagger scene was followed by a "sexually charged" dinner between the pair, the inclusion of the World War II flashback featuring the young Rachel, MacLeod showing Brenda the samurai sword, and the pair kissing before making love and talking.

With the flashback sequence moved, it was now "merely an expository scene for the audience's benefit" rather than a chance for MacLeod to explain who Rachel is to Brenda. Gone completely was Brenda's discussion of Christiaan Barnard and MacLeod's heart troubles, including a mention that "one year of love, though it ends in death, is better than an eternity alone", with Bellwood explaining that the line was "to make the point of the film clear". In the finished film the line was only referenced in the lyrics of the song 'One Year of Love'. According to Bellwood "that alone won't do . . . it's the core of the love story, and it's gone."

For Bellwood, the sequence seen in the film – MacLeod tells Brenda he's immortal, he plunges the dagger in Brenda's hand into his heart, they kiss and make love before he tells her in the zoo that "it isn't going to work" before she comments, "Most people are afraid to die . . . you're afraid to live" – renders their relationship "unintentionally laughable", while Brenda's kidnapping by the Kurgan loses its impact because the audience can't believe that MacLeod has fallen so deeply in love with Brenda.

Bellwood felt that the loss of the love story meant Rachel and Brenda now had roughly the same amount of time on screen with MacLeod, even suggesting that "Rachel's conversations with MacLeod are more intimate than Brenda's" and it might be better to cut out Rachel's backstory completely and make her "merely a secretary . . . her soap opera style is somewhat purple".

Determined to fight the case for an expanded love story, Bellwood suggested that a number of cuts could be made elsewhere in the film, including:

- Shots of the old drunk in the hotel (Prince Howell) who added "beats to scenes that have just finished, killing them"
- The Kurgan's final "It's better to fade out . . ." line from the church
- Some moments of the Kurgan which came across as "Victorian music-hall villain, tongue waggling and 'Heh-heh-heh-heh-heh' . . . a little of this goes a long way"
- Moments from the Ramirez/MacLeod training montage
- Fasil's backflips
- Some of the Scottish battle scenes
- The Boston Common duel, with Bellwood noting that Kastagir's voiceover was "confusing" and that Bassett "runs MacLeod through too many times . . . maybe the film could be speeded up, Keystone Cops style, as in *Tom Jones*".

Other changes that perturbed Bellwood included the removal of the subplot featuring Bedsoe tailing MacLeod, which made the detective's presence in a stake-out car outside Brenda's apartment confusing; the disappearance of Yung Dol Kim from the film; the deletion of the bar sequence featuring MacLeod, Kastagir and Bedsoe, meaning it was now unclear who Kastagir was; the removal of the Rachel/Moran subplot; and the excising of the fire at MacLeod's apartment, meaning there's "no sense of MacLeod, having won it all, disappearing, leaving no trace of himself behind".

One of the major alterations was to the ending, which as filmed saw MacLeod return to Scotland with Brenda in tow, the pair celebrating their love and looking forward to using his powers for good. "Bill [Panzer] and Peter [Davis] did not like that, so we had to come up with something different," laments Larry Ferguson. "I have to tell you that was one of the really beautiful moments that never made it into the film."

Having returned to America, Panzer called the writers and requested new dialogue, with Ferguson explaining that "he said, 'Could you guys write a paragraph just explaining who these people are and what's at stake? We can put it in as a voiceover at the beginning.' I think it was one of those things we needed by five o'clock. Peter and I sat down and wrote that opening statement for Sean: 'From the beginning of time we have walked among you . . .' and sent it to London. Sean liked it and it was dropped into the film." Ferguson and Bellwood's new prologue was sent to the producers in a memo dated 27 January 1986, with their original version running longer than the one seen on the film's opening title card:

> From the dawn of time they came . . .
> From misty mountains, scorched deserts and distant uncharted lands . . .
> Moving silently down through the centuries . . .
> Living many secret lives . . .
> Fighting and surviving . . .
> Struggling to reach the time of the Gathering . . .
> When the few who remain will battle to be the One . . .
> The possessor of the Prize.
> No one has ever known they were among us . . . until now . . .

Also included was an epilogue to be read by Sean Connery for the final scene. Again, the written epilogue differs to what ended up in the finished film:

> Only the Highlander, Connor MacLeod, remains . . .
> To him goes the Prize . . .
> The Prize which unites him with all living things . . .
> Opening his mind to galaxies of secret wishes and dreams . . .

He's at one with generations being born and dying . . .
He senses the thoughts of a faraway dictator plotting a coup
in Central America . . .
The rage of a diplomat in the Middle East . . .
The price of oil on tomorrow's markets . . .
Power beyond imagining . . .

I mention to Bellwood and Ferguson that one persistent story claims Sean Connery was asked to record his lines in his home bathroom, something Ferguson is quick to dismiss. "There are a lot of stories like that, but the truth is there's a lot of misinformation out there. He did not record it in a john. We wrote it and gave it to Bill Panzer. He may have given it to Sean who read it in a bathroom, but that's just apocrypha." In a DVD commentary for the film, Russell Mulcahy clarifies that the sound man was a day late arriving at Connery's home to record the dialogue and that he "did it in three takes. They were played down the phone line to the producers who thought it sounded fine. They couldn't hear the echo [that ended up in the finished film] because of a bad connection."

Evidence of the original ending can be found in the extras for *Highlander* on Blu-ray, which feature some extra frames discovered while the 35mm prints were being processed for the home video release. For the scene of MacLeod and Brenda back in Scotland, the pair can be seen discussing MacLeod's newly won abilities as originally scripted by Ferguson and Bellwood, though the audio is missing.

According to BBFC files dated 15 January 1986, feedback on the film's trailer asks that the editor "remove all sight of apparent decapitation by sword in scene in underground car park" and that they "remove all sight of sword thrust into man's side". By March 1986 the trailer had been passed, though a second was submitted in June and awarded a U certificate.

With a final edit of the film almost finished and a March 1986 release date set for America, over in London plans were underway to launch *Highlander* into the world in grand style later in the year. What nobody could predict at the start of 1986 was just how different things would look at Thorn EMI Screen Entertainment come the spring.

SIXTEEN

SELLING THE STORY

In the 12 months it had taken producers Bill Panzer and Peter Davis to put *Highlander* into production, shoot it in the UK and America and prepare a rough cut of the film, things had been going from bad to worse for their funders, Thorn EMI Screen Entertainment (TESE).

In the spring of 1985, a new head of international marketing had been appointed to TESE in the shape of John Simenon, the Belgian son of Inspector Maigret author, Georges Simenon. Simenon introduced a new concept called 'rollover deals', which caused some consternation amongst TESE accountants and sales people. In traditional sales deals, distributors would pay TESE money up front to have access to a film in their territory. This money was non-refundable, and it encouraged distributors to spend money on prints and advertising; theoretically, the more the distributor spent, the more successful the film would be.

Simenon's new strategy was to negotiate to obtain better financial participation from the overseas theatrical markets. Rollover deals allowed advance guarantees paid to TESE to be refunded to foreign distributors for films which went on to fail at the box office. As 1985 was a less than stellar year for TESE, this new strategy would cause major problems for the company's accountants.

A boardroom coup in June 1985 led to computer entrepreneur Colin Southgate becoming TESE's managing director. Southgate promptly decided to jettison TESE's film and television interests to focus on defence and retail. By September 1985, both TESE and its 50% share in Thames Television were put up for sale. Not only did TESE have a large film library, but it owned both Elstree Studios and the largest chain of cinemas in the UK.

As TESE chief executive Gary Dartnall attempted to raise money for a management buyout, other interested parties made themselves known to the board, including British company The Rank Organisation, and the LA-based Menahem Golan and Yoram Globus, owners of the Cannon Group. As well as producing a string of low-budget titles including *Hercules* (1981), *Enter the Ninja* (1981), and numerous sequels to 1974's *Death Wish*, Golan and Globus owned cinemas in the UK, but they were keen on building a European-wide cinema chain.

With a management buyout the preferred option of the Thorn EMI board, Dartnall was given time to try and raise funds, refusing early advances from Golan and Globus (who were not particularly well thought of by the British film industry) to partner with him on a joint bid. When Dartnall struggled to raise the non-refundable $10 million deposit required by TESE to let him extend the buyout deadline, a saviour came to him in the form of Australian businessman, Alan Bond. Allegedly under the impression that TESE owned *Star Wars* because it had been filmed at Elstree Studios, Bond co-signed a contract worth £110 million in December 1985 to complete the buyout, which would involve another four months of work to raise working capital for the company.

While the executives were taking part in high-stakes deals, staff at TESE were carrying out the daily tasks required to keep the business operating. Planning for *Highlander*'s UK release began in earnest in January 1986 in the London offices of Thorn EMI, under the watchful eye of their head of creative services, Phil Howard-Jones. "I was looking after all the creative development of film campaigns which would be used in the UK and internationally. I was also looking after all the video packaging."

Howard-Jones had been keeping an eye on the development of *Highlander* since early 1985 and was excited by its potential, even if there was some doubt among those involved. "It was an amazingly engaging film . . . I can remember once being at one of the filming sessions and hearing one of the crew saying, 'What a load of old nonsense,' but it was an amazing scene they were filming. It was an unusual film and a lot of people really couldn't get their heads around it and the concept of it, which is a great shame."

In the 1980s, film marketing wasn't as multi-layered as today, with Howard-Jones noting that a campaign was mainly composed of "a poster and a few bits and pieces", but aware of the potential of *Highlander*, including music from Queen and the visual styling of Russell Mulcahy, he was thinking on a grander scale. "When we heard the soundtrack was going to be done by Queen, that was amazing. I actually thought 'Princes of the Universe' was going to be the main number one hit, which was a new way in those days of promoting a film. If you could get a single out there ahead of the launch of a film and build the awareness, that was fantastic."

Following a screening of the film on 7 January for international distributors at the ABC cinema on Shaftesbury Avenue, Howard-Jones began working in conjunction with Bill Panzer and Peter Davis to select clips for a promotional video to be sent out to journalists and cinemas, before putting together briefs for London creative agencies that would help him find some fresh input on the *Highlander* concept. Howard-Jones' personal diaries show a blitz of activity throughout January and February, including a visit to Elstree Studios on 14 February to shoot the promotional video for 'Princes of the Universe'.

On the Monday after the video shoot, Howard-Jones commissioned creative agency Feref to start on artwork for a *Highlander* poster. "For me the whole thing about the promotion was very much the image of the film on the poster. That was always one of the key issues and I think we were very successful with that. After trying out all these other agencies and different angles and fresh approaches, it came down to actually having something which is a classic theatrical poster image, which Brian Bysouth did a fantastic job on."

Bysouth, who had joined Feref's creative team in 1983, had attended a screening of *Highlander* organised by Howard-Jones and been supplied with 35mm transparencies of the film for reference. In designing his poster, the artist latched on to an image from the film's finale, that of Connor MacLeod's reaction to having defeated the Kurgan as spirits start to take over his body. Talking to John Mosby for his 2014 book *Fearful Symmetry*, Bysouth explained that to him, "the image of Lambert, sword in hand, head thrown back in ecstatic triumph, could become the perfect icon for a fascinating film". After supplying initial sketches to Phil Howard-Jones, Bysouth completed the poster in three days.

As work progressed on the marketing, it was becoming clear to staff at Thorn EMI that external factors surrounding Gary Dartnall and Alan Bond's proposed takeover were starting to make their jobs increasingly difficult.

Initially, Howard-Jones was receptive to Bond's involvement. "We were thinking, 'Wow, this is just what we need, huge amounts of money to put behind us,' and we thought we were going to be able to promote *Highlander* and other films much more." His team was already planning ahead to the Cannes Film Festival in May, and one result of having more cash available was spending more at the festival. Says Howard-Jones, "I've got a note about calling an outfit called Airship Industries in March 1986; we thought we could maybe get blimps to go down to Cannes and promote our films."

While the UK marketing team was busy planning for Cannes and a late summer release, over in America 20th Century Fox was gearing up to release *Highlander*, albeit with less enthusiasm than their British counterparts. Although the film's producers had made it clear to editor Peter Honess that their legal dispute with Fox would have no impact on the film's release in the US, Guy Collins, who had helped raise funds on numerous Davis-Panzer productions, wasn't so sure. "When Davis-Panzer took legal action against them, Fox responded by releasing *Highlander* in its minimum 1,000 cinemas, which was the deal, but with zero advertising, so the film actually went out into cinemas with no promotion."

"They didn't promote it properly; they just wanted to sell it to TV," says ex-TESE business affairs administrator David Semple. "It would have been better if Fox had put up a quarter of the budget, then with money at risk they'd have had a reason to promote it. You need to invest money to promote it."

A decision was made that some scenes would be cut from Russell Mulcahy's preferred version of *Highlander* for the American release, with around eight minutes lost in total. Edits included the removal of the first flashback to Scotland while MacLeod is attending the wrestling match, Hotchkiss being shot in the back on Boston Common, and the Kurgan licking the priest's hand. Also removed was the flashback to MacLeod saving Rachel in Nazi Germany, which included his "It's a kind of magic" quip. "I cut both versions, but Russell and I much preferred the European one," says Peter Honess. "The producers never liked the World War II scene and tried to take it out of the European version, but Russell prevailed." The film received an R rating from the Motion Picture Association of America (MPAA).

In addition to limiting the number of cinemas where *Highlander* could be seen, 20th Century Fox also refused to hold press screenings for US critics, meaning no reviews were available for cinemagoers to read or watch in the days leading up to its release on 7 March.

When it did open, it took seventh place in the week's box-office charts, sharing its release date with the John McTiernan-directed horror thriller, *Nomads*, and James Ivory's romantic drama, *A Room with a View*. While Highlander took $2,453,021 on its opening weekend, a release from the previous week, John Hughes' teen comedy *Pretty in Pink*, sat at number one, having made $6,065,870 in its first week and $4,919,668 in week two. *Highlander* fell to 12th place by its second week (taking $1,273,196) and 17th place by week three (taking $807,897), before dropping out of the charts.

Smarting that Fox hadn't allowed him to attend a press screening, film critic Gene Siskel wrote in the *Chicago Tribune* that the reason was they "wanted to prevent us from giving you the word on Friday that *Highlander* was a horror. Sorry, all you weekend suckers." Siskel's biggest issue with the film was that it was "hyperviolent", noting that at his screening some younger patrons walked out of the screening early, with one girl muttering, "Look, there are only men in here," as she left. Bemoaning the lack of "human moments" in the film, Siskel stated that "if [Immortals] are indeed the people who are going to save our planet . . . maybe it's a good time to consider buying an acre in Montana or someplace else remote". Siskel was a fan of the Queen soundtrack, advising fans to "skip the movie and save your money for the album".

Siskel also brought his dislike of the film to television in an episode of the long-running *At the Movies with Gene Siskel and Roger Ebert*, explaining it was "one of the lousiest films I've ever seen in my entire life" that "made no sense whatsoever", while Roger Ebert reckoned it was a "completely silly and very boring movie" that reminded him of 1974's *That's Entertainment*, essentially a series of high points from other movies strung together "with nothing in between". Ebert closed by suggesting *Highlander* be retitled *That's Swordfighting*.

Walter Goodman in the *New York Times* began by praising the presence of Sean Connery – "For his brief time on screen, Mr Connery brings dash and style to the overblown proceedings" – before stating that when he's killed off "we're back with much ado about less than nothing". Unhappy with the film's script and visual style, Goodman opined that *Highlander* was "a cumbersome tale told with noise and flash" that was "not especially funny, and of course it is not serious. What is it?" The critic finished by stating that "since none of the characters makes sense, even on the movie's own terms, *Highlander* keeps on exploding for almost two hours, with nothing at stake".

There was also little love for the film in the *Washington Post*, with Paul Attanasio likening the story's outline to James Cameron's *The Terminator* (1984), and slamming the script as "profoundly derivative, poorly structured and jokey in a dull way". Russell Mulcahy's direction was also taken to task, his style described as "grotesquely overwrought, a relentless exercise in technique for technique's sake . . . as if a 15-minute history of film technique had been compiled by a psychotic". Unsurprisingly, Attanasio wasn't a fan of the actors either, feeling that the "fey, cartoon-faced Lambert is no action hero . . . a French actor, he essays English with a Scottish tinge, and winds up sounding like [Polish-American diplomat and political scientist] Zbigniew Brzezinski".

Bill Cosford in the *Miami Herald* reckoned that "Mulcahy has style to burn, but he may well have used the script to light it, for *Highlander* almost never makes any sense", while the *Los Angeles Times'* Sheila Benson felt that "in spite of a sturdy cast and dazzling production design, *Highlander* is stultifyingly, jaw-droppingly, achingly awful".

Following the film's lacklustre American opening and critical drubbing, *Highlander* was released around Europe throughout the spring and summer of 1986, with France the first country to host a premiere on 26 March. "I remember when the film opened in Paris, there were queues up and down the Champs Elysees because Monsieur Lambert was a huge star in France," says Guy Collins, going on to note that the film was a major success internationally as it slowly made its way to the UK. Thanks to Lambert's star power in France, the film became the country's second-highest-grossing film of 1986.

Reviews also tended to be more positive outside the US, with Australian magazine *Cinema Papers* championing local hero Russell Mulcahy. In Tony Cavanaugh's lengthy take on *Highlander*, he exclaimed that Mulcahy's "camera eye is little short of wonderful" and that the film "becomes a kind of kinetic cross between *Blade Runner* and *Excalibur*". Praising Christopher Lambert as "surprisingly effective", Cavanaugh felt the script was well written and that "there's enough humour to balance the sombre struggle between the Immortals . . . *Highlander* is an exciting, tightly written and beautifully directed thriller".

Back in England, Phil Howard-Jones was still working on his plans for the film's UK release, his notes mentioning that on 14 March he ordered 3,000 *Highlander* posters from National Screen Service, while on 18 March he previewed two *Highlander* featurettes. "On 20 March I had to chase Jim Beach, Queen's manager, for something to do with the promotional video for MTV, and on 4 April I flew to LA, that was all part of the takeover. I had to go to our US offices and talk to people. After that is really when it all started going a bit lairy."

The return of Cannon

By the spring of 1986, Alan Bond and his team had taken a closer look at the finances of TESE and weren't overly keen on what they found. At the same time, the Thorn EMI board now had some doubts about Gary Dartnall, with managing director Colin Southgate unhappy with Dartnall flying to the USA each week by Concorde. On one occasion, he flew from London to New York and back in a day for a haircut. When Dartnall finally admitted he couldn't raise the required cash for the buyout, his partnership with Bond collapsed in March, the latter going on to sign a deal on 25 April worth £125 million.

TESE staff may have been celebrating the takeover, but what they didn't know was that Alan Bond had flown to Los Angeles a few weeks earlier to meet with the Cannon Group's Golan and Globus to discuss their potential involvement in running TESE. When Bond's deal with Thorn EMI was signed, he decided to seal the deal with Cannon just one week later to the sum of £175 million, a profit for the Australian of £50 million. For Golan and Globus, it was a chance to finally take charge of the cinema chain they'd long coveted, meaning they owned cinemas across the European continent, in Israel, in the UK, plus film studios across several countries and a film library with more than 2,000 titles.

Phil Howard-Jones was working at Thorn House in Soho when the news came through about the deal on 2 May. He and his colleagues made their way to the dining area for an impromptu meeting. Also in attendance was film-maker Michael Winner, an ally of Golan and Globus. Says Howard-Jones, "They stood up and said, 'We're here because basically we hate you guys so we bought it so we can more or less destroy you.' It was extraordinary. Imagine if you're working on promoting films and you've got the Cannes Film Festival coming up, which is huge in terms of preparation and getting everything ready, and then you're suddenly wondering, 'Where does that leave us?' We were trying to promote this film and nobody knew if they were going to be gone tomorrow."

TESE's head of international marketing, John Simenon, left the building when news of Cannon's acquisition began to spread, never to return. His leaving meant *Highlander* had one less supporter within the new structure. "He had this big cut-out poster of Christopher Lambert with the sword up in his office on the fifth floor of Thorn House," says David Semple. "The rumour was that he used to play the soundtrack in his office and flash the sword around."

Less than a week away from Cannes, the *Highlander* marketing team now had plenty of plans, but no way to implement them. "[*Highlander*] has wonderful elements, like Christophe Lambert wearing his trench coat," says Phil Howard-Jones. "I remember going out and buying them, wearing the white trainers and everything else. It was an image that really captured people's attention and we were building up extra promotion with a competition where you could win these coats. There could have been a whole load of people turning up at premieres wearing them."

Evidence of the film's promotional material exists in the form of an Exhibitor's Campaign Book and production notes issued in 1986. Stamped with a Cannon logo, the glossy black-and-white Campaign Book offers suggestions to newspapers and magazine editors on how they might promote the film and the soundtrack to their readers, offering them a chance to pay for various pre-designed adverts of different sizes. Usually featuring Brian Bysouth's poster design, and always including a reminder that the film featured original songs by Queen, the ads all had the same promotional text that read:

From another time comes a man of great power, a man of incredible strength, an Immortal about to face his greatest challenge . . . Highlander.

Also offered were "three eye-catching competitions designed for maximum impact in local newspapers, freesheets and magazines", including a game of Spot the Difference featuring MacLeod and the Kurgan; a Time Maze, which asked readers to use a ballpoint pen to follow MacLeod on his journey through the centuries from 1536 to 1986; and a game of Name the Swords, which tested a general audience's knowledge of six types of sword, from a ceremonial sword to a Gurkha's kukri. A five-part serialised cartoon strip was also offered up to newspapers, featuring scenes from the film, with the suggestion to editors to run one or two strips a week in the run-up to the film's UK release.

With *Highlander*'s US release still fresh in his mind, Phil Howard-Jones' hope was that he would have a chance to impress distributors from the rest of the world with the film at Cannes, which was taking place from 8 to 19 May. Although he made it to Heathrow, he didn't get any further. "I had all the publicity arranged and [at Heathrow] a Tannoy went off saying, 'Mr Howard-Jones, report to the main desk.' A telephone was handed to me and it was my PA saying I've been given clear instructions not to fly to Cannes and I'm to come back to the office.' So I had to do a U-turn with the whole process and go back."

According to Guy Collins, the Cannon takeover was a shock to everyone in the UK film industry. "[Golan and Globus] were smart, but Thorn EMI was such a different kind of business. At the first Cannes Film Festival after the takeover, Cannon had all these ex-Thorn EMI people wearing Cannon tracksuits, which did not jive very well with the old hierarchy."

From May 1986 onwards, Phil Howard-Jones' diary emptied as Cannon wound down any work connected to Thorn EMI. "It was almost like, 'You can't do anything, you've just got to be here.' That's why the promotion of *Highlander* fell apart, and we were just left with a poster and a few other bits and pieces. We had lots of other plans. We were hoping that Queen would be doing concerts, we had visions of them being at Wembley and having huge stages looking like [they were from] *Highlander*. These were just thoughts and creative ideas, which would have been amazing in those days, but we couldn't do anything like that because Cannon came in and basically just stopped us from doing anything."

"That would never have happened in a million years," states Queen's Roger Taylor on the subject of *Highlander*-themed concerts. "If we tour, we come first."

Today, Howard-Jones reckons *Highlander* was "one of the most inspiring films" he ever worked on. "The film excited me and other people I was working with. I worked on a whole load for Thorn EMI which were exactly the opposite, they were appalling, and to suddenly get a film that excited you and you could actually see the massive potential. We were looking at trademarking the *Highlander* logo and the catchline 'There can be only one' all around the world so it couldn't be ripped off, but that would have cost a fortune."

Opening in the UK

With *Highlander* due for a UK release in August 1986, it was decided that the final cut would be submitted to the BBFC for classification on Friday 27 June, though it wouldn't be until Thursday 24 July that a decision would be published and sent to Cannon. Comments held by the BBFC note that the examiner felt the film was "A virtuoso action, if not thought packed, movie directed by Russell Mulcahy who must have started in advertising like Ridley Scott . . . *Highlander* is a mind-bending mixture of *Legend*, *Lifeforce*, *The Terminator* and Walt Disney with a dash of *Ghostbusters* in the last reel."

It was on Friday 29 August 1986 that *Highlander* finally opened in UK cinemas, having been awarded a 15 certificate from the

BBFC on 27 June 1986. Though there was little interest from Cannon Films in making the film a success, London publicity agency JAC had been brought on board in the early months of the film's production by Davis-Panzer and they were attempting to drum up publicity as it opened around Europe. As well as interviewing the cast and crew with an eye to creating production notes that could later be sent to the world's press, JAC had been inviting press on set to carry out interviews and experience some of the filming.

JAC's Claire Forbes, one of a small team tasked with working on the film, remembers that securing early publicity wasn't easy due to the "off-the-wall" nature of the story. "I don't think we got the nationals interested in the early stages. Some journalists knew Russell, some knew Christophe and I think we had to go with the more specialist magazines initially in each of the territories. The French press wasn't too difficult with Christophe on board, and the Aussies because of Russell, but we had to build it up as we went."

By the time the film was rolling out around the globe, Forbes and her team were touring Europe with Connery and Lambert to meet journalists for TV, film and magazines. "Christophe did loads of work with the press around the world; he even came to incredibly boring film markets like MIFED in Milan. It's like a shoe fair; you're sitting in a horrible stuffy office and distributors are coming in one after the other for meetings. He was very active in promotion." UK critics took a far more relaxed approach to the film's absurdities than their American cousins had done earlier in the year, embracing the mix of action and humour while appreciating Russell Mulcahy's unique style.

Time Out's Richard Rayner attempted to sum up the film's premise by explaining that "there is this group of gladiators gladiating through the ages to a point in time, 1986 [sic], when they gather in a place, New York, put on Demob raincoats and go out in the rain to club each other to death with samurai swords" before praising Sean Connery for making "tosh dialogue sound like it was written by Noel Coward". Rayner concluded by proclaiming

Highlander was "a lot of utterly preposterous fun, even if it doesn't quite hang together. Scotch missed".

Writing in *Monthly Film Bulletin*, Tim Pulleine likened *Highlander* to both *The Terminator* in its premise ("an immortal hero and villain who travel and battle down through the centuries") and Errol Flynn costume romances, latching on to Russell Mulcahy's rock video background when he noted the film had "been made as a succession of set pieces, extracting maximum mileage from Skycam and Steadicam". Though Pulleine praised the present-day sections as being "sufficiently ingenious in detail and black humour", he wasn't as keen on the historical scenes, dismissing them as descending into "a token level of fancy-dress flummery", concluding that "*Highlander* periodically manages to be quite exhilarating".

Stephanie Billen in *The List* also fell for *Highlander*'s charms, dismissing the fact that it was being promoted as an action film and noting that it was "a curious mixture of romance in the 15th-century [sic] heather and car chases in present-day New York", pulled together by the "magnetic Lambert". Billen also praised Clancy Brown and the "luminous" Beatie Edney, though she wasn't so generous with Sean Connery, stating he was "mis-cast . . . the weak link that threatens to turn the film's gentle humour into unintentional farce". She concluded her review by stating that *Highlander* was "highly enjoyable . . . a film worth seeing on several levels".

Over in *City Limits* magazine, Nigel Matheson began his review by observing that "Russell Mulcahy certainly has a vivid imagination", before detailing elements of the plot and noting that "somehow, the cameras manage to move faster than the plot". Trying to put the film into some sort of context for readers, Matheson described *Highlander* as "an amalgam of a Duran Duran video, '*The Terminator/Mad Max*' school of action and the *White Heather Club* on acid", before concluding it was "the daftest major movie for a while and . . . highly entertaining due to its director's daring in the face of folly".

As with the majority of films released in the pre-digital age, the views of the paying public are almost impossible to gauge, as apart from personal diaries or letters in print publications there were few places to record such responses. Although hardly representative of the thousands of viewers who would see *Highlander* in cinemas, a look at the BBFC's records show that they received a single letter of complaint during its UK cinema run.

[Name and address redacted]
12 October 1986

Dear Sir/Madam,

As a regular cinema goer, and until tonight satisfied with your certification, I feel I must complain at the 15 rating given to the film *Highlander*. I attended the film with my husband and I considered taking my 15-year-old sister-in-law. Thankfully we didn't. From the write-ups given in the local press, we were led to believe it was an adventure film with a 'good guy' fighting a 'bad guy', what was not mentioned were the numerous decapitations and other unnecessary violence. As a State Registered Nurse, who has worked in a busy accident and emergency department close to a busy motorway complex, I feel that I am quite used to the sight of blood and guts, however this film left me feeling physically sick. What has this film done to numerous 15-year-olds who have seen it? I hope these [unclear] will be borne in mind for the future, as these films usually become available in video shops for rental shortly after general release.

The BBFC responded to the member of the public in a letter a few days later:

British Board of Film Certification
16 October 1985

Dear [name redacted],

Thank you for your letter regarding the film *Highlander*. You'll appreciate that film classification is not an exact science and on occasion a film falls between two categories and we have to decide which is the more appropriate. HIGHLANDER is at the top end of the 15 for violence, but our examiners felt it would be wrong to bar the teenage audience from seeing this well-made film. I, personally, have seen it in the public cinema, apart from seeing it at the Board, and I am sure that the 15 decision was correct. This decision was also agreed with the Director who also saw the film. I should explain that we have 11 female and 10 male examiners, all have varying backgrounds, and a number of them have teenage children, so we are aware of the reaction of teenage audiences. HIGHLANDER has been on release for seven weeks and to date no other letter has been received from the public regarding the classification of this film, so I think it is reasonable to assume that the Board's decision was correct.

The BBFC received a second letter of complaint regarding the film following its release on home video.

[Name and address redacted]
24 August 1987

Dear Sir,

My husband's interested in science fiction and recently hired the film Highlander from our local video shop, believing it to deal with the concept of time travel. He was sickened, and I was appalled, at the level of violence contained in this film rated 15. There were five instances of prolonged fighting, culminating in an apparent decapitation. There were two implied rapes and one lovemaking scene which I considered too adult for a 15-year-old. I think seeing this film would have an unsalutary effect on a 15-year-old, even an 18-year-old. I would class this film as a video nasty.

As before, the BBFC replied swiftly to the concerns addressed in the letter:

British Board of Film Certification
28 August 1987

Dear [Name redacted],

I regret that you are disturbed by HIGHLANDER being given a 15 category and consider it to be a video nasty. In the opinion of the Board it is a well-meaning thriller adventure story that by current standards is a top level 15 category tape. This incidentally was the category also given to the film version, which was widely shown. It is now Board policy that the 15 category is a major category, and this is one of the reasons where the age was raised to 15 years, whereas the previous Category AA was 14. In no way would we consider HIGHLANDER to be a video nasty, decapitations consisting of fast cutting with no attempt by the director to linger on the torso or head, while the sex scenes are well within current standards for the 15. While I would not argue that the Board is always right in its decisions, for example I personally did not agree with the decision to pass the film PLATOON in the 15 category, it would appear from the lack of comment from the public that the 15 category was considered the appropriate category for HIGHLANDER. I should explain that we have 11 female and 10 male examiners, all of varying backgrounds, and a number of them have teenage children, so we are aware of the reaction of teenage audiences. Thank you for writing as it is only by receiving comments such as yours the future policy can be defined.

Between August and December 1986, *Highlander* continued to be released in countries such as Spain, Ireland, Japan and Greece, while Poland, Taiwan, Denmark, Mexico and Argentina didn't see it until 1987 and Peru had to wait until 1990 for screenings. In the end, *Highlander* would add $7 million to its US box-office takings, bringing it to a total of $12.9 million globally, a disappointing result considering the initial $16 million budget and the resultant marketing and publicity costs that would have nudged the total higher.

Says Christopher Lambert, "It was huge in Europe and it was big in the States, but not in the beginning. It picked up afterwards due to word of mouth, and people saying it was so different to everything else. In Japan they went to see the movie not for Sean, Clancy or myself, but because I was holding a katana."

Though traditionally the cinema success of any film had been of prime importance to studios, by the mid-1980s home video had become a huge money-spinner. In 1984 there were 10.5 million VCRs in US homes and 9 million in the UK, meaning that when it came time for *Highlander* to debut on VHS in early 1987, fans were ready to pay to watch it again in the comfort of their own home.

The UK's *Video – the Machine* magazine offered two takes on the new VHS in its January 1987 issue, the first from 'MC' stating that Russell Mulcahy's dazzling camerawork "manages to propel the film into the ranks of an instant classic, a film where style and content mix to make the almost perfect fantasy . . . I urge you to rent it – now!"

The second review from 'RM' mentioned that they had watched their tape on a "pleasant Sunday morning following a heavy VTM Glee Club gathering the night before", going on to note that the film was "more of a visual than plotting triumph" while pondering whether the film would "translate to the small screen, often a film that is so impressive will lose its impact within the confines of the average 20' job". Readers were also invited to enter a competition to win either a copy of *Highlander* or 1986's *Clan of the Cave Bear* on VHS.

As *Highlander* became available to rent and then buy at video stores internationally, word soon spread even further about this impressive mix of swords and modern-day action. Fans who had seen it in cinemas could invite friends over to watch it again and again, inspiring others to do the same with their friends and family.

Though Peter Davis and Bill Panzer may have started looking for new projects to produce once *Highlander* was released, the success of the film on home video soon made them realise that they had something on their hands that was taking on a life of its own.

Could there really be only one *Highlander*?

SEVENTEEN

BUILDING A FRANCHISE

When Gregory Widen first sat down to write the script that would eventually become *Highlander*, his aim was to craft an entertaining adventure that somebody might one day turn into a feature film. Producers Bill Panzer and Peter Davis wanted to make that feature film, one that audiences would flock to at cinemas around the world, hopefully making them millions of dollars in the process.

Highlander may have been similar to countless other films in that it featured a battle between good and evil that was resolved in a major action sequence, but screenwriters Peter Bellwood and Larry Ferguson were always uneasy about the ending being planned for their hero. "I remember how hard we fought with Bill Panzer because he came up with this idea that the Prize is that Connor MacLeod could die," says Ferguson. "We had a lot of meetings and Peter or myself said, 'If he dies, what are you going to do if there's a sequel?', and Bill just waved his hand and said, 'There's not going to be any sequel.'"

Once the film had been unleashed on the world and sales of *Highlander* on video and to TV stations grew, it became clear that a follow-up might be something that fans would like to see. Never mind that nobody had planned for such a film, if there was an opportunity to capitalise on the original's popularity, it made business sense for Davis-Panzer to at least discuss the possibility, something they'd begun doing soon after *Highlander*'s release.

One of those involved in discussions was Guy Collins, who had got into film financing a decade earlier. He'd raised production funding for 1978's *The Wild Geese*, going on to do the same for various high-profile independent films including Davis-Panzer's *The Osterman Weekend* in 1983. Introduced to the producers by distribution sales agent Michael Ryan, Collins knew they had a short amount of time to get the finance together so that *Osterman* could enter production. "I was able to do that in about five or six weeks, primarily with an English investment bank that I'd got into some earlier film activity. That's how I met Pete and Bill, and then we did some other films together."

According to Collins, by 1988 regular discussions about a second *Highlander* feature were taking place, but kept stalling. "After the first film was finished, Cannon was bought by Weintraub, and from the producers' point of view the film disappeared into a bit of an abyss. I think that was part of the momentum to actually go again; second time around they might actually get to keep and own something. I think one day I said to them, 'For goodness' sake, let's stop talking about it and go and do it.'" The trio headed to Milan's MIFED film market, grabbed themselves a table and according to Collins "sat there for five days and did about $23 million of pre-sales. I took that and put the banking together, raised some other bits and pieces of finance and then off we went and made a movie."

Bill Panzer worked with veteran British screenwriter Brian Clemens (*The Avengers*, 1961–69) on the sequel's storyline, also bringing back Peter Bellwood from the first film to write the script. "I wrote the sequel, the second film after *Highlander* very competently labelled *Highlander II*," explains Bellwood. "I didn't enjoy the experience because they had to bring Sean Connery back to life, and everything was so tortuous in an attempt to get mileage out of something which Bill thought had finished with the end of the first film."

In the version of *Highlander II: The Quickening* released in US cinemas in November 1991, the story takes place across numerous time periods and locations, initially finding Connor MacLeod in 1994 as the world becomes aware that the ozone layer is disappearing and an ecological crisis is brewing. MacLeod then helps to oversee the creation of a shield that will protect the Earth from the Sun's radiation, though by 2024 the planet is in a dire state and the shield is under the control of the Shield Corporation. It's then revealed that MacLeod and Ramirez (a resurrected Sean Connery) are in fact aliens from the planet Zeist, banished to Earth by General Katana (Michael Ironside). Ramirez must help MacLeod attempt to defeat Katana and shut down the shield.

A slightly different version had arrived in UK cinemas in April 1991, this time featuring eight minutes of extra footage overseen by Davis-Panzer and Nigel Green of Entertainment Film Distributors, the UK distributor of the film.

Though Russell Mulcahy and Christopher Lambert were contractually obliged to return for the sequel, no such deal had been made with Clancy Brown. Despite this, the Kurgan was part of the original draft, which was duly sent to the actor for his consideration. "The second script was horrible," says Brown. "They only showed me 20 pages of it and I could tell it was terrible. I said to my agent, 'This is a piece of shit. I'll do it for $1 million and they can pay me what they paid Sean [on *Highlander*].' They weren't going to do that and it was fine."

"One of the producers insisted on explaining where we came from," explains an exasperated Lambert when we touch on the sequel. "I said, 'Who the fuck gives a shit about that? It's established we're immortal, end of story.' I fought that, but the difference between Clancy and myself is that I was signed to do a sequel so I didn't have a choice, but I battled for months with Bill Panzer, whom I loved, saying, 'Bill, who cares?' He would say, 'No, I think it's important,' and he was the writer and the producer, so it was difficult. But we got Sean back and we got planet Zeist. They didn't even know what Zeist was."

Sean Connery returned with the promise of a $3 million pay packet for a reputed six days on set. *Highlander* editor Peter Honess was working with the actor on 1990's *The Russia House* when he heard he was about to make *Highlander II*. "I said, 'What the hell are you doing another one for?', and he said, 'It's the money, laddie, the money!'" Connery is said to have delayed his arrival on set until his fee was placed in escrow, going so far as to refuse to publicly acknowledge he was even in the film until the money was escrowed.

Production began in Argentina in 1990, but things soon started to go awry as a result of a disastrous economic climate. "For the first and only time in its financial history, the Argentinian currency went up against the dollar," says Guy Collins. "It was something to do with their new president, Menem, and people thinking he was going to do something great to the country." As a result, the cost of using local talent and facilities spiralled, forcing the producers to bring in more crew from the UK and US. "I think the budget was $23 or $24 million, and the film went something like $8 million over budget. That's usually pretty catastrophic."

Having already pulled together a number of international funding deals, Collins was now tasked with finding a way to recoup the unexpected $8 million overspend, deciding the only place they could look was to America. "I think the best offer we got in the US was a million and a half dollars. So we talked about it and said, 'Why don't we do it ourselves?' We raised about $6 million to fund the US release – I think we did the video rights with Sony – and I sold the TV rights to Showtime and Worldvision. From the first cycle in America we did something like $11 million."

Christopher Lambert has always felt that the issue wasn't that the script was bad, but that it was bad as a sequel to *Highlander*. "If it had been called *The Aliens from Planet Zeist* or *Highlander: The Return* or whatever, the movie would have been great. During promotion all over the world, I was saying to the audience, 'If you guys going to see *Highlander II* are thinking it's the sequel to *Highlander*, then it's not.' The producer was saying, 'Are you nuts?' and I said, 'No, I'm telling the truth; the movie's great, but it's not the sequel to *Highlander*.' He said, 'You can't say that,' and I said, 'Well I'm not going to do promotion.' The movie did well, but [fans] were disappointed. At least they couldn't say I was betraying them, because literally at every screening and on every TV show I was saying, 'People expecting to see the sequel to *Highlander* shouldn't go.'"

Russell Mulcahy touched on his *Highlander II* experience in a 1994 interview, stating that it was "a complete disaster. It was done for totally the wrong reasons. I was *tricked* into doing it. No script, no screenwriter. Shot in Argentina to try and do it on the cheap. *That* backfired. By the time I left Argentina, there were whole scenes that *hadn't* been shot. The story wasn't even joined together . . . I sat and watched 15 minutes at the Westwood premiere and walked out. I hear it's shit."

Worldwide, the film grossed just over $15.5 million at the box office, $5.2 million of that in the US, showing once again that the *Highlander* brand was popular internationally, even if it didn't instantly recoup its budget. As with the first film, it would be on video and TV sales that it would see real success, though this would be far from straightforward thanks to the decision to release a different edit of the film on Laserdisc in 1995 and later DVD, *Highlander II: The Renegade Cut.* This version added 18 minutes to the US cut of *The Quickening*, removing references to the planet Zeist and restoring flashbacks lost in the original version.

It's fair to say that *Highlander II* remains the most controversial entry in the franchise, with fans and critics debating the merits of each cut in numerous podcasts and magazine articles through the years, while *Video Watchdog*'s Sean Murphy dedicated a number of pages to painstakingly detail the differences between *The Quickening* and *The Renegade Cut* in a January 1997 feature.

Speaking in 1992 about the film's box-office failure, Bill Panzer told *Starlog* that he "always felt *Highlander II* was a success in telling an exciting, entertaining story and furthering the *Highlander* odyssey. To this point, the *Highlander* films in the US are more of a cult thing, and the second film drew upon that cult. But I'm convinced these films will eventually break through to the kind of audience in the United States that they have elsewhere in the world."

Highlander: The Series

Though fans would have been happy to watch another cinematic outing for Connor MacLeod, it was the small screen that next beckoned for the character when in 1992 plans were set in motion for a TV series.

"It was another one of those situations where Peter and Bill kept saying, 'Why don't we make a TV series?', but none of us knew how to make a TV series," says Guy Collins, who remembered he'd once met The Walt Disney Company's vice president of international television, Sheryl Hardy, who had since left the company. "I was in LA and I called her up and said, 'Any ideas how we could make a TV series about *Highlander*?' She said, 'I know exactly how to do it,' and we did it for six years." The pair became co-executive producers on the series, with the rights owned by the French production company, Gaumont.

"We realised that *Highlander* would have an advantage over other TV series in that there were two other movies that preceded it," explained Bill Panzer. "The movies were hugely successful worldwide, and, while not a huge theatrical success in America, they've done quite well there. We want to make sure the fans of the movies can look at this and say, 'OK, it's on television, but it's still *Highlander*.'"

The original hope for the series was that it would focus on the weekly adventures of Connor MacLeod living in 1990s New York, but Christopher Lambert balked at the idea when Davis-Panzer offered him the series. Initially saying no to starring in every episode, he subsequently agreed to appear in the first episode. "I wasn't ready to commit myself to do 22 episodes a year sword fighting. I don't think I would have stayed; I don't like to be caged. The producers said, 'You'll be paid a huge amount of money,' and I said, 'It doesn't matter; after three years I don't want to look at you and say, 'I want to quit,' and not be able to.'"

Instead of Connor MacLeod leading the show, the decision was made to introduce a new member of the clan, Duncan MacLeod, in the shape of English actor, Adrian Paul. Says Lambert, "I did episode one, handing my sword to Adrian, and he did a great job." Produced in Canada and France and mainly funded with money from Gaumont and other international partners, *Highlander: The Series* ran for six seasons between 1992 and 1998, clocking up 119 episodes. It also utilised Queen's 'Princes of the Universe' for its theme song, ensuring some continuity with the first film. "The series was our saving grace," admitted Peter Davis to *Empire* magazine. "Through all the years the films might not have been appreciated by the fans, and rightfully so, the series was extraordinary."

While Davis-Panzer would go on to make millions of dollars from the syndication of the TV series, undoubtedly the more lucrative deal was done with Gaumont when they negotiated with them in 1992. "Gaumont wanted a bigger piece of syndication – which they've done very well with – and just gave us home video for nothing," explained Peter Davis to *Screen International* in 2005. The deal led to the first season of *Highlander: The Series* becoming the first box set of a US TV series to be released on VHS, leading to sales of 30,000 units in 1995. Christopher Lambert wasn't so happy about the decision to use his likeness during the promotion of the series on video. "What I didn't like was that they put my face on video boxes to try and sell more and to try to scam the audience into thinking I was in *all* those episodes. That makes me *furious*."

Davis-Panzer had first seen the value in retaining the rights to merchandise following their release of *Highlander II* in the US. According to Guy Collins, because they had self-distributed the film, they could license individual rights for short periods of time, making more money on each deal. "People will tell you that with independent films you can't make any money out of merchandising. Whatever else *Highlander* did, it showed that if you got behind it and had some creative ideas, you could do it, and they did."

DVDs from the series would go on to sell upwards of 200,000 units per season, earning Davis-Panzer an estimated $50 million in wholesale revenues by 2005, with merchandise soon becoming a staple part of their income when legendaryheroes.com opened for business, the go-to destination for *Highlander* fans looking to stock up on replica swords and jewellery. The site also sold helmets, armour and other clothing for TV series such as *Hercules: The Legendary Journeys* (1995–99) and *Xena: Warrior Princess* (1995–2001), and films including *The Lord of the Rings* trilogy, the *Conan* films and *Gladiator* (2000).

While the TV series was still on air, *Highlander* also found itself moving into the world of animation, with the debut of *Highlander: The Animated Series* on the USA Network in September 1994. Set in a post-apocalyptic 27th century, it followed the adventures of Connor MacLeod's descendant, Quentin (Miklos Perlos), dubbed 'The Last of the MacLeods', who battled the evil Kortan. In this version, Quentin attempted to gain their Quickening and their knowledge by sharing a sword rather than by a beheading. Forty episodes of the series aired between 1994 and 1996.

Soon after *Highlander: The Series* ended in 1998, a spin-off premiered in the shape of *Highlander: The Raven*, which focused on the character of Amanda (Elizabeth Gracen), who had featured in the parent series. Despite praise for its impressive stunt work and use of flashbacks, the series lasted just 22 episodes and ended in 1999.

Though screenwriters Peter Bellwood and Larry Ferguson weren't involved with *Highlander: The Series* or anything that followed ("I met Adrian Paul briefly," says Bellwood. "I think I was drunk, or he was, or we both were, but other than that I haven't had any connection with subsequent incarnations of *Highlander*"), the credits to each episode mention that the show is "based on characters created by Gregory Widen", despite the fact that all three men had an input into the script that was filmed by Russell Mulcahy.

This stems from a decision by Bellwood and Ferguson to enter into arbitration with the Writers Guild of America over who should receive credit for creating the story in the *Highlander* script. Says Ferguson, "What happens with the Guild is that if there are more than two or three writers on a project, the studio comes up with their recommendations when they submit the script to the Guild. Before the Guild makes a determination as to what the final credits will be on the script, they assign three arbiters. Those arbiters are not supposed to be in contact with anyone else except the Guild representative, who shuttles back and forth between those three people, and they have to have a unanimous decision and that's what the credits will be."

Although the pair received payment for their *Highlander* script, Ferguson points out that they were also keen to receive story credit. "We do make a lot of money when we write a screenplay, more than a writer normally makes because we sell the copyright, which means that the producer can and does hire other writers to work on making amendments to what we've done. That means we lose control over it, and story credit is only important because it means you own the characters."

Explaining that neither he nor Peter Bellwood completely understood the rules of arbitration at the time, especially when dealing with original material, Ferguson tells me that they wrote to the Guild stating their case. "Because we were neophytes at that time, we sat down and said, 'Well, we think we've created the story,' and we made some arguments to that. We recommended the story credit read: 'Story by Peter Bellwood and Larry Ferguson, script by Gregory Widen, Peter Bellwood and Larry Ferguson'. Had we not brought that issue up, the story credit would probably not have been an issue because nobody was claiming it. Because we did, and because the rules of the Guild are what they are, this long article proved ultimately to be an instrument of our own destruction."

In the end, the Guild awarded Gregory Widen sole story credit, meaning he had ownership of the name 'Connor MacLeod' and others. Says Ferguson, "After it went to TV and made everybody famously rich, since we did not have story credit but Gregory Widen did, he was given a percentage of everything that happened in terms of money."

The saga continues

Having an ongoing *Highlander* TV series didn't stop development on a third feature film, with Bill Panzer teaming up with writer Brad Mirman, who had previously penned Christopher Lambert's 1992 film, *Knight Moves*, to develop a story that would see a new Immortal take on Connor MacLeod. Music video director Andrew Morahan stood in for Russell Mulcahy this time around. "To me the real sequel to *Highlander* is *Highlander III*," states Lambert.

Written by Mirman, Paul Ohl and René Manzor, the script to *Highlander III: The Sorcerer* begins after the death of Heather in Connor MacLeod's native Scotland and sees the Highlander travel to Japan to train under fellow Immortal, the sorcerer Nakano (Mako). MacLeod soon encounters another Immortal, Kane (Mario Van Peebles), who kills Nakano and is trapped in a cave as a result of the energy caused by the subsequent Quickening. Centuries later, Kane tracks MacLeod down to New York in 1994 and the pair must fight to win the Prize.

According to Lambert, the director of *Highlander III*, which also went under the title of *Highlander III: The Final Conflict* and *Highlander III: The Final Dimension* among others, was perfect "because of his understanding of the first *Highlander*. I was convinced we could do a sequel that would be good, if not better, than one." With a budget of $26 million, the film grossed just over $12 million at the worldwide box office.

"We did *Highlander III*, which probably was the best of them outside of the original, in Canada," explains Guy Collins, who adds that he convinced Harvey Weinstein to become the film's US distributor under the Miramax banner. "Then Harvey, being true to form, nicked the fourth one and did it through Dimension, which is the Miramax genre division."

The fourth film, *Highlander: Endgame*, was released in 2000, and was an attempt to unite the universe of the Lambert films with Adrian Paul's TV series. Written by Joel Soisson and directed by Doug Aarniokoski, the film sees Connor MacLeod return to the village of Glenfinnan in 1555 to help protect his mother, Caiolin MacLeod (June Watson), from village priest Jacob Kell (Bruce Payne). When his mother is burned at the stake by Kell, MacLeod kills both him and his adopted father, Father Rainey (Donald Douglas), only for Kell to be revealed as an Immortal and to seek vengeance on Connor. Connor must team up with Duncan MacLeod (Adrian Paul) to defeat Kell.

Bringing back Beatie Edney as Heather and Sheila Gish as Rachel, from the original film, *Highlander: Endgame* also featured numerous cast members from *Highlander: The Series*, and was a worthy attempt to unite two disparate elements of the franchise into something resembling a coherent story. "This is a movie about redemption, about two men who are very close," explained Adrian Paul to *Starlog* in 2000. "They've grown together for 2,000 years, and at present both have to deal with problems they had and find redemption in the past."

"In *Highlander: Endgame* I did half of the sword fights," admits Lambert. "I was in great shape but I was tired, not on a physical level, I was tired of all the movies and I wanted to do something else. With the sword fighting, for each movie you trained for 10 to 12 weeks before shooting, by the fourth film I was going, 'You know what, I'll do half the fights and leave the rest to my stunt double,' because I was tired of this sword thing. It shows when you're not happy in a movie." The film was the last *Highlander* movie to be released in cinemas, taking almost $16 million on a $25 million budget and, similarly to *Highlander II*, giving fans an opportunity to see numerous deleted scenes when it finally arrived on DVD.

The franchise lay dormant for a number of years, until 2007 saw two new productions released, beginning with an anime film, *Highlander: The Search for Vengeance*, in June 2007. Written by David Abramowitz, a writer and producer on *Highlander: The Series*, and directed by Yoshiaki Kawajiri, the film takes place in Roman Britain and a future New York, as Colin MacLeod (Alistair Abell) fights his mortal enemy, Marcus Octavius (Nolan North), through the centuries.

The second *Highlander* of the year was *Highlander: The Source*, a follow-up to *Highlander: Endgame*, once again starring Adrian Paul as Duncan MacLeod, but this time destined for a premiere on the Sci-Fi Channel in September 2007 rather than in cinemas. Written by Mark Bradley (a pseudonym for *Highlander: Endgame* writer Joel Soisson) and Steven Kelvin Watkins, and directed by Brett Leonard, the film finds MacLeod searching for a legendary source of immortal power, helped by old friends from the TV series and hindered by the Guardian (Cristian Solimeno).

Unloved by critics – Keith Breese of FilmCritic.com reckoned that "The acting is uniformly terrible, the special effects are hideous, the sets are cheap and grubby, and the direction is uninspired. The film is an utter failure . . ." – and with an audience score on Rotten Tomatoes of just 19%, *The Source* managed to stop the franchise dead in its tracks.

Although screenwriter Larry Ferguson wasn't involved with any of the sequels, at one point he did find time to sit down with Bill Panzer at a Los Angeles bar to discuss his thoughts on where the franchise was going. "I had looked at the sequels and some of the television series and I told him that he did not fully appreciate what the first *Highlander* was. I think that's where I told him what the Quickening was. I tried to explain to him the very subtle difference between science fiction and fantasy, and that the original *Highlander* is a mythical fantasy. It's not about other planets, it has its own myth that you learn about during the film, but it doesn't involve people on another planet. I'm not sure he ever recognised the subtle difference between those two, but they are very different mediums."

Looking back on the films that followed the original *Highlander*, I mention to Guy Collins that it's interesting to watch the trend of none of them doing big business in cinemas while still managing to spawn follow-ups. "It was one of those strange things, in the sense that none of the *Highlander* movies ever took more than $16 or $17 million in the US box office and to make five films where it consistently didn't make money in the cinema . . . it was quite a successful franchise, but it would have been nice if it had worked in the cinema in America."

By the mid-noughties, Collins and his partner Michael Ryan were trying to convince Bill Panzer and Peter Davis that a different approach to the franchise was needed. "Michael and I kept saying to Peter and Bill, 'This is ridiculous, we're making lower and lower tier versions of what was a great, great movie. Why don't we stop fucking about with this and reboot the first film?' It didn't get any traction with Peter or Bill."

Tragically, on 18 March 2007, Panzer fell while ice skating near his home in Idaho and hit his head on the ground, dying in hospital soon after. When Guy Collins next met Peter Davis in Los Angeles, he was given some unexpected news. "He said, 'I have to tell you that I optioned a reboot of the original [*Highlander*] to Summit.' That kind of brought an end to our business dealings with one another."

The deal with Summit Entertainment, then an independent production company before later being bought by Lionsgate, was announced in the trade papers in May 2008, accompanied by the news that the script was to be written by the team behind 2008's *Iron Man*, Art Marcum and Matt Holloway. Summit's co-chairman and president, Patrick Wachsberger, was quoted as saying he was "a huge fan of the original *Highlander* and of its mythology" and that he had "always dreamed of reinventing this franchise; as a brand it is hard to think of one which has greater worldwide recognition with audiences – young and old". Peter Davis, on board as a producer, added that "Summit can now say 'There can be only one.' Again."

The next few years saw a revolving door of talent sign on to the project, including two of the team behind the *Fast & Furious* franchise, director Justin Lin and producer Neal H Moritz; *Twilight* (2008) screenwriter Melissa Rosenberg; *28 Weeks Later* (2007) director Juan Carlos Fresnadillo and actor Ryan Reynolds, who was to star as Connor MacLeod; and *Snow White and the Huntsman* (2012) second unit director Cedric Nicolas-Troyan. Neal Moritz was the only name present in each new announcement, with everyone else departing *Highlander* as the years ticked by.

In 2016 it was revealed that *John Wick* (2014) director Chad Stahelski had signed on to revive the franchise, with *The Hollywood Reporter* quoting him as saying, "I've been a huge fan of the original property since I saw it in high school. Such great themes of immortality, love and identity are all wrapped up in such colorful mythology. I can't think of a better property that gives the opportunity to create interesting characters, mythic themes and action set pieces." In 2018 it was announced that screenwriter Ryan Condal would be providing a new script, with the plan being to leave the ending open for a sequel or potentially a trilogy.

By June 2020, Stahelski was still discussing his plans for *Highlander*, telling *Discovering Film* that he was in "heavy development mode . . . tweaking the scripts, writing, conceptualising sequences, how we're going to do everything."

Then, on 31 October, *Highlander* fandom was rocked by news of the death of Sir Sean Connery at the age of 90, while just four months later it was announced that *Highlander* producer, Peter Davis, had died in his sleep on 21 February 2021. While Connery's involvement with the franchise had ended 20 years earlier, Davis was still very much part of discussions on its future, explains Davis-Panzer Productions' Director of New Media, Kareem Michael Dimashkie.

Dimashkie had met Davis in 2015, connecting with him "because, surprisingly, nobody was working at Davis-Panzer who knew *Highlander* well or agreed with Peter as to the direction it should take creatively. We had the same goals for *Highlander* even though we had a 40-year age gap between us. Bill Panzer was always going to be Peter's one, true business partner in the franchise, but I did my best to continue helping Peter get the franchise on the right track creatively. It's what I continue to do now alongside Peter's son, Josh."

Dimashkie explains that a year before he met him, Davis had been very ill, and that as he recovered thanks to the support of his wife and family, "he reflected deeply on the mistakes he felt were made in the franchise and the personal and business relationships that were strained over the years. He made amends where he could in the time he had left, and I believe he wanted to do more. Through all of it, one thing Peter was determined to get right was the *Highlander* reboot. The first question he'd ask any *Highlander* initiate was, 'What do you feel is the most important aspect of [the first] *Highlander*?' If you said the love story between Connor and Heather, Peter would instantly take a liking to you. It's what he fought for most in all the various iterations of the reboot scripts with the various creative teams that came and went. You'd be surprised how many dismissed that part of Connor's story over the years."

More substantial reboot news broke on 21 May 2021 that actor Henry Cavill (2018's *Mission Impossible: Fallout*) was in talks for a lead role in the new *Highlander*. Now with a script from Kerry Williamson, the film would be produced by Neal H Moritz and Josh Davis, and executive produced by Gregory Widen, Amanda Lewis, and Patrick Wachsberger. An article on *Deadline* explained that, "The plot of this latest take is unknown, as is whether Cavill will be playing a brand new character to the universe or a character from previous projects", while on the same day Cavill excitedly posted on his Facebook and Instagram accounts that he had "Very exciting news today!"

Alongside a small bottle of whisky, a sgian-dubh ankle knife, and copies of two books – *So you're going wear the kilt: All you want to know about tartan dress* and *Those bloody kilts: The Highland soldier in the Great War* – Cavill wrote: "I've been a fan of *Highlander* since I was lad. From the movies in all of their 80s, Queen slathered glory to the TV show with an actor who looked remarkably like one of my brothers. Being not shy with swords, and having a director as talented as Chad Stahelski at the helm, this is an opportunity like no other. Deep diving into franchise storytelling with all the tools at our disposal, is going to make this an adventure I (and hopefully all of you) shall never forget. I've lately been dipping into some of my Scottish heritage, and inadvertently getting my baseline research underway!"

An interview with the actor in November 2021 quoted him as saying, "Stahelski's vision is a more grounded-in-reality take than the original movies and show, and will play a bit more like a modern tragedy", while director Stahelski himself offered more details on his plans. "Henry obviously has the physicality, but that doesn't mean a whole lot if you can't also carry the empathy of a character that's lived 500 years, and I needed somebody who could do both. The character's arc spans hundreds of years and he becomes many different personalities, all of which extend the timeline of his emotional growth."

The director went on to say that during their first meeting, "Henry was immediately riffing on the idea of the burden of immortality and you could see in his eyes that he can transform himself from being a young, vibrant soul to an old, wise soul. He had this combination I was fascinated by. The other thing you could see was his genuineness – he really loves the property and loves what he believes he can do with it, and when an actor has that level of passion, you're going to get something unique."

Despite Kareem Dimashkie's enthusiasm for a new *Highlander* film, any excitement is tinged with sadness. "It hurts that Peter won't be around to see the reboot he worked so hard to make happen, and the same goes for Bill Panzer. I didn't know Bill, but I've heard a lot of stories posthumously about him. He was more instrumental than what is commonly known; particularly with the quality of the TV series alongside creative consultant David Abramowitz. Whatever comes next, we have to remember and respect that it's built on what Bill and Peter began."

Although he's not involved in the franchise today, Guy Collins would still like to see a new film-maker try to redo the first film. "I really hope they do get it together because I think it would warrant a reboot. I mean, so many people plagiarised the immortality aspects of *Highlander* that it would be nice for the audience that wasn't around in the 1980s to see the original remade, I think it could be great."

When I ask Russell Mulcahy about the possibility that his film might be rebooted by a new generation of film-makers, he's more than happy for someone to have a go. "They've been trying to do a remake for ten years. The guy who directed *John Wick* is a brilliant film-maker and he will have a lot more tools at his disposal. My film was done with cardboard and string. When I made the film I wasn't DGA [Directors Guild of America], so I made zip money, but I'm not bitter about that. It's one of the most enjoyable films I've done. I'm not saying it's the greatest film, just that I had a great time making it. I'm proud of it and I wish the remake the best."

Clancy Brown is also open to the idea of another extremely tall actor filling the rather large boots of the Kurgan. "It seems like a pretty simple process. It's not like you wouldn't make the movie better, you would; there's lots of problems with the original. I think you should get Jason [Connery] to play Sean's role, I think that would be fun, he's a good actor. I don't know who you'd get to play Connor. You could go a billion different ways with the Kurgan, you could have him be that *Terminator* guy, or you could have him be Heath Ledger as the Joker."

As for Christopher Lambert, he would give his blessing to a remake, but he questions the need for one. "I don't care, it's fine with me. But what are you going to bring to an audience that's going to be more powerful than Russell's vision, than Queen's music? You can have a voice like Freddie, but on a heart level, Freddie was Freddie, end of story."

On the subject of Queen being involved, Brian May doesn't dismiss the idea when I ask for his thoughts on the subject. "I wouldn't see any point in remaking the first one because it's a classic. I would rather it wasn't messed with, but making a spin-off or a sequel to that would make sense; it'd be something nice to work on. The subsequent films were in a very different kind of place, a very different flavour and we weren't involved, which we were sad about at the time, but they chose to go a different way. But if there were something which was a bit closer to the spirit of the original that we could get involved with, I think Roger and I would be very keen to look at that."

Discussion of a new film brings us to the subject of whether it should even be made for a cinema audience, with Lambert keen on another direction for the franchise. "[Going] to the movies is more and more expensive. Smaller movies are [a good way] to tell a story. All the TV series of the last seven or eight years are amazing. I would love to do a [Netflix or Amazon Prime] show. If they were doing *Highlander* today I'd play Sean Connery and have fun with it, being the mentor."

Should a sequel, prequel, remake or reboot ever happen, one of the most important considerations for the production team will be how to make it appeal to a new generation of viewers, while still attracting the fans that have remained loyal since *Highlander* first graced cinema screens in 1986.

EIGHTEEN

HIGHLANDER'S LEGACY

"I've never done one of these before and I said to my good friend, Clancy Brown, 'Are you going? Did they ask you?' and he said, 'Yeah, but I'm not available, I'm working.' I said, 'I'm really nervous,' and he said 'Don't be, they love *Highlander*, the fans are really fun.' So I thought, 'OK, he wouldn't steer me wrong.'"

It's June 2018 and Roxanne Hart is taking 20 minutes out of an exhausting day of signing autographs and posing for photographs in what could easily be mistaken for an aircraft hangar in Birmingham, England.

The National Exhibition Centre covers some 611 acres on the outskirts of the city, welcoming over six million people to more than 500 events each year, including such diverse events as Crufts (the biggest dog show in the world) and The UK Concrete Show (the biggest selection of concrete products in the UK). Today it's the turn of Collectormania 25 – Film & Comic Con Birmingham, a chance for film, TV, sports, comics and gaming fans to gather and meet actors, athletes, writers and other creative types to make themselves available for autographs, photos and talks for a small – or sometimes not so small – fee.

The fans come from all walks of life, many of them dressing up as their favourite characters to show their allegiance and perhaps make some connections with other fans. Such events are now commonplace around the world, turning what was once a cottage industry of conventions into a large-scale, often cut-throat, business. For a period of time, starting in the late 1970s and lasting well into the noughties, a hundred or so fans would descend on provincial towns to meet stars of long defunct sci-fi shows in hotel conference rooms for conventions.

Fans would bring along their VHS covers to get signed, hearing stories from behind the scenes of their favourite shows at panel discussions. Fans got to shake the hand of their favourite Doctor/Captain/Monster, while the actors collected a few thousand pounds in cash for a weekend's work. As a friend once dryly observed, "Convention rhymes with pension."

While such small-scale events haven't disappeared entirely, they have bred the likes of Collectormania. Rather than focusing on one series, the guest booking policy is more scattergun, with names drawn from numerous films and TV shows as each one tries to bag celebrities beloved of multiple generations of fangirls and boys. If the star of the latest CW show doesn't float your boat, perhaps meeting the cast of *The Dukes of Hazzard* will do the trick.

Queuing outside the hangar to meet Roxanne Hart and her fellow attendees Christopher Lambert and Beatie Edney, I'd spotted multiple versions of The Riddler (both male and female) rubbing shoulders with Wolverines, Jedi, Punishers, steampunk cosplayers and zombies. On entry, it's easy to spot the event's guests, with giant banners hanging behind tables around the hall proudly showing photos of them at the height of their powers, whether that's *Lethal Weapon*'s Danny Glover, *Casino Royale*'s Mads Mikkelsen or Hammer Scream Queen, Valerie Leon. Some of them look remarkably well preserved and almost the same as they did 40 years ago, while with others it's hard to tell if it's them or an elderly uncle looking after their seat while they nip to the toilet.

Thirty years on from playing Brenda, the 65-year-old Roxanne Hart escapes from behind her signing table to meet me in a quiet corner. With so many cosplayers dressing up to meet their heroes, I wondered if she'd encountered any other Brenda Wyatts in her signing queue. "Beatie had a couple of little kids that were dressed like she was, but no, I haven't seen any Brendas."

As she sips from her bottle of water, I ask what it's like meeting fans after more than 30 years. "It's amazing. People come up to me and say, 'I'm old enough to have watched it in the theatre,' and I say, 'I'm old enough to have made it!' More than a dozen people that came up to me said it impacted them in a significant way in their lives. I don't know what it was about that movie."

What has surprised Hart the most is the film's longevity, the fact that fans have embraced it and made it their own, new generations discovering it and passing it on to their own sons and daughters. "I remember the film sort of coming and going when it opened in Los Angeles. My brother was working in Boston and he called me up several years after the film had been released and said, 'You know, Rox, the film has midnight showings and it's like *The Rocky Horror Picture Show*. These people all dress up like Highlanders and they stand around the block to go to these midnight showings. It's a huge cult film.'"

A fandom is born

It was in 1986 that the first piece of *Highlander* merchandise arrived in bookstores, Garry Douglas' 252-page novelisation of the script that took readers deeper into the story. Douglas fleshed out some parts of what was seen on screen – explaining that Connor was away hunting when the Kurgan came to the forge and killed Ramirez, revealing that MacLeod first met Kastagir in the Zulu Wars of 1879, and, most bizarrely, sending Brenda to Miami to meet her father during the events of the film – and gave fans a chance to relive the adventure months before the film would arrive on video cassette.

Also in 1986, Ocean released the first computer game based on *Highlander* for the ZX Spectrum, Amstrad CPC and Commodore 64, allowing players to take on the role of Connor MacLeod as he fought Ramirez, Fizir (Fasil in the film) and the Kurgan. In his

2015 book *Terrible Old Games You've Probably Never Heard Of*, author Stuart Ashen wrote that *Highlander* features "two albino Lego models trying to smash each other apart with sticks" and that the gameplay is so clumsy that "you could only effectively respond to an opponent's attack if he sent you details on a postcard a week in advance".

Ashen's view that playing the game was "one of the least entertaining ways you could possibly spend your time" was backed up by *Crash* magazine in 1986, who said it was "totally boring and quite unplayable", while *Sinclair User* described it as a "Golden Turkey" and awarded it two out of five.

In the decades that followed, *Highlander* merchandise sporadically appeared in stores and online, though with a fan base significantly smaller than the likes of *Star Wars*, there were never any guarantees that the latest item would lead to more. It was following the creation of the 1990s TV series that licensees realised there was a large enough audience willing to buy items stamped with the *Highlander* logo, while Davis-Panzer's own website and merchandise catalogues were popular with fans keen to own the latest clothing, swords or books relating to their favourite show.

A March 2006 branding document produced by Davis-Panzer gives an idea of the situation during the 20th anniversary of the original film's release, noting that by that point over $100 million of merchandise had been sold via the catalogue, over the internet and via telemarketing, and that the database of "hardcore fans" exceeded two million at that point. A re-release of 1986's *Highlander* on DVD in 1999 had stayed in the top 15 DVD sales for 35 weeks and generated sales of one million units. Each of the sequels had also sold in excess of one million units on DVD, while sales of *Highlander: The Series* on DVD had generated a wholesale gross of approximately $30 million.

The first film has been released multiple times on multiple formats, from its earliest incarnation on VHS through to high-definition Blu-rays and streaming versions. Each edition usually brings its own special features offering further insight into the creation of the film. Two commentaries exist for the film, the first featuring producers Peter Davis and Bill Panzer alongside director Russell Mulcahy, the second featuring just Mulcahy, and they're an important record of the decisions taken during filming and in post-production. There are also documentaries, deleted scenes, memos and photo galleries scattered across different DVDs and Blu-rays, with fans snapping up each new release to try and obtain the highest quality sound and picture and perhaps some new nuggets of information in the extras.

Other merchandise produced in the aftermath of *Highlander: The Series* included 14 original novels set in its universe and published by Warner Aspect; action figures of characters from *Highlander: The Animated Series*; numerous 12-inch action figures from the first film and the TV series from Sideshow Collectibles; three comic book miniseries from Dynamite Entertainment released between 2007 and 2009; the first 13 issues called simply *Highlander*; the second four-issue series called *Highlander: Way of the Sword*, and the third called *Highlander Origins: Kurgan*; two seasons of audio adventures based on the TV series from Big Finish Productions in 2009 and 2011; and a five-issue comic book series, *Highlander: The American Dream*, released in 2017 by IDW.

A number of *Highlander* games have also been released through the years, including 1996's *Highlander: The Card Game*, described as "a collectible trading card game of swashbuckling swordplay and dark intrigue"; 2018's *Highlander: The Duel*, a "head-to-head battle game for two players" in which "Connor MacLeod pits his fighting prowess against the massive Kurgan in a battle to the death"; and 2019's *Highlander: The Board Game*, "A fast-paced game of strategy and chance in which up to six Immortals battle to claim the Prize".

Actor Adrian Paul, Duncan MacLeod in *Highlander: The Series*, took what he learned about swordplay and martial arts on six seasons of the show and turned it into *The Sword Experience*, a training course that he tours around the world, meeting fans in person and passing on some of the knowledge he picked up from mentors such as swordmaster Bob Anderson.

Revisiting *A Kind of Magic*

Decades on from the release of *A Kind of Magic* and the death of Freddie Mercury in 1991, Queen are still one of the biggest rock acts on the planet. Not only did the 2018 biographical film *Bohemian Rhapsody* gross over $900 million worldwide, but Brian May and Roger Taylor still perform their songs with Adam Lambert as lead singer at sold-out gigs around the world.

"Adam sings 'Who Wants to Live Forever' like an angel; it's absolutely riveting," says Taylor, before explaining that it's a highlight of every show. "Apart from that we don't really do 'A Kind of Magic' very much these days. I used to sing it after we lost Freddie, but I kind of like being behind the drums. It's not easy having a lead vocalist behind drums. It's doable, but it's not preferable."

Highlander's music supervisor Derek Power is keen to see an official *Highlander* soundtrack materialise after all these years, finally replacing some of the bootleg editions that appear online and at record fairs. "To this day, I have a record company that calls me every couple of years saying, 'Well, is there anything new from Brian May?' I would dearly love to have had a soundtrack album. We had one, but it was called *A Kind of Magic*. It wasn't the soundtrack of the movie, it was six or seven songs from *Highlander* and other material. That was my great disappointment. It would be fantastic to do a remastered version of the tracks from the score and the songs."

One potential stumbling block for such a project could be the whereabouts of the original tapes containing an unmixed version of Michael Kamen's score and longer cues of tracks edited down for use on the film. "The last time we checked, [20th Century Fox] couldn't find them," says Power. "Things moved around in a lot of ways in a lot of places. I'm sure that the Queen tracks exist."

One piece of music fans of both *Highlander* and Queen have long wanted to hear in its full-length glory is Freddie Mercury's rendition of the Frank Sinatra hit, 'New York, New York', a few lines of which can be heard during the car sequence in New York.

Could a longer version ever be released? "It comes up every now and again as a thought, but it's only a snippet as he only sang that little bit, it's not a complete track," explains Brian May. "It would fit very nicely on the soundtrack album of course; that's the place for it. There's certainly a few bits of orchestra underscoring that I worked on with Michael, which I played guitar to and which didn't make it into the cut, so it would be interesting to fish all that out and play around with it."

Would May and the rest of the band ever agree to a release of a complete *Highlander* soundtrack album? Though he feels Queen made the right decision in making *A Kind of Magic* their 12th studio album, May adds that he's "always had a tinge of regret that we didn't do the complete soundtrack album" with Michael Kamen, before stating that at one point he "got as far as putting a rough version together" before he had to move on to other projects.

"It would have been a great thing, and actually when Michael went, I spoke to his wife and said, 'That's still in my mind; it's still a dream of mine to put that album together properly, so that posterity has a complete *Highlander* soundtrack album. I'd love to do it at some point, but it's just a question of finding the moment I suppose and getting on with it. I would definitely like to do that; it's on my bucket list."

The show must go on

For fans not fortunate enough to be able to catch Queen at one of their stadium gigs, there is still a way to revel in their music thanks to a number of tribute bands who keep the union flag flying at their concerts.

"I always remember watching Live Aid in 1985 and seeing Queen," says Joseph Lee Jackson, lead singer of Mercury, the tribute act he formed in 1989 along with the ersatz Brian May, Glenn Scrimshaw. "Prior to Mercury I used to do musical theatre, and I was like a sponge, trying to learn as much as I could. The day after

Freddie died, they showed *Queen Live in Budapest* on TV. I always had so much respect [for Freddie], he was a phenomenal showman, had a fantastic voice, and was a fantastic musician. It was just a shame he had to leave us. I never thought for one minute I'd be doing this for a living, portraying Freddie Mercury as a lookalike."

Jackson and Scrimshaw aim to make their concerts a musical time machine for the audience, transporting them back to when they saw Queen live or experienced one of their songs with a loved one. "We want to make it as close as we can to an original Queen show," says Jackson. "Obviously it's on a smaller scale, but music's a great medium. It brings so many emotions and so many memories back to you."

Just as Roger Taylor feels 'Who Wants to Live Forever' is a show highlight for Queen, Jackson is also aware of the power it has over an audience. "The amount of times we've had people asking for it because it's their husband or wife's favourite, or they had it played at a funeral. It's one of those songs that captures that moment for four minutes. Depending on where the gig is and how you're feeling, it's one of those songs that can take you away as well, you get wrapped up in the music and forget where you are. It always goes down really well."

Although the band are fans of the *A Kind of Magic* album, not every song is suited to being played on stage every night. "'Princes of the Universe' is a phenomenal song, but I don't know if you'd be able to do that live because it's so bloomin' high for a start," continues Jackson. "A lot of Queen's stuff is demanding, it's very complex music and that one is challenging due to how high it is."

As for the song that gets the best audience reaction, Jackson is clear that 'A Kind of Magic' is hard to beat. "We don't do the *Highlander* version that they play at the end [of the film]. I absolutely love that version, but we do it like Queen did it live. It's one of those songs where you can be anywhere in the world having a good time on stage, but you might not have captured the audience. But you bang in 'A Kind of Magic' and all of a sudden it takes it from being 50 degrees to 150 degrees. It's one of those songs like 'Don't Stop Me Now' that always goes down well; it transports the gig to somewhere else."

Getting creative

An aspect of *Highlander*'s legacy that goes beyond the merchandise is its fandom, the tens of thousands of people who are happier having the film and its progeny in their lives.

One of *Highlander*'s most prominent fans is writer and director Adam F. Goldberg, whose autobiographical comedy series, *The Goldbergs*, arrived on America's ABC network in 2013. Set in Pennsylvania in the 1980s, the show follows Goldberg's early life, with each episode riffing on elements of 1980s pop culture. Of particular interest to *Highlander* fans is the presence of Clancy Brown as one of young Adam's teachers, Mr Crosby, who plays an important part in the 2019 episode, 'There Can Only Be One Highlander Club'.

"Ever since *The Goldbergs* began, one of my dreams was to write an homage to *Highlander*," said Adam Goldberg during promotion of the episode. "In high school, I was so obsessed with the movie that I started an actual *Highlander* club with my two best friends Mike Levy and David Sirota. What began as a few geeks hitting each other with swords we made in wood shop soon became a school-wide game with 20 people playing. It became so disruptive that the administration had to shut it down." The episode sees two rival *Highlander* clubs started by pupils and features Queen's 'Princes of the Universe' on the soundtrack. It appears to have been written just so that Clancy Brown can say the words "There can be only one . . . *Highlander* club".

Continued Goldberg, "My *Highlander* obsession never died and it's why I ended up casting Clancy Brown as Mr Crosby the shop teacher two years ago. I've been a long-time fan of his talent and *The Goldbergs* marks his first network comedy. It was perfectly fitting to put Clancy Brown – the Kurgan – in our *Highlander* episode which I've been waiting to tell ever since the show began. We not only perfectly replicated the costumes and sword choreography, we got Queen's approval to use their song from the soundtrack. It's one of my favourite episodes we've ever made, and I can safely say the only *Highlander* sitcom episode that's been made!"

Not every *Highlander* fan produces their own TV series in which they can profess their love for the film, but many of them still go to extraordinary lengths to channel their passion into something that might inspire others.

One fan who saw the film soon after its original release is Grant Kempster, who has a clear memory of standing at a bus stop in Brighton, England with his mother in 1986 and "looking at the gorgeous Brian Bysouth poster, wondering what it was about. Years later, when it arrived on VHS, I rented it when I was staying at a friend's house in the summer and we watched it twice in a row." Noting that it was Russell Mulcahy and Gerry Fisher's visuals that initially hooked him, it wasn't until he spied a poster for *Highlander II* in the lobby of his local cinema that he "felt a rising excitement and anticipation. I think that this might have been the moment that I knew that *Highlander* was it for me. I'd found the film that would be my BFF (Best Film Forever)."

Around the same time as Kempster found out there was a *Highlander* appreciation society, 'Clan', he also discovered it was closing down. This led him to contact the organiser, Joe O'Callaghan, and *Highlander* rights holders Davis-Panzer to ask for their blessing to start a new society, Clan: The Renegade Highlander Appreciation Society, along with its own magazine, *Highlander Heart*. By the mid-nineties, Kempster was writing articles and designing the magazine using his work PC. "I absolutely loved creating the magazines. It was a way of pouring my love for the franchise into something physical."

Each issue included the latest news from the *Highlander* universe, discussing developments on the long-mooted reboot or giving updates on stars from the franchise, before reviewing the latest spin-off novels or audio adventures. Interviews with high-profile cast and crew were also regular features, alongside fan artwork and fresh takes on elements of the films and TV series that particularly irked or enamoured the writers.

One of Kempster's most memorable experiences was visiting the Romanian set of *Highlander: Endgame*. "It was so incredibly immersive; standing in the graveyard, surrounded by Peter [Wingfield], Jim [Byrnes], Adrian [Paul] and Christophe [Lambert], and watching them shoot scenes in character. There's no amount of convention attendance that could rival that in my mind. The final day I was there, Christophe was shooting the flashback scene where he was imprisoned and I'll forever have the sight of him emerging in full Highland dress and walking towards me etched in my mind."

Though Kempster enjoyed the creativity and the chance to bring people together, the logistics of running a club and magazine weren't so much fun. "Getting the copies made at the local photocopy place and sending them all out or getting in membership fees to cover costs, which they never did, was time-consuming and as life became more complicated, I became less and less able to continue." As technology moved on, *Highlander Heart* left behind its physical form and moved online, with the print magazine ending and a Facebook page taking its place. Today the group boasts in excess of 5,000 members, with daily discussions covering aspects of *Highlander* lore, favourite moments from the series and where copies of Connor's sword can be bought online.

"This gets bandied about a lot, but at this point the fandom is like a family for me," says Kempster when I ask him to explain what *Highlander* fandom means to him. "When I attended the last *Highlander Worldwide* convention in LA, I was equally looking forward to meeting friends I'd made in the group as much as I was seeing the cast and crew. And for good reason. When a group of people share a love and passion for anything, there's an immense pleasure in being around them."

The convention referenced by Kempster, *Highlander Worldwide: The Gathering*, took place in Los Angeles in October 2017 and allowed fans of *Highlander: The Series* to quiz their heroes at panels and meet them over coffee and at the bar. The event was the tenth organised by a small team of fans headed up by the Australia-based Carmel Macpherson, whose *Highlander DownUnder* events in the 1990s morphed into the *Worldwide* conventions in 2004 and soon went global.

Another popular Facebook group is *Highlander Rewatched*, the online presence of the podcast of the same name that was established in 2015 by three Philadelphia natives: Eamon Dougherty, Keith Garabedian and Kyle Garabedian. The trio set themselves a mission to watch every episode of *Highlander: The Series* and then record an episode detailing their thoughts for the podcast. All three hosts discovered the franchise through the television show and the weekly exploits of Connor's cousin, Duncan.

"I remember being drawn to the entirely romantic concept of people in modern-day fighting with swords," says Keith Garabedian. "Something seemed noble about it, likened to Obi-Wan's quote in *Star Wars* about a lightsabre: 'An elegant weapon for a more civilised age'. In Duncan MacLeod I found a hero who always tried to do what was right. I wanted to be that sort of person."

For Dougherty, it was the opening credits and Queen's 'Princes of the Universe' theme song that captured his imagination. "I would often sing it to myself even before we started the podcast. The mysterious imagery of Duncan MacLeod, the Highlander, stalking through a steamy city wearing a trench coat, sword in hand, was more than enough to capture my young imagination forever."

"The thing that really captured my imagination initially was the sword fights," explains Kyle Garabedian. "I thought it was so cool that this relic of another age was transported into modern times. It was almost like the flashbacks in reverse. *Highlander* not only transports you to the past, it brings elements of the past into a modern context in a really fun way."

It was after rewatching the first season of the TV series on DVD that Keith Garabedian decided a podcast could work, with Kyle and Eamon enthusiastic enough to join him. Says Keith,

"*Highlander*, the film and series, asks potent questions about our existence and the human condition. Those questions are always worth revisiting at different stages of your life." The team has now recorded hundreds of episodes and covered numerous aspects of the *Highlander* universe, boasting thousands of listeners in over 50 countries worldwide.

As well as interviewing key members of the cast and crew, including Christopher Lambert and Adrian Paul, in some cases they've become friends with them. "My biggest highlight of this podcast adventure was interviewing *Highlander: The Series* actor Stan Kirsch," says Keith Garabedian, adding that the pair became friends when he helped produce a podcast for Kirsch's acting studio. "The circumstances in life that lead me down a road to eventually become friends with a childhood hero are pretty amazing." Tragically, Kirsch, who played Richie Ryan, passed away in 2020 at the age of just 51. "I miss hearing Stan's voice and laugh on our weekly phone calls. I will always treasure those memories."

As well as being fans themselves, the team now have their own fan base who listen to the episodes, buy the badges and follow their progress on social media. "We've met many generous, kind people who have welcomed us with open arms, sent us cool *Highlander* facts, goodies, snacks and well wishes," adds Dougherty. "It's very humbling, in a good way."

"You could probably write a whole book on just the *Highlander* fandom," states Kyle Garabedian, referencing the fact it's composed of such a diverse group of people. "It spans all ages and every fan seems to be pulled in from something completely different, from the romance to the martial arts. I feel like you can tell a lot about each fan by looking at what episodes or facets of the franchise speak to them and from their take on the moral decisions. As some kind of remake moves forward, I'm excited to see who it brings into the fandom."

Evidence that there can't be only one *Highlander* podcast comes in the shape of *Blood of Kings*, founded by the US-based Kevin Reitzel in 2016. Reitzel first discovered *Highlander* on VHS at his local video store, intrigued by the cover featuring Connor MacLeod wearing a trench coat and brandishing a sword. "I asked myself, who was this present-day dude using a sword? It's such an iconic look." On watching the film, Reitzel began to wonder how he might handle immortality if the gift, or curse, was given to him. "I also loved the romance in the film, and how Connor honoured his mortal wife Heather till her dying day."

Reitzel was already podcasting about other pop culture subjects when the idea to launch a new show about *Highlander* came to him. "I knew my good friend Norman was a big *Highlander* fan too, as we both played the *Highlander* card game. So in early 2016 we started the podcast. Highlights have been interacting with the wonderful fan base and interviewing many *Highlander* celebrities and wonderful people behind the scenes. My other highlights have been attending several conventions. My original co-host Norman has moved on to other podcasts and my new co-host Lee is also a huge fan of *Highlander*, martial arts with swords and has visited Scotland."

Indeed, visiting Scotland is almost a prerequisite to work on *Blood of Kings*, with Reitzel also having made his way to Connor MacLeod's homeland with his fiancée in 2018. "We took a special trip to England and Scotland to visit as many of the *Highlander* filming locations as we could. Our three favourite locations were Eilean Donan Castle, the church where Connor and the Kurgan meet, and the beach where Ramirez teaches Connor about the Quickening."

Eilean Donan Castle remains something of a Mecca for *Highlander* fans, with general manager David Win telling me that while they've had around 28 different movies filmed there over the years, "there's no doubt *Highlander* is the one everybody recognises. We get a lot of *Highlander* fans, but some are more extreme than others. One couple comes here maybe eight to ten times a year and they have all sorts of *Highlander* memorabilia. You wouldn't believe the number of people that run across the bridge shouting 'MacLeod!' A couple of years ago we had a *Highlander*-themed wedding, and guests came to the castle bedecked in a variety of interesting outfits."

For Kevin Reitzel, being part of *Highlander* fandom is "a special thing. *Highlander* fans are a smaller fandom, but we're very close and love this world that the original 1986 *Highlander* film introduced us to. It's an honour that I get to be part of the fantastic fandom and bring our fans closer together as we share our stories, memories and podcasts with others."

Looking to the future

One subject that regularly comes up in *Highlander* fandom is the future of the franchise, with regular news items regarding reboots and remakes fuelling discussion in Facebook groups and podcast episodes.

For Kevin Reitzel, the first film holds a special place in his heart and is one of his top five movies of all time. "It's something that my fiancée and I love and share together. It's beautifully shot by director Russell Mulcahy, with wonderful locations. It has one of the best musical scores by Michael Kamen, and a great soundtrack by the legendary band Queen. This movie transports you back in time in a fantastic and memorable way."

Despite his love of the original film, he's keen to see the franchise return from the dead. "The universe that the original *Highlander* movie, sequels and the TV show gave us is too rich to never be explored again. *Highlander* should return in movies or television, as long as it honours the original source material. I don't mind if certain details change, as long as it originates in Scotland around a Highland clan."

"The first film is a masterpiece and a classic film, not just a cult classic," reckons *Highlander Rewatched*'s Eamon Dougherty. "The characters are iconic, the story timeless. The phrase 'There can be only one' has entered our shared lexicon, people reference it and don't even know where the phrase originates from. Who knew you could take fantasy, history, action, romance and film noir, smash them all together, and come out of the other side with a hit movie?" Dougherty would welcome a new film in the franchise, not necessarily a remake of the original. "I would like to see another movie, but I think there is great potential in another TV series, a big budget one that explores other Immortals, or another Immortal protagonist."

"The first film still holds up incredibly well," adds Kyle Garabedian. "The music, both Queen and the score, is second to none and it might boast the best training montage on film. It is definitely still essential viewing even decades later. I tend not to have much of an issue with sequels or remakes; if it sucks, just ignore it. I think epic shows like *Game of Thrones* have really shown what is possible and that audiences have the patience to follow a fairly complicated narrative embracing lots of characters. Showing a diverse group of Immortals through different times and conflicts could be pretty amazing TV."

As for Keith Garabedian, he's also happy to sit and watch the 1986 film today, explaining that while it may not be a perfect film, "it's a film that came together perfectly". He's excited about the idea of a return of the franchise, though he feels it's essential that it retains its humanity. "The original script is so rich with meaning regarding the eternal battle between good and evil, oneness with nature, and ponders the great questions of the human condition. As long as *Highlander* keeps that human core, that romance, that loss and sadness, I believe it will be a franchise that will once again captivate new generations' hearts and minds all over the world.

For *Highlander Heart*'s Grant Kempster, watching the first film is "almost like sitting down with an old friend for a few hours and catching up. My eldest two watched it a year or so ago and they got what I saw in it, but the visuals that I loved then were very much of their time and as a result they've dated. That said, *Highlander* exists as perhaps one of the most eighties movies ever made and I think it can be enjoyed by a younger audience with that in mind."

Like the other fans I've spoken to, Kempster has strong feelings about the world he's committed so much of his life to. He's in no doubt that the franchise should return in some shape or form.

"The greatest thing about the movie and the franchise as a whole is that it is, in a very real sense, immortal," says Kempster, adding that the themes and ideas of splicing the past with the modern day in such a visceral way "will always be exciting". He feels that simply ignoring the events of the first film would be a shame and that "there is always a way of explaining away the concept that the original still exists in continuity. The franchise as a whole is so disjointed that the only way you can explain it as a whole is to imagine separate timelines and in a way, a reboot is just that. Another timeline where Immortals battle and a different Connor wins the Prize; that way everyone wins and a new generation can enjoy the story that we grew up loving without laughing at the dated aesthetics and effects."

Though most fans can see some of the cracks in the veneer of the first film, it's clear that elements such as Russell Mulcahy's vibrant direction, a script that easily shifts gears between comedy and drama, the music of both Michael Kamen and Queen, and, perhaps most crucially, a central love story that resonates with anyone who has lost a loved one, keeps them coming back time after time.

As Eamon Dougherty says when asked about his feelings regarding the film, "Like Connor MacLeod at the end of the film, us fans are all inheritors of the Prize. The Prize is *Highlander*."

EPILOGUE

For an actor with a long-held policy of not discussing *Highlander*, celebrating the film's 30th anniversary at a Scottish red carpet premiere in front of an eager press pack must have been a strange situation for Clancy Brown.

An email had dropped into my inbox in May 2016 to announce the premiere of *Highlander*'s new 4K digital restoration at the Edinburgh International Film Festival, quoting Brown as saying that it had taken a while "but I swore to myself that I would return to Scotland after filming *Highlander* 30 years ago where I first learned of Robert the Bruce, James Macpherson, The Fortingall Yew and, most blissfully, single malt Scotch whisky."

I was standing outside Edinburgh's Cineworld to film a short YouTube video with the actor, waiting in line with other journalists. Suddenly he was in front of us in full Highland dress, looking comfortable in his kilt and rocking some shades as he posed for photos with his wife, son and daughter. For his children, that night's screening of *Highlander* would be the first time they had ever seen the film. Brown's hair may have been greyer, but he was still recognisable as the Immortal who had terrorised New York in 1985.

A notoriously private man, when Brown had spoken of *Highlander* through the years, it wasn't always with pleasure.

Journalists knew not to probe too deeply on the subject, so I was uncertain how he'd respond to my questions on camera. Not that they were particularly probing, designed to elicit a few soundbites that could be easily edited into my three-minute video.

One thing I was keen to know was what it was like being back in Scotland after so many years. "It's weird," admitted Brown. "I've stayed away from the *Highlander* universe for a long time, so it's a little strange that it's 30 years and it won't go away and that it's getting this kind of treatment. It's astounding. And that I'm the only guy here. Where the hell is Sean, where the hell is Roxanne, where the hell is Chris and Russell, where are those guys? Maybe they don't like me, maybe that's why they're not here, they knew I was going to be here . . ."

He may have been joking, but he'd made a valid point. It felt odd that Brown was the only member of the cast or crew in attendance and on his triumphant return to the *Highlander* fold, nobody else that he'd worked with was there to welcome him back. He then moved on down the line of journalists, each waiting to ask him roughly the same questions, before meeting a gaggle of fans and professional autograph hunters clutching DVD covers and posters to be signed and asking for selfies.

It wasn't until the next day that I got the opportunity to speak to him properly. Sitting down at Edinburgh's Caledonian Hotel, the actor was open about why he's kept away from conventions and events through the years. "I didn't like the producers much. They weren't really film-makers, they were just salesmen. If Panzer and Davis were involved I wasn't interested. I think [the fans] have been exploited in a bad way until now."

He looks back on his time as the Kurgan with something approaching bemusement, happy to know that it still holds up as a piece of entertainment and that the fans love his character, even if he is unable to put his finger on the exact reasons behind its longevity. "It's a weird alchemy," he muses, before touching on the central theme of the film. "That was one of the things that really worked, the romantic idea that love lasts forever. What the fuck?

What if it doesn't last forever? You last forever but your love dies? Can you find it again? And he finds it again, apparently."

As for his reasons for coming to Edinburgh, it's mainly to do with the decision to create a new 4K edition of *Highlander*. "I'm flattered by the treatment. The 4K restoration stuff, I always thought that was for films of weight and significance within the art form; I never thought it was going to be for *Highlander*. Since then, I've heard arguments about it being a film of weight and an artistic film . . . it's a very strange film, it works in a very odd way; next thing you know it'll be *Friday the 13th*."

****

It may have taken Clancy Brown more than 30 years to feel comfortable discussing *Highlander*, but Christopher Lambert made his peace with the role of Connor MacLeod early on in his career. "I feel loyal to all the characters I've played, but *Highlander* is more omnipresent. I did four because it became a cult movie all over the world. If you say Mel Gibson you think *Mad Max*, Clint Eastwood you think *Dirty Harry*."

As a French-speaking actor, Lambert's success in an English-speaking role gave him opportunities many young actors could only dream of. "When Michael Cimino cast me in *The Sicilian* he went to see *Highlander* and said, 'I saw that movie and I nearly didn't cast you.' He was in shock, thinking, *What the fuck is this movie?* [because] he wasn't aiming for an action audience. We talked about it and I said, 'Michael, this movie is a romance before being an action movie.' He watched it again and said, 'It's more interesting to watch the movie and consider the immortality aspect,' but it's impossible to explain that to all the people that don't like the movie."

I mention the moment that Ramirez tries to convince MacLeod to leave Heather as he'll only feel pain when she dies before him. The fact that the words are spoken by the then 54-year-old Connery to a man almost 30 years his junior, adds gravitas to the scene. Looking in his eyes it's possible to see that he's lived through difficult experiences rather than just speaking the words from a script. Is that getting too deep about what was promoted as an action fantasy film?

"No, no, there is something deep in *Highlander* if people want to see it," retorts Lambert. "This movie is in many ways very complete; you can watch it over and over again and find something you didn't see the time before."

As our conversation comes to an end, we linger on the themes of love and loss that are so prominent in the film. Lambert has strong feelings on the subject, something to be expected from a man in his sixties who has lived a full life.

"My father died, my brother died, my mother's going to die. I've prepared myself coming from the fact I've lived it in movies because I'm not playing the character, I'm becoming the character, it's written in the scripts, you're a different person between action and cut. Is it good training? It might be. For three years when my father died, I did my mourning, the same for my brother. When they died, in some ways I was happy for them because it was painful for them. I can manage my pain. Their pain, physical and mental, that's awful. My pain is my problem. I tell myself, you can crawl or you can walk."

Something that can get overlooked while watching *Highlander*, thanks to the speed the film rattles along at, is the fact that the character of Connor MacLeod in 1986 is more than 450 years older than the Connor MacLeod viewers first meet in 1536. With the only concession to the passage of time being a shorter haircut, one reason to rewatch the film is to spend some time focusing on Lambert as he flips from young Connor to older Connor.

"I've always mixed the childish quality in all the characters I've played with the adult or heavier side when they get older," says the actor when I ask him about his approach to the MacLeod we're introduced to at different points in his life. "I don't think that just because they're older they have to become a 'boring adult'; you can have fun, you can be a kid and be responsible. So for me to play a young and feisty Connor MacLeod and to then go back to a heavier MacLeod, the only thing I saw was that he had this weight of being hundreds of years old on his shoulders."

The final word on the film has to go to Lambert, who has spent more time than most pondering what it means to live forever. Without his portrayal of Connor MacLeod, the franchise wouldn't have outlived its poor box-office takings and succeeded in an industry that is slow to forgive failure. Perhaps there's something we can all learn from the character of MacLeod, as we each face our own mortality.

"MacLeod's still walking in 1986, he has a mission, he cannot fail, he has to be the only one in order to save the world, to sense different things, and be allowed to grow old and die. That's where I think the movie is powerful. It's not because you lose a loved one, which happens to everybody. *That* life stops. Stand up and walk; life goes on for *you*."

AFTERWORD

It's a rare and sometimes strange thing to have a story you've written live on in the way *Highlander* has.

Just last week I heard some version of "like the *Highlander*, there can be only one" used in the context of an economics argument about German exports, a podcast on the philosophical works of the 10th century philosopher Avicenna, and a description of someone in Netflix's *Tiger King*.

It's certainly nice to hear when someone likes a script you wrote, but I'm always impressed by how many people say *Highlander* is their favourite film. For a movie that was considered to be a box office failure in the US when it was released, it's been a unique and gratifying journey to see it become over time the sort of demi-classic it is now.

That such simple ideas as a time travel movie where no-one actually travels in time, in which immortality is at best a mixed bag where you bury everyone you ever knew, could still resonate 30 something years later has meant a lot to me.

That and, of course, avoiding having anything to do with the sequels (ha ha).

Gregory Widen
Los Angeles
September 2020

ACKNOWLEDGEMENTS

Thank you to everyone who took the time to talk about *Highlander* in person or via email, phone, Skype, or Zoom: James Acheson, Andy Armstrong, Edwin "Itsi" Atkins, Peter Bellwood, Andy Bradford, Neil Brand, Clancy Brown, Garrett Brown, Lois Burwell, Roger Chiasson, Guy Collins, James Cosmo, Frazer Diamond, Eamon Dougherty, Richard Easson, Beatie Edney, Larry Ferguson, Alistair Findlay, Claire Forbes, Matt Forrest, J.D. Freedman, Anthony Fusco, Keith Garabedian, Kyle Garabedian, Tim Gallin, Roxanne Hart, Joe Haidar, Peter Honess, Tim Hutchinson, Joseph Lee Jackson, David James, Jim Jenkins, Phil Howard-Jones, Vincent "Ginger" Keane, Grant Kempster, Paul Kenward, Christopher Lambert, Clyde Lawson, Bill Little, Richard MacLennan, Nick Maley, Brian May, Tony Mitchell, Campbell Muirhead, Russell Mulcahy, Derek Power, Hugh Quarshie, Mark Raggett, Ian Reddington, Kevin Reitzel, Adam Samuelson, John Schoonraad, David Semple, Keith Short, Mike Smith, Robin Squibb, Michael Stevenson, Ian Sutherland, Ravi Swami, John Swinnerton, Roger Taylor, Richard Walter, David Win and Ian Woolf.

Thank you to Gregory Widen for writing both the script that started all of this and the coda to this book. I owe you a Glenmorangie.

Thank you to Peter Briggs for your last minute help. Social media can be a force for good.

Thank you to the team at Edinburgh International Film Festival, Zoe Flower and Tim Mosley for helping to make my interview with Clancy Brown happen.

Thank you to Claire Connachan, Dorothy Connachan, Robert Girvan, Ian Hoey, Ross Maclean and Ron MacKenzie for reading the early drafts, correcting my mistakes, and suggesting so many improvements.

Thank you to Pete Burns at Polaris for nurturing this book to completion (and for the hamper), and to my agent Kevin Pocklington for all the advice and assistance.

Thank you to Ben Morris for the book's stunning cover.

Finally, thank you to Claire for helping cement the idea that I should write a book on *Highlander*, and for putting up with anecdotes about the film for four years. You brought it on yourself . . .

If you enjoyed this book, please consider leaving a review on your favourite online bookseller or book review site.

Also by Jonathan Melville:

Seeking Perfection
The Unofficial Guide to Tremors

Local Hero
Making a Scottish Classic

REFERENCES

Prologue

x It was on 29 October, 1994: *The List*, 21 October 1994, p. 30.

xiii "stultifyingly, jaw-droppingly, achingly awful": Sheila Benson, *Los Angeles Times*, 11 Mar 1986, p.5.

xiii "making a sci-fi, thriller, horror . . .": Anon., *Variety*, 31 December 1985, https://variety.com/1985/film/reviews/highlander-1200426907/

xiii "little more than an everlasting . . .": Jay Scott, *Highlander* review, *The Globe and Mail*, 10 March 1986, p. C9.

Chapter One

1 To walk through the corridors . . . : Tower of London blog, 30 April 2020, https://blog.hrp.org.uk/curators/the-tower-of-london-a-thousand-years-of-resilience-and-strength/

1 "They have the world's largest collection of armoury": *The Projection Booth*, Episode 300, http://www.projectionboothpodcast.com/2016/12/episode-300-highlander-1986.html

2 following stints as a disc jockey: *Highlander* production notes, 1986.

2 "On the one hand, I was going into burning buildings . . .": "T*he Making of Highlander*: Part I: A Legend is Born", (Fiction FACTory Filmproduktion, 2007), *Highlander* Blu-ray, StudioCanal, 2016.

3 "To me, that was a very classic dilemma . . .": Ibid.

3 In his 1992 book . . .: William Froug, *The New Screenwriter Looks at the New Screenwriter*, (Silman-James Press, 1992), p. 99.

10 "I was always taught . . .": Ibid.

11 Davis was a former: *Highlander* production notes.

11 "Early on we recognised . . ..": Ross Johnson, "The Pioneers: A tale of two franchises", *Screen International*, 2005, p29.

11 Bill Panzer's introduction to Gregory Widen's script: "*The Making of Highlander*: Part IV: The Producer's Point of View", (Fiction FACTory Filmproduktion, 2007), *Highlander* Blu-ray, StudioCanal, 2016.

12 "We like adventure movies . . .": Alan Jones, "Rock Video Stylist Russell Mulcahy Films Epic Fantasy of Swashbuckling Immortal Warriors", *Cinefantastique*, May 1986.

12 option the rights for $1,500: Johnson, "The Pioneers: A tale of two franchises".

12 from Widen in 1982: *Highlander* production notes.

12 "the option money for *Highlander* . . .": Froug, *The New Screenwriter Looks at the New Screenwriter*.

Chapter Two

13 After graduating from the University: "Hollywood screenwriter shares the stories behind his biggest films", http://www.uoalumni.com/s/1540/uoaa/index.aspx?sid=1540&gid=3&pgid=3417

14 English-born Peter Bellwood had studied: "Ojai Valley Museum Town Talk - A Conversation with Peter Bellwood", May 20 2018, https://www.youtube.com/watch?v=H8Nep-ueEuA

14 The aptly named *St. Helens*: https://en.wikipedia.org/wiki/St._Helens_(film)

15 "I was a young, green college kid": Jones, "Rock Video Stylist Russell Mulcahy Films Epic Fantasy of Swashbuckling Immortal Warriors".

19 "The Legend of The Prize": Still Photos, *Highlander* 10th Anniversary DVD, Republic Pictures, 1999.

Chapter Three

28 MTV didn't even have them all: Rob Tannenbaum and Craig Marks, *I Want My MTV: The Uncensored Story of The Music Video Revolution*, p. 44.

29 "I learned everything . . .": Alan Jones, "Director Russell Mulcahy on Razorback", *Starburst*, Vol 7 No 5, Issue 77, January 1985.

29 "My early promos were like . . .": Anne Billson, "Out of Kilter", *Films and Filming*, September 1985.

29 film a batch for him: https://en.wikipedia.org/wiki/Music_video

29 "they had a freedom . . .": Gail O'Donnell & Michelle Travolta, *Making it in Hollywood: behind the success of 50 of today's favorite actors, screenwriters, producers, and directors*, (Sourcebooks, Inc, 1995).

29 "I invented the pop promo in Australia.": Nina Davies, "Highland hurdy gurdy", *City Limits*, 28 August to 4 September 1986.

30 Jon Roseman: Alan Jones, *Starburst*, January 1985.

30 "It really was . . .": Paul Rowlands, "Interview with Russell Mulcahy (Part 1 of 2)", http://www.money-into-light.com/2016/07/an-interview-with-russell-mulcahy-part.html

30 becoming Billboards' biggest hit of 1981: https://en.wikipedia.org/wiki/Billboard_Year-End_Hot_100_singles_of_1981

30 "It broke every rule . . .": Rob Tannenbaum and Craig Marks, *I Want My MTV: The Uncensored Story of The Music Video Revolution*, (Plume, 2012), p. 81.

30 "Russell was a visionary": Ibid.

31 "Indiana Jones is horny . . .": Andy Taylor, *Wild Boy: My Life in Duran Duran*, (Orion Publishing Group, 2008). p. 100.

32 soon being shown four times a day: Roy Shuker, *Understanding Popular Music*, (Routledge, 2001), p. 171.

32 On arriving in the outback: Alan Jones, *Starburst*, January 1985.

33 At one point during the shoot . . ., . . . rest of my life.": Ibid.

33 "looked like someone had told me . . .": Ibid.

33 Unlike the producers, he never: Ibid.

34 "very aggressive basis": *Highlander* production notes.

34 Michael Ryan, who started his career: http://www.dinglefilmfestival.com/film-festival-ireland/producer-michael-ryan-joins-dingle-iff-ltd/

34 "they took the world outside . . .": Johnson, "The Pioneers: A tale of two franchises".

34 "thought it was terrific": *Highlander* production notes.

35 A press release announcing: Still Photos, *Highlander* 10th anniversary DVD.

35 television broadcasting, retail/rentals: https://en.wikipedia.org/wiki/Thorn_EMI

35 on a budget of $1.5 million: Paul Moody, *EMI Films and the Limits of British Cinema*, (Palgrave Macmillan, 2018), p. 136.

35 the decision to invest: David Semple, *Rollover and Die*, http://www.iridescentvillage.com/politiclass_blog/?p=368

36 a more substantial payment of around £250,000: Froug, *The New Screenwriter Looks at the New Screenwriter*.

36 "We were socially comfortable . . .": "T*he Making of Highlander*: Part IV: The Producer's Point of View", *Highlander* Blu-ray.

36 "many of my favourite directors were dead": Ibid.

37 "There were certain aspects . . .": *Highlander* production notes.

37 "*Highlander* cried out . . .": Ibid.

37 "In *Highlander* [Russell] got his first chance . . .": "*The Making of Highlander*: Part IV: The Producer's Point of View", *Highlander* Blu-ray.

38 A press release announcing the hiring of Mulcahy: Still Photos, *Highlander* 10th anniversary DVD.

Chapter Four

40 "I'd never met him before . . .": "*The Making of Highlander*: Part II: The Visual Style", (Fiction FACTory Filmproduktion, 2007), *Highlander* Blu-ray, StudioCanal, 2016.

41 A memo from Peter Davis dated Tuesday 19 February: Still Photos, *Highlander* 10th anniversary DVD.

41 "Allan came in early and we sat down . . .": *Highlander* production notes.

41 "That wasn't going to work . . .": "*The Making of Highlander*: Part IV: The Producer's Point of View", *Highlander* Blu-ray.

41 Contemporary production notes claimed: *Highlander* production notes.

42 "really wild, kind of like a pop video . . .": "*The Making of Highlander*: Part II: The Visual Style", *Highlander* Blu-ray.

44 Building the apartment in London also: Edwin Atkins interview, Highlander Rewatched Chronicles 19, https://soundcloud.com/highlander-rewatched/chronicle-19-edwin-itsy-atkins

45 "Russell and I . . .": Ibid.

45 The rewrite was accompanied: Still Photos, *Highlander* 10th anniversary DVD.

46 "We realise it may not be practical . . .": Still Photos, *Highlander* 10th anniversary DVD.

48 Taking up fencing: Chris Riemenschneider, 'A Master Who Teaches the Rhythm of the Sword', *Los Angeles Times*, 11 July 1995.

48 "In order to be a stunt coordinator . . .": Adam Pirani, "On location with *Highlander*", *Starlog* 104, p. 28-31.

48 Frazer maintains a website: http://www.peterdiamond.co.uk/

50 Jacob Street Studios: http://www.thestudiotour.com/jacobstreet/index.php

50 "Jacob Street wasn't really a studio,": "*The Making of Highlander*: Part II: The Visual Style", *Highlander* Blu-ray.

53 A memo from Peter Davis: Still Photos, *Highlander* 10th anniversary DVD.

53 Sean was always known for his love of money: Michael Ryan, American Film Market LIVE Broadcast, November 7, 2016, https://www.voiceamerica.com/liveevents/episode/95655?name=american-film-market-live-broadcast&segmentId=56752

53 because another project fell through: *Highlander* production notes.

53 "When I heard it was Russell Mulcahy doing it . . .": Ibid.

55 "I saw every American living in England . . .": Commentary, *Highlander* 10th anniversary DVD.

56 "bogus": Ibid.

56 In later years, Polito looked back: Jon Polito interview by Nathan Rabin, http://www.avclub.com/article/jon-polito-60244

57 "pretty much the next day": Beatie Edney interview, Highlander Rewatched: Chronicle 4, 28 June 2016, https://soundcloud.com/highlander-rewatched/chronicle-4-beatie-edney

Chapter Five

59 Born in Great Neck: https://www.imdb.com/name/nm0000483/bio?ref_=nm_ov_bio_sm

59 kicked out of school five times in six years: Stephanie Billen, Christopher Lambert interview, *The List*, 22 August - 4 September 1986.

59 "interesting for the first three weeks": Ibid.

59 "highly intellectual and boring.": *Highlander* production notes.

59 Due to the intense physical nature of the film . . .": Ibid.

60 "We could open ourselves up. . .": "T*he Making of Highlander*: Part IV: The Producer's Point of View", *Highlander* Blu-ray.

60 "I thought it was great to be an Immortal. . .": Adam Pirani, "Immortal Highlander", *Starlog* 105, April 1986, p 28-32.

61 "We put our hands out. . .": "*The Making of Highlande*r: Part IV: The Producer's Point of View", *Highlander* Blu-ray.

61 "He is charming. . .": Ibid.

61 An announcement was made: Still Photos, *Highlander* 10th anniversary DVD.

62 "I think so long as . . .": *Highlander* production notes.

64 When asked in 1995: Chris Riemenschneider, 'A Master Who Teaches the Rhythm of the Sword'.

65 "You should talk to this big American . . .": Ibid.

65 with confirmation of the deal: Still Photos, *Highlander* 10th anniversary DVD.

65 "I envisioned him as a guy who . . .": "*The Making of Highlander*: Part I: A Legend is Born", *Highlander* Blu-ray.

66 "The Kurgan in the movie is . . .": Ibid.

66 "pretty much like Freddy [Krueger] . . .": Ibid.

66 Discussing the character with *Starlog* in 1986: - Adam Pirani, "On location with *Highlander*".

68 "I said, 'Bob, come and live with me . . .": Clancy Brown Q&A, Edinburgh International Film Festival (EIFF), 18 June 2016.

68 "Chris would steal all the cool moves . . .": Ibid.

Chapter Nine

124 "I was 25 when I was doing that show . . .": Clancy Brown Q&A, EIFF.

124 Both the first glimpse of the Kurgan: Commentary, *Highlander* Blu-ray

124 Lightning was added: Ibid.

Chapter Ten

138 "the relationship didn't work . . .": Commentary, *Highlander* 10th anniversary DVD

138 Clancy Brown was particularly enamoured: Clancy Brown Q&A, EIFF.

138 "There could have been wonderful dialogue . . .": Adam Pirani, 'Call him the Kurgan', *Starlog* 106.

139 "The Kurgan is in a heavy metal sort of get-up . . .": Ibid.

141 "When you do extreme make-up . . .": Ibid.

158 "Cold and wet and a night shoot . . .": Mark Newbold, "Vintage Interview: Christopher Malcolm: 19 February 2006", https://www.fanthatracks.com/interviews/vintage-interview-christopher-malcolm-19th-february-2006/

Chapter Eleven

155 a memo dated Wednesday 3 July: Still Photos, *Highlander* 10th anniversary DVD.

162 "Russell wanted everything covered in rain . . .": Edwin Atkins interview, Highlander Rewatched Chronicles 19, https://soundcloud.com/highlander-rewatched/chronicle-19-edwin-itsy-atkins

Chapter Twelve

167 In preparing the roof for filming: Edwin Atkins interview, Highlander Rewatched Chronicles 19, https://soundcloud.com/highlander-rewatched/chronicle-19-edwin-itsy-atkins

168 hired by Itsi Atkins because: Ibid.

170 The match filmed involved: Eric Rhodes, "Highlander: 10 Hidden Details Everyone Missed in the Original Movie", https://screenrant.com/highlander-hidden-details-original-movie/

171 According to production designer Allan Cameron: "The *Making of Highlander*: Part II: The Visual Style", *Highlander* Blu-ray.

Chapter Thirteen

179 "Queen were absolutely the best band of the day . . .": Daria Kokozej, http://www.mercury-and-queen.com/liveaid.htm

181 "That was a really stupid thing . . .": Eamon O'Neill, 'Steve Rothery, Marillion, Uber Rock Interview Exclusive', *Uber Rock*, http://www.uberrock.co.uk/interviews/60-september-interviews/12333-steve-rothery-marillion-uber-rock-interview-exclusive.html

181 The band's lead singer: Mick Wall, *Appetite for Destruction: Legendary Encounters with Mick Wall*, (Orion 2010).

182 recording music for *Highlander*: Still Photos, *Highlander* 10th anniversary DVD.

185 According to Russell Mulcahy: Commentary, *Highlander* 10th anniversary DVD.

186 Studio A on 22, 23, 27 November – Grant Kempster, *Highlander Heart*, Issue 1.

193 selling more than 100,000 copies: https://en.wikipedia.org/wiki/A_Kind_of_Magic

Chapter Fourteen

199 A post-production schedule: Still Photos, *Highlander* 10th anniversary DVD.

200 Contemporary production notes for *Highlander*: *Highlander* production notes.

201 a notoriously troubled production: Sam Weisberg, "'A Snake Pit Gig": The Making (and Undoing) of Abel Ferrara's "Cat Chaser"', *Hidden Films*, https://hidden-films.com/2015/09/09/a-snake-pit-gig-the-making-and-undoing-of-abel-ferraras-cat-chaser/

Chapter Fifteen

211 a letter dated 24 January: Still Photos, *Highlander* 10th anniversary DVD.

213 memo dated 27 January 1986: Ibid.

214 "did it in three takes . . .": Commentary, *Highlander* 10th anniversary DVD.

Chapter Sixteen

216 In the spring of 1985: David Semple, *Takeover at EMI London*, https://therepublicrecordings.wordpress.com/2020/08/19/takeover-at-emi-london/

219 Talking to John Mosby: John Mosby, *Fearful Symmetry: The Essential Guide to All Things Highlander*, (JM2, 2015), p. 15.

220 it took seventh place in the week's box-office charts: https://www.boxofficemojo.com/release/rl1280935425/weekend/

221 "wanted to prevent us . . .": Gene Siskel, "Highlander takes low road of superhero violence", *Chicago Tribune*, 10 March 1986, https://www.chicagotribune.com/news/ct-xpm-1986-03-10-8601180411-story.html

221 "one of the lousiest films I've ever seen . . .": *At the Movies with Gene Siskel and Roger Ebert*, https://www.youtube.com/watch?v=qZKBvC0Kols

221 "For his brief time on screen . . .": Walter Goodman, "Highlander with Sean Connery", *New York Times*, 8 March 1986, https://www.nytimes.com/1986/03/08/movies/screen-highlander-with-sean-connery.html

221 There was also little love for the film: Paul Attanasio, *Washington Post*, 19 March 1986, https://www.washingtonpost.com/archive/lifestyle/1986/03/19/movies/31170141-de95-4749-b790-10fe920cfb49/

222 "Mulcahy has style to burn . . .": Bill Cosford, *The Miami Herald*, 11 Mar 1986, p.B4.

222 "in spite of a sturdy cast . . .": Sheila Benson, *Los Angeles Times*, 11 Mar 1986, p.5.

222 Second highest grossing film of 1986: Owen Williams, "Highlander: A history", *Empire*, https://www.empireonline.com/movies/features/highlander/

222 In Tony Cavanaugh's lengthy take: Tony Cavanaugh, "Clan destined", *Cinema Papers*, September 1986, p48.

223 By the spring of 1986: David Semple, *Takeover at EMI London*, https://therepublicrecordings.wordpress.com/2020/08/19/takeover-at-emi-london/

227 "there is this group of gladiators . . .": Richard Rayner, "Highlander", *Time Out*, https://www.timeout.com/london/film/highlander

228 "an immortal hero and villain . . .": Tim Pulleine, "Highlander review", *Monthly Film Bulletin*, August 1986, Vol. 53 No. 631.

228 "a curious mixture of romance . . .": Stephanie Billen, "Highlander review", *The List*, issue 23, 22 August 1986.

228 "Russell Mulcahy certainly has a vivid imagination . . .": Nina Davies, "Highland hurdy gurdy".

232 In 1984 there were 10.5 million VCRs in US homes: Ross Johnson, "The indie raiders who struck gold", *Screen International*, 28 January 2005.

232 "manages to propel the film . . .": Video reviews, *Video – the Machine*, January 1987.

Chapter Seventeen

236 Sean Connery returned: Owen Williams, "Highlander: A history".

237 Connery is said to have delayed his: Johnson, "The Pioneers: A tale of two franchises".

238 "a complete disaster . . .": Will Murray, "Master of Death", *Starlog* 205, August 1994.

238 dedicated a number of pages: Sean Murphy, "Highlander II : Three Versions Of A Film In Search Of Its Identity", *Video Watchdog* No. 37.

238 "always felt *Highlander II* was a success . . .": Marc Shapiro, "Battle of the Immortals", Starlog 185.

239 "We realised that *Highlander* would have . . .": Ibid.

240 "The series was our saving grace ": Owen Williams, "Highlander: A history".

240 "Gaumont wanted a bigger piece of syndication": Johnson, "A tale of two franchises".

240 "What I didn't like . . .": Dan Yakir, "Higher Ground", *Starlog* 212.

240 DVDs from the series: Johnson, "The Pioneers: A tale of two franchises".

241 moving into the world of animation: https://en.wikipedia.org/wiki/Highlander:_The_Animated_Series

243 According to Lambert: Dan Yakir, "Higher Ground".

243 With a budget of $26 million: https://www.imdb.com/title/tt0110027/

244 "This is a movie about redemption": Dan Yakir, 'Beloved Immortal', *Starlog* 279, October 2000.

244 taking almost $16 million: https://www.imdb.com/title/tt0144964/?ref_=nv_sr_srsg_0

245 "The acting is uniformly terrible . . .": http://www.filmcritic.com/misc/emporium.nsf/reviews/Highlander-The-Source

246 The deal with Summit Entertainment: Jeremy Kay, "Summit Entertainment to remake 1986 hit Highlander", *Screen Daily*, 21 May 2008, https://www.screendaily.com/summit-entertainment-to-remake-1986-hit-highlander/4039106.article

246 director Justin Lin: Peter Sciretta, "Justin Lin, Fast & Furious Director To Remake Highlander", *SlashFilm*, 22 September 2009, https://www.slashfilm.com/fast-furious-director-to-reboot-highlander/

246 screenwriter Melissa Rosenberg: Adam Chitwood, "TWILIGHT Screenwriter Melissa Rosenberg to Tackle HIGHLANDER Remake Script", *Collider*, 9 February 2011, https://collider.com/melissa-rosenberg-highlander/75464/

246 Juan Carlos Fresnadillo: "Ryan Reynolds Confirmed as Highlander", *MovieWeb*, 27 June 2012, https://movieweb.com/ryan-reynolds-confirmed-as-highlander/

246 second unit director Cedric Nicolas-Troyan: Mike Fleming, "Summit Sets Cedric Nicolas-Troyan To Helm 'Highlander' Feature Reboot", *Deadline*, 28 October 2013, https://deadline.com/2013/10/summit-sets-cedric-nicolas-troyan-to-helm-highlander-feature-reboot-622113/

247 director Chad Stahelski had signed on: Boris Kit "'John Wick' Director Chad Stahelski Tackling 'Highlander' Reboot (Exclusive)", *The Hollywood Reporter*, 22 November 2016, https://www.hollywoodreporter.com/heat-vision/john-wick-director-chad-stahelski-tackling-highlander-reboot-949693

247 screenwriter Ryan Condal: Peter White, "'Highlander' Reboot Gets Moving After 'Colony' Writer Ryan Condal Hands In Script", *Deadline*, 1 March 2018, https://deadline.com/2018/03/highlander-reboot-gets-moving-after-colony-writer-ryan-condal-hands-in-script-1202307522/

247 By June 2020: Andrew J. Salazar, "Chad Stahelski Talks Stunt Recognition & Upcoming Projects – Exclusive Interview", *Discovering Film*, 24 June 2020, https://discussingfilm.net/2020/06/24/chad-stahelski-talks-stunt-recognition-upcoming-projects-exclusive-interview/

247 Peter Davis, had died in his sleep: Dino-Ray Ramos, "Peter S. Davis Dies: Producer Of 'Highlander' Franchise Was 79", *Deadline*, 23 February 2021, https://deadline.com/2021/02/peter-s-davis-dead-the-highlander-producer-of-highlander-franchise-obituary-1234699557/

248 More substantial reboot news broke: Justin Kroll, "Henry Cavill To Star in Lionsgate's 'Highlander' Reboot From Chad Stahelski", *Deadline*, 21 May 2021, https://deadline.com/2021/05/henry-cavill-lionsgates-highlander-reboot-chad-stahelski-1234761916/

248 posted on his Facebook and Instagram accounts: Henry Cavill, Facebook, 21 May 2021, https://www.facebook.com/henrycavill/posts/318335612997420

249 An interview with the actor: James Hibberd, "Why Henry Cavill Basically Already Is James Bond", *The Hollywood Reporter,* 10 November 2021, https://www.hollywoodreporter.com/feature/henry-cavill-interview-witcher-superman-1235044553/

Chapter Eighteen

255 "two albino Lego models . . .": Stuart Ashen, *Terrible Old Games You've Probably Never Heard Of,* (Unbound 2015).

255 "totally boring and quite unplayable": Ibid.

255 A March 2006 branding document: http://davis-panzer.com/HighlanderBrand.pdf

256 three comic book mini-series: https://www.ign.com/articles/2005/12/20/highlander-the-comic-book

256 two seasons of audio adventures: https://highlander.fandom.com/wiki/Big_Finish_Highlander_Audio_Series

256 a five-issue comic book: https://www.idwpublishing.com/product-category/highlander-the-american-dream/

256 *Highlander:* The Card Game: https://www.boardgamegeek.com/boardgame/9161/highlander-card-game

256 *Highlander*: The Duel: https://www.kickstarter.com/projects/bnbgames/highlander-the-duel

256 *Highlander*: The Board Game: https://www.kickstarter.com/projects/1428582690/highlander-the-board-game

256 The Sword Experience: https://swordxp.com/

260 One of *Highlander*'s most prominent fans: Joey Paur, "THE GOLDBERGS Will Have a HIGHLANDER-Themed Episode with Clancy Brown!", *Geek Tyrant*, https://geektyrant.com/news/the-goldbergs-will-have-a-highlander-themed-episode-with-clancy-brown

262 a Facebook page taking its place: https://www.facebook.com/groups/highlanderheart

263 *Highlander Worldwide*: http://www.highlanderworldwide.com/

263 *Highlander Rewatched*: https://www.facebook.com/HighlanderRewatched

264 passed away in 2020: Greg Evans, "Stan Kirsch Dies: 'Highlander: The Series' actor was 51", *Deadline*, https://deadline.com/2020/01/stan-kirsch-dead-obituary-highlander-actor-friends-1202830035/

265 *Blood of Kings* podcast: https://fpnet.podbean.com/